In A Perfect World:

Interpersonal Skills for Life

Pat Hirst

 **FriesenPress**

Suite 300 - 990 Fort St
Victoria, BC, Canada, V8V 3K2
www.friesenpress.com

ISBN
978-1-4602-5621-3 (Hardcover)
978-1-4602-5622-0 (Paperback)
978-1-4602-5623-7 (eBook)

1. Language Arts & Disciplines, Communication Studies

Distributed to the trade by The Ingram Book Company

Table of Contents

Preface
Interpersonal Skills: My Own Experience

If you continue to think what you've always thought...
You'll continue to get what you've always got! — *Anonymous*

In 1993, when I was a leader in an international corporation, I attended a communication workshop that changed my life. Until that point, I had believed adages such as "The one with the biggest stick always wins," "In every situation someone is right and someone is wrong" and "To change your mind and consider a different point of view is a sign of weakness" were effective principles to live by. That day, I realized that many of these beliefs were causing problems in my most important relationships. I had always thought the problems were because of other people's behaviour. That day I realized the way I communicated was not working. I was part of the problem! It was a monumental tipping point. I also discovered my calling, which is coaching people to foster their interpersonal communication skills to use their capacity to create the life they choose. I have pursued that passion ever since. This book is intended to be of service to those who are reflecting on their interpersonal skills and their relationships with others.

Having spent thousands of hours as a trainer, speaker and mediator, I continue to be energized by the many clients who, like me, have found an opportunity to change the quality of their relationships by employing effective communication practices. These people have learned to use different approaches when interacting with others, achieving positive results at home and at work. People have said things like: "That person really isn't difficult. It is the way I was approaching him that was creating the problem." Or "I can't believe how eliminating certain words from my vocabulary and being more aware of my tone and body language has improved my interactions."

That workshop was a real wakeup call for me to challenge my own limiting beliefs. In fact, a friend of mine kept telling me that when things aren't going right in your life, "Change your mind!" I never understood what she meant until that moment in the workshop.

When you allow yourself to change your judgments and attitudes, you create an opportunity for your behaviour to change. When your behaviour changes, you invite others to engage with you differently, which creates richer interactions. You can be the spark that creates a new culture in your family or workplace. Your relationships will be enhanced and you may find that those difficult people or interactions just don't matter as much as they did before.

As you read through these pages, examine your own thoughts and beliefs. Self-examination may affirm your approach and confirm that you are already on the right track. Allow yourself to release the beliefs that stop you from moving forward and engage thoughts that allow you to create an abundant future.

Best Wishes,
Pat Hirst

Note: For pronoun use the traditional rule suggests the use of he when there is not a direct reference. In the interests of simplicity this practice has been followed and the masculine has been used except in cases where the example refers to the feminine.

Dedication

This book is dedicated to every workshop participant and audience member who has participated in my sessions over the last two decades. Your generosity and graciousness has helped me understand how learning and change happen. You have inspired me to write this book and have helped me create my own perfect world.

Introduction
A Perfect World

A conversation never takes place in isolation.
Each conversation you have with someone takes place
in the constellation of all the other interactions you have
had with them.[1] — *Dr. Louise McNaughton-Filion*

What is perfection? Today we are in constant pursuit of the impeccable. We strive to find our soul mate, orchestrate the perfect wedding and raise perfect children, all the while working at the perfect job and living in a perfect home. We pursue these goals in a world that is not perfect.

In my perfect world the sun would shine, everyone would have enough to eat and there would be peace in our families and nations. We would always be understood and supported by those we count on. Our lives would be happy and fulfilled. In the real world, things do not always go the way we want. Storms rage, people starve and there is war. Our world spins out of orbit when those closest to us betray or disappoint us.

No single event or relationship has to define our lives. We have the opportunity to create the best and most perfect life on our own terms and by our own design.

For the majority, what brings richness to our lives is the quality of the relationships we have. In his book, *The Moral Molecule*, Paul Zak notes that in life:

> The things people rate most highly when pursuing happiness
> are having a good romantic relationship and many friendships,
> having a job you like, enjoying the community you live in and
> having a level of income good enough to reduce the stress of
> just getting by.[2]

The quality of our relationships rests largely on our interpersonal skills, which include communication skills, listening skills, assertion skills, problem-solving skills and conflict resolution skills. The quality of our relationships is affected by 1) our ability to assess when to use each skill, and 2) our proficiency in using them. Our primary circle of relationships contains family and friends, our work network and the people in our community. On a daily basis we have the chance to interact with each person in a way that is rich and meaningful.

Relationship building is not an event. It is a process. As Dr. McNaughton-Filion suggests, no conversation we have with another person occurs in isolation. It occurs within the constellation of all the interactions we have had with them before. Each time we speak with others, work with them, laugh or cry with them, hurt or demean them, that singular experience becomes another point of memory in the relationship. The collection of these experiences reflects the quality of a relationship that can be described as good or bad, as loving and supportive or fractured and estranged. When evaluating relationships, we tend to remember not what people say to us, but how we feel after we have had an exchange with them. We gravitate to those who make us feel happy and loved. We shy away from people who make us feel judged or uncomfortable. Unlike a constellation that is fixed, we can change the nature of our relationship with another person — for better or for worse — by having other interactions.

Doubting Thomas

For everyone who is open to trying new approaches, there are those who aren't. One day I had a conversation with Thomas, a workshop participant. At the end of a session on communication, Thomas gave me a dubious smile, shook his head and said, "Pat, this is really good stuff! There is no doubt in my mind the ideas and strategies you have shared could work somewhere. You don't understand our reality here. In our organization, here in the *real world*, this stuff just won't fly! There is no point in even trying this because, frankly, I don't think people would respond to it." He went on to say, "These practices and strategies can't work unless *everyone* uses them and buys into them. These ideas are fine in a classroom like this — but in the real world — no way. This stuff only works *in a perfect world.*"

The Myth

There are many people like Thomas who believe there is no point in trying to enhance their interpersonal skills, because certain things work only in a *perfect world.* And because the world is not perfect, there is no point in trying. This logic disempowers people from taking control of their lives. It is this thinking — believing there is no point in trying — that prevents a person from making changes that could have big results in their relationships. So they stay stuck in a bad work environment, a bad relationship or situation and complain but they don't do anything about it.

What value is there for you in working on your interpersonal skills? In order to evaluate this question it is useful to take a quick inventory of your current situation:

- Who are the people that constitute the most important relationships in your life?

- How could you transform these relationships if you improved the quality of your interactions with them?

- What are you missing out on in life because you are waiting for everything and everyone else to be perfect?

Through your own thoughtful consideration and intentionality, you have the opportunity to decide what your own perfect life looks like. Don't relinquish your opportunity for a happy life and meaningful relationships because of beliefs that do not serve you. If you wait for a "perfect world," you will be waiting a long time! You have an opportunity here and now to realize this is the only world you have and to decide how to make the most of what you've got.

This book is designed to help you reflect on your interpersonal skills and key relationships and to encourage you to take the time and effort with those relationships that matter. Evolving your communication skills and resolving differences with others will improve your relationships. It is important because your relationships define your destiny.

In the following chapters you will be introduced to or reminded of a number of concepts and practices that promote effective interpersonal skills, deepen the trust and understanding that you have in your key relationships and enhance your life.

This book is like a smorgasbord. There are some concepts or practices you may choose to consume now; other things that aren't palatable at the moment, you might leave for another day.

I believe our life and experiences in this world are a self-fulfilling prophecy generated by our thoughts. Be open to new ideas and thinking. Give yourself a chance to experiment and practise interpersonal skills. And don't be surprised when they lead you where you want to go. As they say, practice makes perfect!

PART ONE
Starting with Ourselves

All the interactions we have start with us —
what we think about ourselves, the world and others.
How we feel and what we believe affects every interaction
and relationship we have.
Our perfect world starts with us. — PH

Chapter 1
Making Smart Choices

The Bank Robber

What is a smart choice?

At sixteen, I started working part time as a bank teller. In the 70s times were tough and robbery was a common risk in the banking industry. During a training session we were told if we spent an entire career in banking, there was an excellent chance of being held up at gunpoint. The typical scenario is that a robber comes in with a weapon, walks up to your counter and shoves a note across the counter that reads, "Give me all your money now!"

The trainer then asked us, "How might you react when you read this note?"

We all brainstormed ideas that included:

- Faint

- Cry

- Remain calm

- Tell him you will get the manager

- Try to talk him out of it and press the alarm

- Jump the counter and try to overpower him

- Give him the money

The trainer asked us, "What is your primary goal when a robber is holding up the bank?"

Someone said, "To stay alive."

Another trainee added, "To make sure we *all* stay alive."

"Exactly!" said the trainer.

The best way to keep everyone safe was to give the thief the money as quickly as possible because the longer he stayed in the building the more likely it was that someone would be mortally wounded. If we were to pick another choice, such as jumping the counter to overpower him, it would be more likely that we would get hurt. That is because behaving with the robber in a way he did not ask would make him more nervous. Choosing to hand over the money is the most sensible way to keep the robber calm, get him out of the building fast and keep everyone from harm. So, the smart choice is the strategic choice — the one that gives you the best odds of achieving your goal.

This example illustrates the many options we have at our disposal in any given situation. How our own life turns out is a direct result of the choices we make in what we say and what we do. Many decisions are made in haste or out of habit. We tend to go with our knee-jerk reaction without due consideration of our own goals and then wonder, "What happened here? How did I get into this mess? How come things never go my way?"

Most of the time the answer is: "*We* happened!" The choices we make during interactions with others influence their behaviour because people react to what we say and what we do and what we don't say and what we don't do. Often we choose wrongly.

THE THREE PRINCIPLES OF CHOICE

Principle One: Choices Have Consequences

Our choices have consequences. Consequences can be positive and enhance our interaction or they can be negative, creating problems and damaging our relationships. The process of making "smart" choices begins with thinking and assessing *before* speaking or doing to consider the consequences your choice may trigger. Smart choices are the ones that give you the best odds of achieving your goals and creating good consequences.

In our daily interactions with others we often experience the bad consequences of ineffective communication. I regularly ask people in workshops, "How do you know when your communication has been *ineffective* with another person?"

People will respond to my question by saying that the other person might:

- Get mad

- Become confused

- Misunderstand

- Give the wrong result

- Walk away

When people misunderstand us it is often a result of how we have interacted with them. We habitually communicate in ways that cause negative consequences.

During every conversation we make a staggering number of choices that can either improve communication or derail the conversation. We make these decisions consciously or subconsciously. We choose:

- The words we say

- Our tone, pace and volume

- Our facial expression and the amount of eye contact we make

- How close we stand to the other person

- If and when to stay silent and listen

- How we respond to what someone says to us

To communicate well you need to make conscious choices about all these elements throughout an interaction. Further, you need to continually assess the impact of what you say or do in terms of how the person might perceive what you are saying and how he might react.

An effective approach engages the other person, creates understanding and enhances the relationship. Good relationships help us to work well with others and achieve results. Our conversations and interactions are what move us either towards life goals or away from them, affecting our ultimate success.

The challenge with communication is that once words leave our lips, they are no longer ours. Other people interpret what we say and do and put meaning to what they've heard and how they heard it, regardless of our intent. They are deciding what is effective for them or not. So a major part of our choice process is assessing who we are communicating with, what role we have, what our relationship is like, what their style of communication is and how we can communicate with them in a way that works.

Below are some scenarios and possible responses. Which choice do you think would be the most effective to invite good consequences?

1) Your son has been struggling with math and getting what you consider to be low grades in the 50-55% range. Today he comes home with a test where he got 69%. He studied hard and is proud of himself when he presents it to you. You respond by saying:

   a) *"You did a great job and I am proud of you. Your hard work helped you get a higher grade. Keep up the good work!"*

   b) *"69% is still not high enough — try harder!"*

   c) *"I do not have time to look at this now — show me later."*

   d) *"Good job. Now that you have improved in math, maybe you can do better keeping your room clean."*

2) You arrive at work at 7:45 a.m. and are rushing to your office to prepare for an 8:00 meeting. As you near your door, an employee who likes to talk smiles and says, "Good morning!" You respond by:

   a) *Replying to her with a pleasant "Good morning" and a smile and keep walking to your office.*

   b) *Pretending you did not hear her and rush into your office without saying anything.*

c) *Replying with a terse "Good morning" in an unfriendly tone and an eye-roll so you do not invite any chitchat.*

d) *Putting up your hand as you walk by and saying, "Not now, I'm busy."*

3) You work at a customer service counter handling customer returns and inquiries. A customer approaches you with an item for return. You respond by:

a) *Asking (with a smile): "How can I help you today?"*

b) *Asking (with a frown): "What is your problem?"*

c) *Saying: "Hi, I have had a terrible day. Two people phoned in sick so I am shorthanded. What do you need?"*

d) *Saying nothing, holding out your hand and waiting for the customer to put the item in it, then asking, "Where is your receipt?"*

4) Your friend just got a haircut. You think it does not look flattering and no one else mentions it. You:

a) *Remain silent on the point, as it is not an issue and no one is asking your opinion.*

b) *Say: "Wow! Your haircut looks great!" (said sarcastically)*

c) *Say: "Did you pay for that haircut or did you lose a bet?"*

d) *Say: "I noticed you got your hair cut. Do you like it?"*

Given each situation, can you imagine the possible outcomes associated with each choice? Did you get a sense of how the other person might react to each approach? How would each option affect your relationship with that person? What are the probable consequences? Which choice is the most effective?

In each of these scenarios the best option is (a). The other choices could lead to unhelpful reactions and create unnecessary animosity in the relationship.

This exercise illustrates the importance of understanding a situation, thinking through the choices you have at your disposal and selecting one that takes the situation and your relationship with the other person in a direction that you want it to go.

We are often more careful about choices when we are interacting with strangers than when we are interacting with those who are closest to us. If we go out on a first date, we are on our best behaviour. We put on our nicest clothes, our best face and our biggest smile. We are very conscious of what we say and do in order to make a good impression. However, in our closest relationships how often do we choose to say things that are hurtful or condescending, controlling or judgmental? When we do these things we act in a way that undermines the love and trust in our relationship.

In making strategic choices, it is not about what is good or bad, right or wrong, but rather what is effective or ineffective in the situation that you are in with the person you are with. — *PH*

People can react to us in ways we do not anticipate or intend; we don't live in a vacuum. Behaviour has a cause-and-effect dynamic. As we develop relationships with others, we learn how they react to us. This knowledge and understanding allows us to be more effective. We will inevitably make mistakes and say things that are misunderstood or offensive. In that case we can make the choice to apologize for errors we have made and try other approaches in communicating. The opportunity is to be strategic in how you communicate. Approach others in a way that works for them. Communicating with thought and care is especially important in our closest relationships.

Principle Two: There is Power in Choice
Often the reason we don't make effective choices for ourselves or don't take the high road is because others don't. We believe that if others are unwilling to be effective, it relieves us of our power and responsibility to choose. We absolve ourselves with the thought, "Why should I try when other people aren't?" As President Barack Obama has been credited with saying, "Change will not come if we wait for some other person or some other time. We are the ones we've been waiting for. We are the change we seek."

This reminds us that at some point in our lives we need to take control and be in the driver's seat to choose to live, think and do for ourselves. We are accountable. We don't blame others or make excuses. Often we get sidetracked by the power we *don't* have and all the things we *cannot* do. Our opportunity is to focus on what we *can* do and not be stopped by what we *can't* do. We can focus on the power we have, which is the power of choice.

> Don't let what you can't do stop you from
> doing what you can do. — *PH*

When I was a child the rare opportunity arose for the entire family to go out for dinner at a restaurant. It was for Mother's Day so that Mom would not have to cook. With eight of us at the table, the bill was hefty. Dad paid and we left. The next morning my dad said he had to go back to the restaurant. Although he did not have a receipt with him, he said he'd thought about how much he had paid and he concluded that we had not been charged enough, as he and Mom had enjoyed a bottle of wine with dinner. He believed that the bill total did not include the wine. Sure enough, the manager, someone my father had known for years, appreciated him coming back. At closing the night before, the staff had discovered they had not charged for the wine. They were not going to phone Dad because it was their mistake. Dad, however, always believed in choosing to treat others as he would want to be treated. He did not say, "I won't worry about it unless they call me." His view was that he and my mom had enjoyed the wine and that he needed to pay for it.

We have choices every day. Do we remain silent? Do we say something? Do we step up and do things that make a difference to other people and the relationships we have with them? Are we doing the best that we can do?

My friend and I cajole each other when faced with challenging circumstances that call for maturity and reason. We call it, "Putting on our big-girl pants." Putting on the "pants" is exerting your power. It's about taking responsibility and consciously deciding to either take action *or* let things be. Exercising responsibility also means accepting the consequences with peace and graciousness, knowing that we made the best choice we could at the time. So? Dare to create your own version of your perfect life. Put on your big-boy or big-girl pants!

Principle Three: Choose Now

There is some urgency and value in deciding to exercise your power of choice right *now*. Our time on earth is limited and finite. This can be a sobering thought. We don't know when this extraordinary adventure will be over. We don't know how many more chances we are going to get to cherish or improve the relationships we have.

How are your relationships now? Are you surrounded by loving friends who respect you and who you enjoy spending time with?

Your children grow up and experience the tumultuous teens. Are you spending quality time with them now to establish strong relationships that will carry you all through the challenging times? Sooner is better than later. You have no doubt heard comments like, "His wife left him and he just didn't see it coming." Or "Their daughter was on drugs and they didn't have a clue." Or maybe you've heard a friend lament that her dad passed away and the last interaction they had was a horrible fight and she didn't get to tell him she loved him.

What you do with your time here is up to you. The life experience you have is simple. It will depend on the choices you make. The things you do. The things you don't do. The things you say. The things you don't say. The relationships you develop. The ones you let slip away. Choose now.

Chapter 2
Our Primary Frame of Reference: Ourselves

You yourself, as much as anybody in the entire universe
deserve your love and affection. — Buddha

The Chocolate Bar

I grew up in a competitive family that included six children. Right was determined by might. The oldest, strongest or favoured one prevailed. I was none of these and at times was unsure of my value or place. I frequently heard messages that I was awkward, troublesome or ugly. I have a poignant memory of a childhood incident that left me questioning my value and what to expect from those closest to me.

At four years old, while watching my brothers target-practice with their BB guns, I was shot in the face. The BB lodged in my cheek and it was a week before I was taken to the doctor. By that time the entry point had healed over. The doctor suggested that the bullet not be removed until my teeth came in because surgery might inhibit their arrival.

Fast-forward to a summer afternoon three years later just after the surgery to remove the bullet from my face was completed. My mom and I went to our local pharmacy to buy post-op antibiotics. I spied a chocolate bar at the counter while we were waiting.

I asked my mom, "Could I please have a chocolate bar?"

She gave me a strained "yes," paid for the bar and the prescription, took me solidly by the wrist and yanked on me as she strode out to the car.

Once in the car, she dropped the bar onto my lap with an angry face and audible huffs, and said, "There's your bar! Don't you *ever* ask me for something *in front* of someone again! You have *five* brothers and sisters at home, and if I get you something, I should get them something too. I just couldn't do it today — so enjoy that bar!!"

It was the least satisfying bar I ever ate. You might say, at that moment my mother became one of the top travel agents for booking guilt trips!

For me, the interpretation was: Even though most people get special treatment when they are ill, I didn't deserve the chocolate bar and I should not be afforded any special consideration. When we expect others to show us love and consideration and they instead show us contempt, it can leave a mark.

As we go through life, all our experiences combined with the feedback we receive from others contribute to our self-perception.

Parents Impact Esteem
How we nurture and treat our children will have a profound
impact on their self-esteem. It is a balance of loving and
supporting and empowering and letting go. — *PH*
Children cultivate 85% of their intellect, personality and skills
by age five.
Wisconsin Council on Children and Families [3]

OUR SENSE OF SELF

In our various roles in life — as parents, siblings, friends, neighbours and professionals — most of us, at one time or another, wrestle with our egos and wonder if we are up to the task. We struggle with questions like: Am I competent? Am I a good person? Am I loveable? Am I doing the right thing? Is it really my place to say something?

Our ego is our sense of self. It is one part of our frame of reference that influences how we send messages and how we interpret information from others. The ego can seem like a pulsing energy, a voice that provides a running commentary on what we should believe about ourselves, about others and their motives and what we should or shouldn't do. Our opinion of ourselves can change over time and with the situation. The good news is that our self-perception is something we can adjust.

Whatever our inner voice says to us has an impact on how we communicate and interpret information, so communication really starts with our own self-image. If we have received good messages from others that we're fast enough, smart enough and good enough, we tend to feel positive and competent to take on life's challenges. We will also be more likely to communicate effectively with others, as we will not be so inclined to misinterpret slights that aren't there, or take things in a negative way that are not intended. We can be more empathetic and thoughtful, not needing to put others down in order to elevate ourselves. If we have received less than favourable feedback from others — "Why can't you be more like your brother?" "Why are you so stupid?" "You did okay but you can always do better" — our self-image may unnecessarily be stuck on low.

The value in reflecting on our sense of self is that it allows us to examine the experiences that put us where we are, and then to choose what to think here and now in a way that lets us move on productively with life. It also informs us about how we want to treat others. Why would we do something to someone else that had a negative effect when it was done to *us*?

CHOOSING A MINDSET

Self-perception is like a volume-adjustment control on a computer. On a continuum from LOW to HIGH, you can move the volume control up or down. Likewise self-perception is on a continuum from passivity to aggression. You can adjust it depending on your circumstances and situation. You get to choose.

The first step in communication is to be aware of your self-view and how it affects your communication.

The second step is for you to choose a perspective that serves and supports you. At any time you can choose to move along the continuum below:

PASSIVE   ASSERTIVE   AGGRESSIVE

Passive

People whose dial is set on passive see other people's interests and needs as being more important than their own. They tend to believe other people's rights should be respected more than their own. They may appear to be reserved and aloof, not sharing their views, beliefs and needs. They can come across as unsure of themselves. They may make little direct eye contact and seem content to accommodate others.

These people communicate in quiet ways and are often ignored or misunderstood. When they receive messages from others, they may misinterpret what is said and take things as an insult or criticism where none is intended.

In this case the dial may be set here on the continuum:

PASSIVE   ASSERTIVE   AGGRESSIVE

Aggressive

People on the other end, at aggressive, communicate from a belief that their own interests and needs are more important than other people's. If they need something, they do not hesitate to take it even at the expense of someone else. Their view is that it is a dog-eat-dog world. Their communication approach is to share their views whether they are invited to or not. Their preference is to talk rather than listen. They tend not to validate others. Others see them as overly direct, forceful or rude. They move and stand in ways that intimidate others and infringe on people's personal space. Aggression is communicated through blaming, attacking, name-calling and threatening.

Aggressive people are often seen as egotistical or arrogant, coming across to others as demanding and loud.

Their dial is set here on the continuum:

PASSIVE   ASSERTIVE   AGGRESSIVE

When our dial stays constantly at either end of this continuum, it can leave us in a rut. If we are always passive, we will acquiesce to others and never get what we want. Others won't bother communicating with us because we are "yes" people who agree and don't contribute to decision-making. If we stay at the aggressive end, many people will avoid us because we must always have our way and can be seen as exhausting, bullying and overbearing.

Assertive

A helpful and productive mindset for interacting with others is *assertion*. Assertive people believe in basic principles that form a foundation influencing their interactions with others. When we are assertive, we are in a place where we feel good about ourselves. We know and trust ourselves to pursue our own needs and interests. When we ensure that our own needs and interests are taken care of, we have the ability to think about the needs and interests of others. As assertive people, we pursue our right to:

- Be respected just because we are human beings

- Share our opinions

- Say *no*

- Change our minds

- Be treated fairly

- Make mistakes, because we are, after all, not perfect — we are human

- Look after our own needs and interests, because no one else will

These rights are not exclusive. Everyone is entitled to them. Along with the assertive person's belief in rights comes the responsibility to honour these rights for others. For many people who have lived through challenging circumstances such as war, prejudice, neglect, violence and abuse, moving towards assertion can be a challenge. Some approaches are shared in Chapter 24, The Freedom of Forgiveness.

Communicating with this mindset helps us be productive, control our emotions, and experience empathy. It inspires us to be cooperative when we consider we are not alone in this world. When we recognize we belong to a larger group such as a family, organization or neighbourhood, an assertive point of view reminds us we are only *part* of a community and that others have ideas and needs to be considered.

Assertive people recognize the needs of themselves and others, have a positive self-image, and create healthy boundaries for themselves while respecting the boundaries of others. They consider their own interests and needs to be equally important with those of others.

An assertive setting on the continuum looks like this:

PASSIVE   ASSERTIVE   AGGRESSIVE

SUMMARY

If we come at things from a *passive* mindset, we believe other people have rights but we don't; therefore we do not honour ourselves.

If we come at the world from an *aggressive* mindset, we believe we have rights but others don't and we will not honour or respect them.

When we act from an *assertive* mindset we choose to honour ourselves as well as others. We have a more peaceful countenance and manner. We live and let live. We are able to accept the mistakes we make and feedback from others without being self-critical. We can be kinder to ourselves and others realizing that in most cases, people are doing the best they can do. With this mindset we assume responsibility for our own well-being. We do not belittle others or ourselves. We are happier and can move more easily toward our perfect life.

CHOOSING YOUR PLACE ON THE CONTINUUM

Where are you on the continuum? How does your position influence your communication and relationships with others and your own pursuit of happiness? At a workshop with administrative assistants we discussed the common problem of people standing by their cubicle, talking loudly while the assistant is trying to talk to someone on the phone. "What should I do?" someone asked, "Do I have a right to tell them to be quiet?" My answer is, sure you do! How you say it depends on where you are on the continuum.

If someone is passive, they worry about bothering the talkers, even though the talkers are interrupting them. A passive person will usually cover the receiver with her hand, remain seated and say quietly and apologetically, "I am sorry to bother you, but could you please talk a little more quietly. It is kind of hard to hear this person on the phone." Others may not pay much attention to this passive request.

When the pendulum swings to the other end of the continuum, an aggressive message would be delivered by the admin standing up and yelling, "Hey, would you guys, shut up? I can't even hear myself think let alone the person on the phone! Get out of here!" Although the aggressive approach may clear the office, it does not do much for relationships.

Finally an assertive approach would be for the admin to say to the person on the phone "Excuse me, may I put you on hold for one moment?" Then she would stand up and look directly at the people in front of her cubicle. She would pause and then say (in a firm and strong voice), "Excuse me, would you please move your conversation away from this area? Your talking makes it difficult for me to hear the person on the phone." As they move she could say thanks, sit down and resume the telephone conversation. An assertive approach focuses on one's own needs while respecting others.

Am I a Horrible Person?

If you live your whole life being passive or aggressive, it is probably hard to be you, always coming at things from an extreme. This can make you feel unbalanced. However, it is perfectly normal to move along the continuum, given various situations. Some days when we "get up on the wrong side of the bed" our setting can be near to the passive end and we may think, "Nothing will go right today." Or from an aggressive perspective: "No one is going to get in my way today."

Lift up your heart. — *Yoga instructor*

It is important to know when you are consciously adjusting the setting on your continuum. For example, if you have children, pets or are taking care of an elderly relative, you will be more passive in those situations, because you need to care for others. At those times, their needs and interests *are* more important than yours. (Even in these situations, you need to balance your responsibilities with your own need for self-care, and seek help if you are getting run down.)

There are times when others will be aggressive with you and you may need to become aggressive with them for your own good. Backpacking in Europe after university, I was attacked by a gang who started hitting me and trying to take my possessions. I became aggressive — kicking, punching and eventually running to get away. I would not normally hit anyone; however, I felt threatened — it was either them or me. So I chose to defend myself.

People often ask me: When is it appropriate to be aggressive, other than when your safety is at risk?

My personal bias is to use aggression as a last resort. I do feel myself moving to a more aggressive stance when others are aggressive with me. For example, telemarketers who just keep on talking, even when I have said that I don't have time to talk to them, may find the line going dead.

When people ignore our rights, it is common to engage in a more aggressive manner. For example, if someone assaults us we may call the police and be satisfied if they are charged and forced to deal with the consequences of their aggressive behaviour. In a divorce situation with a former spouse not paying child support, we may involve the courts to force him to honour his obligations.

Be aware that some people may see assertive behaviour as being aggressive if it is behaviour that they are uncomfortable or unfamiliar with. For example, some people would never dream of sharing their opinion at a meeting or asking for a raise. These assertive behaviours can be viewed as aggressive when observed by those with a passive outlook.

Think about how a particular incident may affect your *position on the continuum*. If your boss chews you out and the interaction is a blow to your ego, how likely are you to be aggressive with others because that is what you just experienced? Often the bullied become the bullies.

We don't need to be stuck on the continuum, but rather be aware of where we are and be willing to shift along it as the situation warrants.

Where Can You Start?

In workshops, people often ask when they have a right to say something or do something to tell others that they are crossing boundaries. "I'm not sure if it is my place to say something" is a concern that is regularly shared. All of us have roles. At work we have our job role and the responsibilities that go with it. At work you have the right to be assertive in carrying out your role and responsibilities. If others are infringing on your ability to do your job, or make you feel uncomfortable, it is probably time to be assertive and discuss matters.

At home with our family, as parents and partners, we have the right to communicate and behave in a way that allows us to fulfil our roles as we see fit. As a parent, that may mean setting curfews and expecting our children to contribute to the family.

To give yourself the best odds of successful interactions a great place to start is with an assertive mindset. The benefits include being:

- Able to pursue your own interests and needs

- Open to honouring the rights and interests of others

- Better able to be an effective listener because it allows you to pay attention to what others say without having to agree with them

- More confident in sharing your own point of view

- Better able to deal with life's ups and downs, even laughing at yourself

Your Choice

We all have our own chocolate bar story and have experienced circumstances that left us feeling bad. We do not have to be defined by one single moment or interaction, or by the opinion of one person. Each of us has the ability to *choose* how we see ourselves.

So even though the words of the haters, the doubters, the bullies and the critics echo in our memory we can choose to silence them. Ultimately, it is not how others perceive us or what they say about us. It is what *we* choose to believe about ourselves that will allow us to live abundantly. Choosing to be assertive is one of the most powerful choices that you can make.

EXERCISE: Creating Your Own Perfect World

1) If you encounter a difficult situation, ask yourself: Where am I on the assertion continuum?

2) Is my mindset helping me be effective in this situation?

3) What can I think or do in order to move to where I need to be?

Chapter 3
Our Foundation: Personal Characteristics

It is true that we shall not be able to reach perfection, but
in our struggle toward it we shall strengthen our characters
and give stability to our ideas, so that, while advancing
calmly in the same direction, we shall be rendered
capable of applying the faculties with which we have
been gifted to the best possible account. — *Confucius*

Who Are You?

Sonya is a perfectionist. Her home always looks ready for a photo shoot. Mark has a terrible temper. He does not handle bad news well and tends to lash out at others. Simon is a flirt, quick with a compliment for the ladies. Abe is so dependable you could trust him with your first-born. Felicia is extremely self-centred, always looking for what she can get out of a situation. Dawn is the most hospitable person I know — friendly, welcoming, and the first to offer you a cup of coffee and a warm smile.

Has anyone ever asked you what someone else is like? If so, chances are you have provided some responses like these. When we think of others, we tend to define them by the characteristics they display through their words and actions.

What are *you* like? How would someone describe you? What characteristics are you noted for? You can ask other people what they think about you, or you may possess self-awareness and already understand how others view you and the characteristics that you are noted for. These characteristics go beyond aggression, assertion or passivity.

Our characteristics and talents are not all genetic. As we progress through life, each triumph or trial provides an opportunity for us to develop into the best person we can be. For those who are committed to personal development, this is a conscious process. When we experience a situation, we assess whether it went well or badly. Then we decide what we have learned from the situation and what effect it will have on our future behaviour in a similar situation. This process of living and learning is the essence of character building.

Some people seem to be totally unaware of how they come across to others. They appear not to care, nor do they make adjustments in their behaviour that would benefit their relationships.

Consciously or subconsciously we lay down a foundation of values and ideals that form our character and influence the decisions we make and actions we take.

To be effective communicators and have fulfilling relationships, I believe there are a few vital characteristics we need to cultivate.

CHARACTERISTICS AND VALUES

Here are my top five picks and how I define them:

1) **Patience**

> A boss of mine used to say that stress is the confusion created when one's mind overrides the body's basic desire to choke the living crap out of some jerk that desperately deserves it. Life comes at us so fast today, that it is easy to be stressed and hard to be patient. Patience is the ability to remain calm and even-tempered in situations that could easily make us frustrated. Patience encompasses perseverance and the ability to endure challenging or difficult circumstances. It is a quality that is required to do the things we need to do in order to realize long-term goals. For example, it takes patience to complete a post-secondary degree, raise a child or work on a project with others. When we don't use patience, we lose our temper, "lose it" and lash out at others.

> One day I was waiting at a red light, several cars away from the intersection. The light turned green and the lead vehicle did

not move. Other drivers began to honk, and even rolled down their windows, swearing and yelling at the car to move. They were impatient! The lead car did not move for some time, and a woman from another car finally walked up to the vehicle. What she discovered was that a young mother was in the car and she had not driven forward because her child in the back seat was choking. The mom had turned to assist him. Luckily, the child stopped choking and was fine. It is very easy to be frustrated by anything that takes us away from our own agenda. But what is the cost to us and our relationships when we do not display patience?

Patience is a quality that is required throughout the day as we interact with a variety of people. How often have you had to wait in line for a cashier? How difficult was it to be patient?

It helps to exercise patience with our friends, our family and with people at work who have styles and approaches different from ours. Those who are the most impatient condemn others who do not conform to their beliefs or expectations. Other people are entitled to make choices and do things we would not necessarily do.

Exercising patience means tapping into the practices of tolerance, open-mindedness and fairness. It means quieting one's inner voice and being willing to see things from a different perspective. After all, if we are patient with someone else and their differences, we expect them to be patient with us.

Patience is required as we communicate and connect with others. It takes great patience to listen well, to be fully present and to understand what is meant.

We can't tolerate everyone and everything. It is difficult to be patient when others are infringing on our quality of life at work or at home. Think of the co-worker who takes your lunch without asking. It takes patience to have a discussion with him and ask for a change in behaviour.

People who have patience know it takes time to develop relationships, to solve problems and to rebuild trust when there has been a breach in a relationship. Having patience allows us to think calmly and assess each situation so we can choose well. Saint Augustine suggested patience is the companion of wisdom.

2) **Respect**

Respect is another word that can be defined in many ways. At a basic level, we all have the right to be respected regardless of our wealth, rank, talents or position, because we are human. Being respectful to others means showing them they are valued as human beings. It also means treating others in a way that maintains their self-esteem and does not embarrass, humiliate or judge them. The tricky part about respect is that it is in the eye of the beholder. Respect is a feeling. We know when we feel respected and we know when we feel disrespected.

Our family hired some movers. They worked hard and were clearly exerting themselves. I offered them their choice of water, pop or juice. One worker stopped and said, "Thank you so much for this water. Moving is not only a physically demanding job it is also difficult because I think some people don't even see us as being human. We're like hired mules."

"One day," he continued, "we were doing a move in a 5,000-square-foot house in a wealthy neighbourhood. A neighbour came with a bunch of coffees he'd picked up and didn't offer any to me or my co-workers. Hey, I can buy my own coffee. It's not that. It's just the way this guy looked right through me as if I wasn't there. There was even enough coffee left for us. But it's like we didn't count — as if we didn't matter. It left me feeling disrespected and it made me feel a lot less happy to do the move for those people."

Respect can be conveyed in our tone, our facial expression and the words we choose. One powerful lesson I learned about respect was the first time I did a workshop for a First Nations group. I was making my opening remarks and inviting the group to introduce themselves. When I made eye contact with one man he said to me, "Before we continue, can you please stop looking at me?" He went on to explain that in his culture, direct eye contact is a sign of disrespect.

I said, "Thank you so much for your coaching. I was not aware of that." I went on to say, "From my perspective making eye contact is a sign of respect. So can you tell me what you would prefer me to do when I speak to you?" He said, "Sure, just look away from me. It doesn't really matter where, but I would prefer it if you did not make eye contact."

I knew that just because one particular cultural group — in this case, a First Nations people — subscribes to a belief, it does not mean all members of the group do. So in the interest of respect, I asked them, "Who else would prefer that I don't make eye contact?" A few people put up their hands while others said they felt more comfortable with eye contact. This experience reinforced the principle that to respect people is to treat them how *they* want to be treated. That takes some trial and error and the willingness to learn.

Using manners, addressing people in a tone that is open, choosing neutral words and being mindful of others' possessions and personal space are all elements of respect. Respect is a two-way street: if you want to get it you have to be willing to give it.

3) **Good Judgment**

Throughout this book, I caution against judging others, especially in making negative and critical judgments. But in another context, I see judgment as a skill and practice. Using judgment means that you can look at a situation, analyse the factors, assess and process what you have seen and draw conclusions. From this you can make decisions on short-term and long-term actions. This ability to process and synthesize information and draw conclusions is the skill of judgment. If we cannot assess a situation, it is difficult to put our learning into practice. We will always be looking to others to help us make decisions and decide what course of action is the best.

Every day, we are faced with situations that call for judgment and assessment skills. When my daughter started taking driver education classes, she developed judgment skills in driving. Through trial and error, she learned how to drive at a safe speed, how much room to leave between her car and the vehicle ahead and when to change lanes. She also learned how to judge whether or not a parking spot was the right size.

To be effective communicators and have successful relationships, we need to use similar assessment skills. A woman named Claire mentioned she was once taking a group of potential clients on a tour through her company's facility. This group saw her as an expert in her field. Claire's colleague, John, came up to her and, in front of her prospective clients, said she had made some significant errors in a sales report and she needed to get it corrected as soon as possible.

Claire felt her colleague had shown incredibly poor judgment by giving her feedback at that time. She was okay with getting the information about her report. Her issue was that the feedback should have been given to her privately. The feedback embarrassed her in front of her prospective clients. It may have made them wonder whether she was the most competent person to be showing them the facility and handling their account.

As she assessed the situation, her best judgment was not to pursue a discussion with John in front of the clients. She decided it would be better to talk with him in private, not only to discuss the report, but also to negotiate an agreement to approach her privately in the future.

Good judgment is about saying things and doing things at the appropriate time and place, and with carefully chosen words and tone to give ourselves the best odds of a good outcome. We know that our judgment is effective when the choices we make have positive results. Will Rogers said that good judgment comes from experience, and a lot of that comes from bad judgment.

4) **Sense of Humour**

A sense of humour is our ability to laugh at things that we perceive as funny. A basic sense of humour is being able to laugh at jokes and being able to share funny stories and ideas. An enriched sense of humour is when we are able to recognize the irony in complex situations and, more importantly, to laugh at ourselves. Humour is another attribute that is in the eye of the beholder.

We encounter situations in our lives that can feel very grave. Other situations allow us to rejoice. A sense of fun and a willingness to laugh at our foibles will prevent us from taking situations too seriously.

A wonderful gift our mother instilled in us was a sense of humour. A few years ago, she was diagnosed with dementia. On one hand, there is nothing funny about a slow deterioration of one's abilities. On the other hand, you cannot stop it. All you can do is laugh or cry. Laughing is one strategy and it can help us move forward in difficult situations.

At the onset of her disease, my mother had enough awareness to admit that she was scared about losing her skills and independence. Then she joked that the upside was that at some point she would make a lot of new friends and be able to hide her own Easter eggs!

Humour is the emotion we feel when we appreciate the irony, comedy or positive aspects of a situation. It is not about making a joke at someone else's expense. Cultivating a sense of humour can have a positive impact on our health and physiology. Dr. Lee Berk is a preventative care specialist who has researched the connection between the mind, body and spirit for over 30 years. According to his research, humour associated with mirthful or joyous laughter produces a decrease in detrimental stress hormones such as cortisol and adrenaline impacting our biology at a molecular level. When we reduce these hormones, we improve our immune system. Laughter also helps our bodies produce endorphins, which create a happy and euphoric feeling. Most importantly the brain engaged in humour or mirth produces gamma waves that are associated with improved thought processes, memory, recall and an elevated emotional state. Gamma waves are also produced during meditation. So in times of difficulty, laughing and humour can actually sustain us. Dr. Berk sees humour as part of our brain's hardware that provides a tool for us to use throughout our lives to optimize our health and performance.[4]

I always marvelled how a neighbour, Russ, could turn a child's tears to laughter. When one of his girls stubbed her toe and cried, he would make her laugh by saying, "Oh, oh, we'd better call a "toe-truck!" Having a sense of humour can keep us grounded. Humour also gives other people permission to loosen up and see things from a different perspective.

5) **Graciousness**

The culmination of mastering the other skills with unconscious competence, is achieving a state of grace. When we are gracious we respect others and treat them with dignity. Graciousness allows us to accept and receive what others offer us.

I went to a ninetieth birthday party for a woman, Muriel, who is well regarded in her community. To me, this woman epitomizes grace. She is a thoughtful and patient woman. I have not heard her speak ill of others. The feedback she provides to others is given sparingly, lovingly and only with permission. She treats everyone with respect and courtesy. She speaks about others with a kindness and regard as if they were seated beside her listening to her every word. She is tolerant of others and is always aware that people do what they do because it is what they think is best. She is willing to ask questions of others to learn and understand.

This does not mean that Muriel agrees with everything everyone says. She respects people's free will to choose. If others' actions affect her or infringe on her life, she assertively shares her own perspective to problem-solve collaboratively with them. Her judgment on what to say and how to say it is impeccable. I believe that in 90 years she has learned a thing or two about communicating and maintaining healthy relationships.

Muriel's strength is her loving kindness and regard for others. She believes that everyone has much to offer. She has a willingness to let others do for themselves so that they can learn, grow and understand their abilities.

Her life and behaviour is an example of what one can achieve through one's character. I believe there are many people in our lives who can act as a role model for us. Muriel is one of mine.

SUMMARY

We judge people's values and assess their characteristics by observing their behaviour. I read the book, *To Kill a Mockingbird*, every summer because of the protagonist, Atticus Finch. This character demonstrates values and behaviours that model patience, understanding, fairness, integrity and exceptional judgment. Who are your role models when it comes to behaviour?

The five characteristics shared above are the ones I find to be the most important in terms of influencing my words, actions and behaviour. They provide me with a foundation to interact with others and develop and sustain meaningful relationships.

When I am decision-making and communicating, I consider these qualities and what they embody as a touchstone to guide my actions. Developing these traits and behaving in a way that exhibits them is a way for me to live the expression of my deepest values.

The characteristics I have shared here may be meaningful to you. Because of your life experience, outlook or culture, you may subscribe to other key characteristics that reflect other values.

EXERCISE: Creating Your Own Perfect World

1) What are your top five values or characteristics?

2) What ideas do you have to help you develop them?

3) What characteristics do you possess that get in the way of your most important relationships?

Chapter 4
Choosing a Positive Perspective

In the Greek language, Zoey is the word
for life. — George Poritsanos

The Story of Zoe

Author's Note: The parts of this chapter appearing in italics are quoted from a speech given by Zoe Peckover in December of 2010 at a cancer fund-raiser. Thank you to Zoe for sharing her story. Used with permission.

One of the most common communication problems people mention in workshops is dealing with negative people. We all have an aversion to gripers and complainers who whine about their lives, jobs and circumstances. While we all experience problems and need to vent, there are people who are chronically pessimistic and self-centred, who see the glass as half-empty and seem to enjoy a good moan-fest. Such people suck the very life essence out of us and are difficult to be around. What amazes me is that many people who are negative have so much going for them that it is puzzling why they complain so much.

What about the people who really have something to complain and worry about, yet handle their circumstance with a positive outlook? What can we learn from such people to help us in our own lives and interactions?

Such an example is the case of a young lady named Zoe Peckover. When she was 16 years old, she found herself feeling tired, bruising easily and looking overly pale. Coming from an optimistic family who did not indulge in whining, Zoe's family suggested that she get more sleep and stop "faking sick." Then Zoe became alarmed when she noticed two lumps, one on either side of her neck.

Within a few days, two lumps became eight and Zoe was frightened. Thinking it might be mononucleosis she went to the doctor.

A blood test revealed that her hemoglobin was abnormally low and she needed a transfusion. Her family was notified that she must get to the emergency centre at a major hospital immediately. When they followed the instructions of where to find the recommended doctor, they found themselves in the CK5 Cancer Ward and wondered what was happening.

The doctor broke the news to Zoe, her parents and her aunt.

The news that every parent fears and every teen thinks won't happen to them: *"Zoe, you have cancer, specifically, leukemia."*

I knew that it was serious when my dad and auntie both shed tears, something that I had very rarely seen in my life.

Through tears of my own, I asked the first of many questions: "Am I going to die?"
Just short of a laugh, the doctor replied, "We like to live around here."

That positive remark from the doctor was a game changer for Zoe. She told me that she never forgot what he said. A single, uplifting remark became her anchor and mindset in what was to be a long and gruelling treatment regimen. Although she knew death was a possibility, she never felt afraid or dwelt on the idea. Throughout her treatment, Zoe and her family engaged in four practices consistent with a positive outlook:

1) **Do what you can do to help yourself in the situation**

    Many people, when faced with difficult circumstances, find it challenging to grab the bull by the horns. Zoe said her path was clear; she had no choice but to take the treatment or risk dying.

    The first phase of treatment consisted of ten months of intensive chemotherapy. Zoe's family lives in a rural area about 80 kilometres from the major city and hospital where she was treated. Twice a week she made the long drive to sit in a room in the hospital for hours on end to receive treatment. She endured spinal taps, blood tests, transfusions and bone marrow testing. As Zoe said herself, it is much easier sometimes to be the patient than it is to be the one watching and worrying. She said that her parents were always diligent and present through her treatments.

This first phase brought on increased appetite, water retention and insomnia. I lost my hair and puffed up. Through my illness, I was determined not to let my life slow down and to retain as much normalcy as possible. Despite 76 absences and a failed attempt at pre-calculus in my grade twelve year, I was able to get enough credits to graduate.

Zoe also passed her driver's test. She tried to keep up with the girls on the soccer field. Attempting to maintain a normal schedule sometimes gave way to days where she was incapacitated, as the effects of the treatments took their toll. She was often bedridden, with a bucket for a best friend. Yet she kept on doing what she could every day.

Once Zoe started her maintenance program, her doctor gave her the green light to give hockey a try.

Despite many protests that it was too rough and there were too many germs, I hit the ice literally, and fell flat on my face. I was ready to give up, but teammates, coaches and parents gave much needed encouragement that convinced me to play again.

Many people in Zoe's condition would have put life on hold until they were cured. Zoe lived life as fully as she could throughout her illness. She never let what she couldn't do stop her from doing what she could do.

2) **Find the positive**

Zoe said it was so easy to find the positive in her situation. The initial diagnosis was very optimistic. Her cancer, acute lymphoblastic leukemia, is a highly curable type. The doctor told her she was at higher risk because she was already sixteen when she got the disease; most children who get this cancer do so by age ten. Still, she felt fortunate that she had a curable type of cancer. She also felt very blessed to have such an extraordinary community of family and friends.

Her parents and two siblings were supportive and loving throughout. Her extended family of aunts, uncles and cousins visited her and drove her to hospital appointments. The community helped out in surprising ways. In the first phase of her treatment, more than 25 friends and family members showed their support by shaving their heads and wearing "Zoe bracelets." The money raised from the sale of the bracelets and the efforts of the girls' softball team allowed her to buy a wig.

At Christmastime, her grandma rallied Zoe's large family. Instead of exchanging gifts with one another, more than 50 adults on her dad's side gave Zoe Christmas cards with money enclosed. She was unable to work during much of her illness, so saving for university was difficult and parking at the hospital was expensive. The money so generously shared was a Christmas miracle for her and a testament to the family's love and care.

An Attitude of Gratitude

When everything seems to be going wrong, stop and take some deep breaths and list all the things and people you are grateful for. This positive pause allows you to reflect on what is good. Your blessings can become an anchor and fortify you when things are not going well. — PH

During her last week of intensive treatment, she experienced a severe fever and found out she had viral meningitis. She suffered terrible headaches and had to be hospitalized for six days until the fever broke. By the time she was released, she had a blind spot in her right eye due to the chemo's influence on the meningitis. The bad news was that the blind spot would remain; the good news was that it would not get any worse.

During that horrible week, Zoe's hockey team "blind-sided" her (Zoe's word) with a fund-raising event in her honour. Her girls' hockey team played the old-timers. It was an inspiring experience. Zoe was overwhelmed by the support and love of so many people. She believes that her family's positive approach and the optimistic view of the hospital staff helped her through her illness. That positivity was expressed though a sense of humour she believes helped her more than anything. Her family members all possess a dry wit. One evening, a number of Zoe's and her siblings' friends and acquaintances gathered at the Peckover home. The decision was made to take the gathering to a local bar. Someone asked, "Who will be the designated driver?"

Zoe's sister said, "Don't worry, Zoe has cancer and she sure can't drink. She's our perfect DD!"

The Peckover kids laughed but a visitor in the group glared at Zoe's sister intensely and criticized her for making fun of cancer. He said, "Cancer is something you never joke about!" Zoe's family, however, believes that you have to make light of it because you either laugh or cry at such a life-changing situation. They prefer to laugh.

To Zoe, positive thinking was at the root of her healing. During my interview with her, she constantly said she had *lucked out* with a treatable disease, a loving family and community and the best medical team she could hope for.

The entire family maintained a positive focus with the vision of the celebration party they would have "when this is all over."

3) **Be open to what you can learn**

I asked Zoe what she had learned while she had the disease. She said, "So many things." The hospital gave the family a huge binder that contained information about cancer. The doctor had told her that virtually any question she or her family had would be answered in the binder. She said the binder had space to write down appointments and keep track of information. It helped them manage and make sense of a surreal situation. It gave them a focal point and a touchstone.

She said she learned it is important to keep a healthy mindset. That means *not* doing things that *don't* help you. For example, the doctor recommended that she *not* spend time Googling *cancer*. He said the disease affects each person differently and to obsess and worry about what other people have experienced would not help her. He felt patients could make themselves sicker by worrying about what *might* happen. She stayed away from worrying and obsessing and dealt with what was actually happening right in front of her. The family creed was: *Don't worry about what might happen, just deal with today.* Don't dwell on the negative. Keep moving forward. Zoe said though the diagnosis and the prospect of death were daunting, half the battle was coming to terms with the reality of it. Zoe believes accepting reality made the situation easier to deal with.

She learned we are *never alone*. Throughout her experience, help and comfort came from unexpected places.

For every time I got sick, there was a family member to help me hold my head. For every assignment I missed, there was a friend to catch me up. For every test I missed, there was a teacher to allow it to be written later. For every game in which I fell ill, there was a teammate to help me to the bench. For every hospital night I spent, there were friends and family to keep me company. For each question that I and my family had, there was a doctor or a nurse who could answer it.

One special source of inspiration and support for her were the other children in the cancer ward, who became her friends. Although each person experienced the disease in his or her own way, Zoe said nothing matched talking to someone who was going through the same type of treatment and who was experiencing the same types of side effects, hopes and fears. She and her friends in the ward experienced loss and grief when one of them succumbed to the disease.

Zoe said sometimes we have to give ourselves time to adjust to the situation and to try new things.

I was excited about the wig that I got. However, it turned out to be hot and uncomfortable and I ended up ditching it. I was upset and emotional about having no hair and it was something that I had to learn to deal with. I did come to terms with it and my bald head is forever documented in my graduation picture.

Zoe learned the value of telling it like it is. She appreciated that everyone around her openly communicated about her disease and what was happening. She credits her doctor for always being frank with her and making things easy for her to understand. He shared the treatment plan, risks and test results and didn't hide anything. Being honest and open about the situation made it easier for her to manage. There was no whispering and protecting her. She was fully informed. Honest and open communication helped the whole family deal with it.

4) **Celebrate milestones and transitions**

Once Zoe's cancer was considered to be in remission, the family decided to have a celebration. They booked a local community centre and invited anyone who wanted to come to a potluck dinner. There was live music, decorations, a spirit of togetherness and relief at the good news of her progress.

Zoe's mom made a moving speech to thank all of those people who supported Zoe and the family throughout her illness. For the family, it was a time of celebration and a signal of a new phase in the family's life. The worst was over and the disease did not take front and centre any more.

Zoe said she was torn over the idea of a party and would have preferred to do without it. She felt bad celebrating her own recovery when she had an aunt who was sick with cancer at the time and knew so many others who had died. At the same time, the thought of the celebration was something that had sustained the family in the worst of times and she knew it was important, especially to her mother.

I attended the party and thought it was so lovely that everyone could come together this way. An event that marks a milestone is important. It lets us acknowledge the past, allows us to make a transition and prepare for a new phase in life.

Zoe said her doctor told her repeatedly to live her life. There are many people who have experienced a life-threatening disease who never move forward because they are scarred by what happened to them. They dwell on the past and are afraid to try anything new or different because of the bad experience. Zoe said she was amazed at how powerful the mind is, how it can help us heal or make us sick even when our bodies have healed.

LESSONS FOR US ALL

Zoe is still a happy, healthy, vibrant woman, now in her twenties. She has beautiful blue eyes and an infectious smile. She has not changed much since her illness, although her once wildly curly hair has grown back straighter. For her young age she has experienced more than many people do in a lifetime. She is self-effacing and prefers to see cancer as a past chapter in her life. She does not want to be defined by this one thing. The journey she took with her family is an example of how people faced with a devastating situation can confront it with grace and dignity.

Zoe, her mom, dad, siblings, aunts, uncles, extended family and community are role models for what we *can* do in everyday life: be more patient; seek to learn; see the positive side; do what we can; and embrace the love and support that is all around us.

Zoe said it best: *Life is what you make it. It is a privilege to live it. Some days are really bad, but good days are always on the horizon.*

We will all experience the ups and downs of life. There are days when things go so well, it's as if we are standing on top of a mountain, full of energy and possibility. There are also times when things go very wrong and we are in the bottom of the valley, mired in mud, and we must plough through, one foot in front of the other, until we come up on the other side. Focusing on the opportunities for learning and on the positive ways we can connect with others helps us find our own grace as we navigate the troubles of life.

EXERCISE: Creating Your Own Perfect World

When you experience difficult circumstances, consider how you can use this framework to think through your situation from a positive perspective.

1) **Do what you can do to help yourself in the situation**

   - What productive steps can you take to move forward in this situation?

2) **Find the positive**

   - What is there to be grateful about in this situation or who are you grateful for?

3) **Be open to what you can learn**

   - What have you learned from the situation and circumstances you are experiencing? How can this learning help you or others in the future?

4) **Celebrate milestones and transitions**

   - When this is over or as you transition through it, what are ways you can celebrate or acknowledge the short- and long-term milestones?

PART TWO
The Anatomy of Communication

Communication has parts. My part. Your part.
Our inside thoughts that we keep to ourselves.
The outside parts that we share with others.
Words. Tone. Body language.
Communication works effectively
when we balance these parts. — PH

Chapter 5
Because Cows Eat Grass: Communication Basics

Effective communication connects us, helps us build relationships with others, reduces stress and allows us to achieve goals and results with relative ease. — PH

That's Your Hobby?!

Years ago when I was a rookie facilitator, I worked with a seasoned pro to deliver a workshop to a group of nurses. As planned, my partner opened the workshop. I was totally focused on her, carefully observing her delivery style and technique, but not thinking about contributing anything until my section of the program came up in thirty minutes. Then she surprised me during her introductory comments by saying, "Hey, Pat — why don't you get us started by sharing your name and a hobby that you have, and then we'll rotate around the circle as a way of getting to know each other?"

I was completely blind-sided and a little flustered. I said, "Okay, my name is Pat —" and since I had just begun learning woodworking from my father-in-law and we were crafting small footstools, I said, "— and my hobby is making stools."

I said that to a group of nurses! There was a pregnant pause. They looked at me strangely and then broke into hysterical fits of laughter.

When I realized how they had interpreted "stools," I blurted out, "No, no — I mean, wooden stools!"

That only made them laugh harder and someone said, "Ouch!"

That experience taught me to think about my audience and their point of view before sending a message. Knowing your audience is important when you are communicating to crowds, but it is equally important when you are communicating with individuals.

The vehicle we use to do almost everything in life is communication.

COMMUNICATION BASICS

Although everyone is familiar with at least some of the components of communication, the following section supplies an overview of its basic elements and processes, and pulls them together for a review and reference.

The key concepts include:

- Communication is an interaction between two or more people.

- Effective communication happens when we understand what someone else means and/or they understand what we mean.

- The most effective communication is a two-way process.

- Both or all involved parties share responsibility to ensure the communication is effective and understanding has taken place, the challenge being that the message sent is not always the message received.

- Information is conveyed through words, tone and body language.

- Communication happens through various media including face-to-face interaction, telephone, emails, social media, instant messaging, as well as more traditional methods such as notes, cards and letters.

- We all see things differently because of our frame of reference.

- We communicate not only by what we say and do — our actions — but also by what we *don't* say and do, i.e., when we don't do anything at all.

Effective communication occurs when others understand us and we understand them and are able to share information and feelings. Effective communication connects us, helps us build relationships with others, reduces stress and allows us to achieve goals and results with relative ease. When communication is ineffective, interactions are difficult or draining, people feel stress and other negative emotions and it is difficult to achieve results and have good relationships.

The process of understanding is not always obvious. When my son was four years old, he came downstairs one morning rubbing his eyes, and said with a little pout, "Mommy, you *beat me up!*"

I was dumbfounded at the thought that he would think I would ever harm him. I asked, "Matt, what do you mean?"

He replied, "You got up before me, Mommy. You beat me up!"

As I mentioned, the tricky part about communication is that once the words leave our mouths, they are no longer ours. In order to be effective communicators we need to understand the process and why others do not always understand exactly what we mean.

A Model of the Communication Process

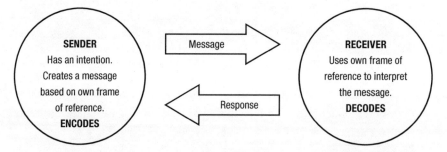

The sender has an intention and sends a message to the receiver. Spoken messages are sent through words, tone and body language. The receiver takes the words, tone, body language and other observations and interprets the meaning of the message.

FRAME OF REFERENCE

One reason we don't always understand one another is we all have our own frame of reference: the accumulation of knowledge, beliefs and information we have acquired in our lifetime. It consists of an abundance of data, including, but not limited to:

- Attitudes
- Beliefs and biases
- Cultural affiliations
- Experiences

- Talents
- Past and present roles
- Professional affiliations
- Self-perception

- Emotions
- Education
- Communication style
- Hobbies

- Values
- Trust
- Interests
- Linguistic skills

We build a frame of reference in our memories just as we accumulate files on our computer hard drive. When we process information as a sender or a receiver, it is our own frame of reference that acts as a sorter or filter through which we attribute meanings to messages we take in. We also access it to encode or formulate messages for others. This frame of reference is what makes the difference in how we encode and send messages and how the receiver decodes or interprets the message.

For example, in a workshop exercise I ask participants what they think of when they hear the word *terminal*. Often someone will respond with "illness." Other responses have included *the end, computers, trains, grain elevators, battery* and even *death*. The reason so many responses arise from one simple question is that each person is accessing his own frame of reference to assign meaning to the word *terminal*.

Because Cows Eat Grass

My friend George, who is of Greek and Trinidadian descent, is married to a woman of Chinese heritage. George told me early on in their marriage he and Cynthia would often disagree. At one point, they both came to the conclusion the other was disagreeing just to be difficult.

Then George came across an article that highlighted research done by Liang-Hwang Chiu, a professor of educational psychology at Indiana University at Kokomo. Professor Chiu tested both Chinese and American children by showing them pictures of three items. In one case, given three pictures — a cow, a chicken, and grass — the children were asked which two items of the three went together. The American children typically grouped the cow and the chicken together because they were both animals.

The Chinese children were more likely to pair cows with grass, because cows *eat* grass. This difference in pairing items arises from what researchers have concluded is a cultural view. The American mindset is one of independence and tends to group items by their similarities. The Chinese view is one of a holistic mindset that looks at the interaction and interdependence of things, thus the connectedness of cows and grass.[5]

It is therefore important to keep in mind that culture plays a huge role in how we send messages and how we interpret information. Culture includes many more elements than just our country of origin or our religious background; it also includes our gender culture and our professional culture and a long list of other affiliations. At the root of my miscommunication with the nurses was their professional culture.

George says now when he and Cynthia see things differently they no longer get frustrated at the discrepancy but savour the richness of their worldviews. They smile because they understand it is all because cows eat grass.

INTERACTING WITH OTHERS

In interactions we are both sender and receiver intermittently and simultaneously. We are constantly sending and receiving data through words, tone and body language. As senders of communication we need to be aware of our own frame of reference and the similarities or differences we have with the receiver, so we can adjust and adapt our message and the delivery of it as necessary. To be the most effective, the sender of a message needs to use the words, tone and body language that will be easily and accurately interpreted in the way we intend by the receiver. As the receiver, we want to check for understanding and accuracy. Understanding the elements of our frame of reference is imperative.

For many of us, our most effective interactions are with people who share a common frame of reference. Think about your best friend or a sibling. Sometimes one look, one word or phrase or gesture is all it takes to convey a wealth of information and context.

The situations where there is the biggest potential for misunderstanding is when we have a frame of reference very different from the person we are communicating with. The most obvious challenge can be when we literally cannot speak the same language. In this circumstance, it is challenging to convey a message.

The key to effective communication is to take the focus off ourselves and our own view and preferences, and focus on the receiver. If we adapt our style and communication to give the receiver the best odds of understanding the message in the way we intend, we create the opportunity to be understood and to get results.

Considerations

- Understand communication is an interactive process.

- Be mindful of the receiver's frame of reference and communication preferences.

- Adapt your style to be more like the receiver's to increase the possibility for understanding.

- Remember it is an imperfect process.

- Be aware of your own frame of reference.

Communication and interpersonal skills go hand in hand, and we will consider other factors and practices to help hone interpersonal skills and make communication as effective as possible.

Key Skills and Characteristics of Effective Communicators

In workshops I have asked hundreds of people, "What skills and characteristics do the most effective communicators possess?" The list of responses includes:

- Is articulate — speaks clearly and concisely

- Is prepared, has thought about the situation

- Doesn't patronize

- Puts me in the driver's seat — asks me what I think

- Uses proper words — ones I understand and are descriptive

- Speaks at the listener's level of understanding

- Respects others and their opinions

- Paraphrases to clarify and confirm

- Uses positive body language — appropriate hand gestures, posture and eye contact

- Doesn't fidget

- Has confidence

- Uses humour when appropriate

- Listens well and effectively

- Asks questions

- Pauses to allow me to process information

- Smiles at people and is polite

- Is open, approachable and non-judgmental

- Is personable and appears comfortable

- Uses the face-to-face medium as much as possible

- Does not use a lot of verbal fillers like "ums" or "uhs"

- Uses proper tone and volume

- Shares information and ideas

- Is calm and patient

This list is a compilation of feedback from all sorts of people in many professions and industries. It is a real-world list of skills that everyday people appreciate and value in the most effective communicators. Before you go any further in this book, do a quick self-assessment to see how you are doing with each skill or characteristic and determine what you are doing well and what you want to work on.

Effective communication takes preparation, awareness and flexibility.

Chapter 6
The Trinity of Talk:
Words, Tone and Body Language

Whatever words we utter should be chosen with
care, for people will hear them and be influenced
by them for good or ill. — *Buddha*

Great Coffee, Bad Karma

One morning I waited with anticipation in the line at a local coffee franchise, excited that I was close to obtaining my first hit of the day of the sweet elixir of life. As I approached the woman at the cash register, my mood was slightly dampened as I noted her angry, unwelcoming face. She said, "What do *you* want?"

Wow, I thought to myself, she seems unfriendly. What happened to the traditional "How may I help you?" and a smile?

Not to be deterred, I placed my order. She held out her hand, so I passed her my credit card. She then shoved the card back at me and said, "Use the machine!"

I had not noticed they had changed their process and equipment. Up until that time the cashier had run the credit card through the machine on her side of the register. Now the machine was situated in front of the register for customer use.

I swiped the card and got an *Error* reading. "You put it in the wrong way!" the woman sneered. "Turn your card around!"

She was practically yelling at me and was staring at me with a look of frustration and impatience.

I said in a very quiet and calm voice, "I don't know if you are having a bad day or what, but I don't appreciate how you are speaking to me. You're talking so loudly people are starting to stare."

I continued, "I am not sure how to use this machine and I have not had the benefit of the training you had. Would it be possible for you to show me what to do?"

She looked slightly embarrassed and held out her hand. She then said, "You turn the card this way, and you have to swipe it fairly quickly."

I did as she'd instructed and the transaction went through.

"Thanks," I said.

She said nothing more. I felt her word choice, tone and body language contributed to a negative interaction.

Face-to-face communication is composed of three basic elements: 1) the words we choose to say, 2) the tone of our voice as we say it, and 3) the body language we reveal. Each of these elements has an impact on how a message is conveyed and understood. So, *how* we say something is as important as *what* we say. To send a message effectively and accurately, we must be aware of this trinity of talk.

Words express the content of our message. The words we choose say much about who we are and what we believe and think. Our tone provides information about our mood, feelings and opinions and what we think of the person we are communicating with. Pace means the speed at which we speak. We choose the volume and how much we inflect or emphasize words or phrases. Pause is an important tool in our effective speaking. Finally, body language gives us cues about a person's feelings and thoughts through facial expressions, eye contact, hand gestures and posture.

CHOOSING OUR WORDS

Words convey the content of our message. The biggest challenge is that we use many words today that people simply don't understand. In a workshop recently some participants had an argument about whether or not "enabling others" was an attribute. Some reasoned that when we enable others, we empower them, giving them the means or the authority to do for themselves. Other people interpreted "enabling others" in the context of addiction, where *enabler* has a negative connotation, because enablers support the addictive behaviour.

Clearly, word meaning is contingent on context and one's frame of reference. The point is that we may take for granted the meaning we understand as the only one that makes sense. It's not so in today's culture, where many words mean the opposite of their common definition. Bad can actually mean good!

Sharing our definition of key words or phrases helps others to understand us more clearly. It also can be helpful to ask others how they interpret certain words.

Know your Audience

Whether you are a manager addressing an executive group to obtain project approval or a hockey coach speaking to the Saturday-morning peewees, it is imperative to keep the recipient of your message in mind and use the words and expressions that will be understood.

Check in with your Audience when using Abbreviations

In today's fast-paced environment we do everything quickly and we like short-cuts. Many people use abbreviations and Three-Letter Acronyms (TLAs) in their communication. While this practice is widely accepted, it is wise to check with the audience to ensure they subscribe to the same definition you do.

Bridge Idioms across Generations

We all use the colloquial language of our era in our communications. The veteran and boomer generations, notably, use certain idioms — "The early bird catches the worm," for example — that have meaning to the user but baffle the receiver who has not grown up with them. The biggest gap in communication regarding idioms is between baby-boomers (people born in the two decades following the end of WWII) and subsequent generations. It is not obvious to everyone that "putting your foot in your mouth" is not actually referring to a show of amazing dexterity, but rather that you regret something you said. Similarly, new words have evolved out of the social media phenomenon. *Life-hacking* isn't someone wrecking your life, it is a tip that if applied can provide a short cut or create an improvement. The challenge is for people of different generations or cultures to share the meaning of words and ask for clarification.

Use Words to Express Meaning

Words don't just express meaning; they express our feelings. My son spent several years playing hockey and I got to know the other hockey parents like family. One Saturday the boys were playing in a tournament far across the city during a blizzard. As I was waiting to watch the boys play, after a harrowing drive to the rink, one of the moms came up to me very distressed. She had driven her hockey-player son and her two younger children to the rink in the storm. Before she'd left home, her husband had cautioned her, "Don't drive like an idiot." The comment stung her. She said sarcastically, "Of course, my first instinct was to floor it and try to get us killed!" His remark left her upset. I believe he said what he did because he was worried about her and the safety of their children. Imagine the difference if he had said, "Honey, please drive carefully — you are all precious cargo."

Every word we choose conveys a meaning. If someone likes to save money, we could say he is frugal, cheap, cautious or disciplined. The word we choose to describe things says more about us than it does about the other person. Using neutral words that are nonjudgmental is more effective in a conversation.

In my encounter at the coffee shop, the cashier chose words — "What do *you* want?" — that expressed her mood. Perhaps she was frustrated with having to deal with many customers who did not know how to operate the machine. By using negative and uninviting words, she tainted her interactions the second she got started. Choosing to say, "How may I help you?" would have been more inviting and appropriate.

Ask yourself when you choose words, are you really focusing on your interaction with the person or are you letting your own mood and thoughts leak out?

Be Aware of Trigger Words

Trigger words are words that stimulate someone's anger response. Effective communicators try to avoid this. People do not do their best when they are angry. One of the trigger words that most people agree creates a breakdown in communication is the word *but*. If you listen to someone and then respond with, "Yes…BUT…" it is like discounting everything they just talked about. Instead of using "but", share your opinion without the word.

Another phrase that can create problems is "You are confusing me," which blames the other person. A better choice would be "I am confused," which takes responsibility for one's own situation. Other words that create problems are *can't, won't, should* or *shouldn't*.

Tips on Words:

- Choose your words carefully with the receiver in mind.

- Don't make assumptions about how your audience is interpreting the word — check it out.

Considerations:

- Think about the interactions that you have with others that don't go well. What specific words do they use that you find unhelpful or offensive?

- What specific words do you use with others that do not express what you really mean, or convey information in a way that is not productive?

TONE TALK

When people talk, their tone conveys a feeling that affects how others interpret and react to the message.

Often people will comment on an interaction they didn't like and say, "I didn't appreciate his tone." We prefer communication that has a pleasant, positive, open and nonjudgmental tone. When someone has a negative tone, which can be judgmental, angry, accusatory, questioning, stressed out or exasperated, we tend to react to the tone rather than listen to the content.

Para-Verbals

Tone is more than a positive or negative sound. Para-verbals or paralinguistics refers to the *way* words are said. Tone is conveyed through four elements:

1) **Volume**

   Some people are quiet talkers and some are loud talkers. When people are quiet, it can be difficult to hear what they are saying. Similarly some people speak so loudly it is intrusive to those around them. Some people crank up the volume when they are on the telephone and everyone nearby can hear them. When people around us whisper, we pay attention because they may be saying something important or confidential.

Many people have almost pre-set volume controls. I worked with a man who had a very quiet and calm demeanour. He couldn't understand why people didn't take his advice. Then he related a story from when he was sharing a house with a number of roommates and there was a fire in the house. He calmly walked from room to room, knocking on people's doors and calmly saying, "Better get out — there's a fire." He was so calm and quiet, his roommates thought he was joking because *they* would have yelled at the top of their voice, "GET OUT OF HERE, THERE'S A FIRE! R-U-U-U-N!!"

Tips:

- Be aware your volume impacts the meaning of your message.

- Use appropriate volume for your audience/receiver so they can hear you.

- Adjust your own volume, trying not to disturb others who don't need to hear your message.

2) **Pace**

Pace is the speed at which we deliver a message. How quickly someone speaks conveys meaning. If someone speaks slowly most people would say the speaker is not excited or doesn't have much energy. Sometimes people speak so quickly it is hard to keep up with them.

People who speak quickly may be excited to share what they have to say. We tend to speak quickly when we are frustrated, stressed or angry. Pace is also affected by the complexity of what we are conveying, our culture and the type of communicating we are doing. For example, normal conversation falls in the range of 110 to 140 words per minute while an auctioneer may exceed 200 words per minute. Pace needs to be a measured part of the communication.

3) **Pause**

Have you ever had a conversation with someone who talked non-stop and you wondered if they actually breathed through their ears because they never stopped to inhale? Pausing allows others to absorb and reflect on what is said and provides a natural pivot point for the conversation to turn over to the other party. Pausing allows for a moment of silence where processing can happen. Pausing is another element that we can adjust as appropriate in a conversation.

It is imperative to be open to pauses when we are on the listening end of someone's communication. Without pauses, we cannot absorb and comprehend information.

4) **Intonation**

Intonation is the inflection we use in our communication. If we speak in a monotone it means we are not using inflection. Listening to a monotone speaker can be boring and can make concentrating difficult. It is also challenging to interpret what is really important and what is not when everything is expressed with the same level of emphasis.

To be effective, we need to use a style that supports the message we are sending. If you are telling someone that they did a great job, you want your tone to be positive and upbeat, your pace to be quick and your inflection to emphasize the important words.

The importance of intonation is that it can change the meaning of the message. For example, say these sentences out loud emphasizing the word that is in bold type. As you say these sentences, note how it changes the meaning of the sentence.

- Yes, I *really* value Bob's opinion.

- Yes, *I* really value Bob's opinion.

- Yes, I really value **Bob's** opinion.

One of the most notable problems related to tone is the audible sigh. Many people use it consciously or subconsciously when they do not believe what someone is saying, or when they are in disagreement or disbelief. Sighs can also show impatience. Be careful about sighing, as it is perceived as negative. A sigh can be positive when it is a sigh of relief.

Tip:

Remember that tone conveys meaning. Make sure your tone is communicating what you want it to.

BODY LANGUAGE

Body language is what we do with our body as we communicate. As I wait in my car at traffic lights, I have the opportunity to observe people on the sidewalks. Even though I cannot hear what they are saying, I can deduce what is happening by the way they are positioned and their proximity to each other, by observing their facial expressions and by what they are doing with their bodies. You can assume that a pair is more than just pals because they are holding hands as they cross the street.

Whatever we are thinking tends to be reflected subconsciously through our body language. It is only through practice that we can control the natural tendencies of our body to reflect what we are thinking.

Common Signals

Your face is your billboard. Eighty percent of body language comes from our facial expression.

We say so much before we ever utter a word. As we approach other people to have a conversation, they are already looking at our facial expression, assessing our mood and making assumptions about our message. In my workshops participants tell me the most effective communicators have a neutral or pleasant facial expression. People comment they tend to shy away from people who have angry or stressed-out facial expressions.

Across all cultures, people share the facial expressions of happiness, surprise, disgust, anger, fear and sadness.

Eye Contact and Facial Expressions

In European-North American cultures, we expect people to make eye contact with us up to six times a minute. Effective eye contact depends on how well you know someone and what is appropriate culturally.

In workshops, participants have commented on the facial expressions they notice the most.

Facial Gestures:	Common Interpretation:
Rolling of the eyes	disagreement, disapproval, disbelief
No eye contact	disinterest, not paying attention
Frown	displeased, unhappy, angry, concentrating, stressed
Smile	open, friendly, happy
Raised eyebrows	surprised

Body Gestures

Body language conveys a message. How we place our hands, legs, and the proximity that we stand to one another, all have meaning.

Gesture:	Common Interpretation:
Pointing finger	lecturing, scolding, bossy
Hands on hips	authoritarian, bossy
Crossed arms	closed to the message or to change, unhappy
Hugging another	affection, support, closeness of relationship
Shaking hands using both hands	shows special affection, respect, or warmth, a little less formal than a regular handshake

Proximity to Others

Most people do not want us in their personal space. Our personal space extends around us in a circle that is the distance of our arm extended fully in front of us; in other words, comfortable hearing range. Only loved ones or friends are normally welcomed into our personal space. When we are communicating it is helpful to be on the same spatial level as the other person. For example, if the person with whom you are speaking is sitting, it is better to sit beside them rather than stand. Sitting on the same side of a desk or table as the other person is more welcoming than having a desk or other barrier between you. Appropriate proximity and body language varies from culture to culture. I enjoy my Latin friends who have a smaller personal bubble then North Americans. They welcome others into their personal space.

Our Physical Appearance

On top of everything, we notice people's appearance. Appearance includes everything from haircut to clothing, jewellery and accessories, birthmarks, tattoos and shoes. Appearance is related to body language. It will be interpreted by other people. Considerations of appearance:

- Are you dressed appropriately for a situation or occasion?

- What are your clothing, hairstyle, tattoos and make-up saying about you?

- Have you thought about your appearance and how others may interpret it?

- Is your appearance conveying what you intend?

Emoticons

A further testament to the importance of *how* words are said and their intended meaning is the use of emoticons. *Emotion* plus *icon* have been merged to create a word to describe a graphic representation of a facial expression. The smiley face is the first of such representations. Emoticons are commonly used in electronic communication because words alone, without any tone or body language, can be misinterpreted depending on who is reading them. :) or : (can convey the emotional intent associated with a message. Further, we now often use abbreviations to describe our emotional intent, such as "LOL" (laughing out loud) or "JK" (just kidding).

PUTTING IT ALL TOGETHER

When our words, tone and body language are consistent, people will tend to believe our message. If our words are saying one thing and our tone and body language are saying something else, people will not believe our words but our body language and tone. When there are inconsistencies, it is usually feelings and attitudes that are leaking out, distorting the meaning of our message.

For example, when you walk into a store and a salesperson slumps and says flatly and unenthusiastically, "How can I help you?" one tends to think that he probably can't, because from his tone, it seems as though he really doesn't want to help and is annoyed by the intrusion. If he says, "How can I help you?" with a smile and an enthusiastic tone, we will believe that he is ready and willing to assist.

Tips for Effective Communication:

- Whatever you think in your inner voice will leak out in your tone and body language unless you manage it.

- What you say matters — so choose effective and appropriate words that people will understand.

- How you say something influences the message — so use a positive and appropriate tone and speed.

- Does your appearance convey what you intend?

Chapter 7
Two Realms: Inside and Out

What a wee little part of a person's life are his acts
and his words! His real life is led in his head, and
is known to none but himself. — *Mark Twain*

The Line Up

One day my daughter and I were shopping in a clothing store. The clerk was frantic because she was not only acting as cashier, but she was letting people into change rooms and answering the phone. Because there was only one clerk the line to pay was slow. A woman standing behind us suddenly asked, "Can I go ahead of you?"

My daughter and I were surprised. We wondered why she thought she should go ahead of us. Did she feel she was entitled because she was older than us? Was she feeling ill or at the end of her patience? We didn't know and she didn't tell us. This led to all of us feeling a little uncomfortable and there was an awkward pause.

Often during our interactions with others, we do not share what we think in our heads. Nor do we inquire what the other person is thinking. When we do not share information we run into misunderstandings and conflict.

Finally my daughter asked, "Why?"

The woman explained that she was volunteering at a cancer ward and had to catch a bus within ten minutes, so she was hoping to go first. Of course we let her go before us.

THE PUBLIC AND THE PRIVATE
SIDES OF COMMUNICATION

Communication has its own anatomy. There are parts we can see and parts that are hidden. What we think in our head is our private realm. The outside part is the public realm. This realm consists of information that is available to all, and in an interaction, it includes the things that are said and done that others can observe. The public realm exists outside of our own minds and can be shared. Lorella DePieri first introduced the concept of realms to me.[6]

Private Realm

The private realm is our "inner voice," a dialogue of our own thinking and processing, our own feelings, opinions and interests that we keep to ourselves. After we observe things, we formulate what we choose to communicate to others, concealing our thoughts until we are ready to share them. Only someone like *Star Trek's* Spock could determine others' thoughts without being told.

Our thoughts are formed in our inner voice. We process our observations and interpret the world and others in our own silence and privacy. No one will ever know for certain what we think until we release the information from our thoughts and share it in the public realm.

Public Realm

The public realm exists outside our own minds. It includes the observable elements such as what we say and do in front of others, the words we choose, our body language and our tone. It also includes the things that we do *not* say and do *not* do. For example, if my phone rings, I may not pick it up because I want to finish something I'm doing. In that case, my action was *not to answer the phone*. If I say good morning to someone, for reasons unknown to me he may not reply. These non-actions are also noticed. This visible part of communication is known as the *public realm* where things are said and done that can be interpreted by others who are observing us. People tend to notice what we say and do, and what we *don't* say and *don't* do, and interpret our words and actions based on their frame of reference.

The public realm is the area of communication that includes other people. Simply put, once you open your mouth and speak, or share information on the Internet, or walk through a store, you are putting information out into the public realm. Any time you have a conversation in your workspace, in a meeting, in the cafeteria, in an airport, at a party, in a store, at the club or at school you are in the public realm. Facebooking, blogging, and other online formats are public. Any time you are out amongst other people or sharing information electronically you have entered the public realm and are putting information out for others to consume.

The challenge of communication is that so much is hidden. If we don't share information from our own private realm to the public realm, effective communication cannot happen, and that's where we run into problems.

We can be most effective in our communication when we close the gap and share what is in our thoughts. Our opportunity is to make our hidden thoughts public so that others can understand us. We need to encourage others to share their thoughts so we can understand them.

Here is a diagram showing the public realm and private realm in an interaction between two people:

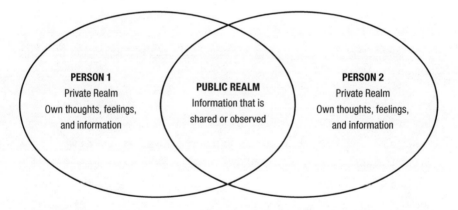

ASSUMPTIONS

When we keep private information to ourselves, we force others to act on their assumptions about what *they* think *we* mean or expect. An assumption is a point of view or a piece of information we take as accurate without having verified it.

For example, my friend, Laura, said she would send me an email letting me know about an upcoming function, in the event I wanted to attend. She said she would send it that day. I waited for a couple of days and still had not received it. I did not want to hound her, but I knew the event was coming soon. Finally, after two days, I called her to check in. Laura said, "I've been waiting for you to reply to my email for three days! What's up?"

I said, "I didn't receive your email and was just following up, as the event is close."

Laura: "But that's crazy! I sent it...oh...wait...here it is, still in my draft basket. Oops — my bad! Can you come?"

In this interaction, I assumed Laura didn't have time to send the message and she assumed she had sent it and I was slow to respond. It is important to share our private thoughts with the other person to clarify our assumptions.

We assume so many things: why people do what they do; how people will interpret things; when people will agree or disagree with us.

THE HIDDEN PARTS

We have the right to keep information to ourselves. However, when we don't share certain information, it creates a gap in understanding with others that leads to misunderstandings and conflict. This leads to a breakdown in our personal and professional relationships.

As a mediator who has helped people work through their differences for two decades, I have seen the disastrous effectives of not sharing what we think. Therefore I maintain there are three types of information that are the most crucial to share with others. They are *expectations, intentions* and *effects*.

1) **Expectations**

    One big problem I have observed as a mediator is that people don't usually talk about expectations until someone has breached them. In every relationship we have expectations of others and we believe others should live up to them. When they don't we get angry or disappointed. Then the fight begins with, "Why did you do that? You were supposed to…"

    Expectations are the beliefs we have about what should happen. Our expectations are what *we* think is proper or improper, right or wrong. We judge others' behaviour based on our own frame of reference.

The bottom line is if you want others to live up to your expectations, then you need to let them know what your expectations are. That means telling people what is on your mind.

The other consideration about expectations is just because we communicate them to another person doesn't mean they will be fulfilled. Sometimes people disagree with our expectations and will not comply. There are then two parts to communicating about expectations: a) what *you* think they are, and then b) negotiating with the other person to get his agreement.

If we don't discuss expectations, lots of problems can occur. For example, what expectations do you have of a spouse? I have seen disputes when a couple was fighting because she went out and bought a brand new car without consulting him. He was upset because he expected to be consulted. He felt it was an implied "no brainer" that any major purchase would be a joint decision. She felt she was making her own money and she didn't have to answer to anyone. This is just one example of very different expectations that create disharmony.

Another couple met online. He lived in the United States. She lived in Canada. They had a lovely wedding in the United States but two months after the honeymoon they couldn't agree on where to live so they broke up. It seems incredible they did not talk about where they were going to live before they got married. Each had simply expected the other one to move to his or her home.

In a marriage there are a number of expectations to discuss. Will both spouses work? What about children? How many? Who looks after them? Who cooks, cleans and does house maintenance? Who pays what bills? Who hosts family meals? What about vacations? How do you show your love and appreciation to each other? The list is endless. But working through expectations is critical to having a healthy relationship.

Likewise at home it is important to work out expectations with your children. I used to tell my kids that I expected them to keep things clean. However, their idea of clean and mine were different. So, we wrote out a sheet listing expectations of what "clean" meant and taped it on the cupboard just for clarity. These included:

- If you take something and use it, put it back so others can find it later.

- Clean up after yourself (put dishes in the dishwasher, wipe counters and put food away).

- We expect everyone home for dinner; if you are not going to be home, let us know and tell us where you are.

- If you are going out, let us know where you are going and who you are going to be with.

Take every opportunity to discuss expectations with your children regarding home, chores, friends, manners, cell phones, school and extracurricular activities.

What expectations do you have in the workplace of your boss and co-workers? What do they expect from you? At work, it is imperative to discuss performance expectations. What targets are we shooting for? By when? With what resources? Who is responsible for what? How often do you discuss expectations with others? What processes do you have set up to do so?

Leaders in organizations will often ask me, "How do you get people to meet expectations?" and they tell me about someone who disappointed them. Then I ask, "How did that person know what your expectations were?" The answer is often, "Well, any professional should know what I expect because it's obvious." In my view it is necessary to have a conversation about expectations. We need to tell others what we expect and check for their understanding. After a conversation, we can document details and specifics to highlight what was agreed to so that there is a written record.

In many workplaces, people rely solely on one-way emails, guidelines, methodologies, processes or policy and procedure manuals to clarify expectations. Even if expectations are in writing, we can't automatically assume people are going to follow them or understand them just because they are written down. If you want people to follow processes, specifications or guidelines, make sure you verbally highlight these items. Check in with them and give them a chance to ask any questions they may have.

Written contracts are the ultimate attempt to clarify expectations. When agreements last over a long term it makes sense to document expectations and obligations in a written contract. Such contracts are common in the business world. Some couples about to wed enter into prenuptial agreements.

The best part of writing up any agreement is not just having things in writing. The real opportunity is the process of having a discussion to understand each person's point of view. For example, writing a prenuptial agreement provides a catalyst to air issues that may not be very enjoyable to discuss. However, I believe that it is better to discuss such items when you are feeling good about each other and have time to process it, rather than waiting until problems arise.

Tips about Expectations:

- Share your expectations with others.

- Ask for agreement and be prepared to discuss, negotiate or modify your expectations in light of the other person's perspective.

- Ask other people to clarify their expectations if you don't know what they want, or just to confirm your understanding, using the following key phrases:

- What is your expectation regarding this situation?

- What specifically would you like to see as an outcome?

- So if I understand you correctly, your expectation is…

- It is unrealistic to think we can ever clarify every expectation up front, so when someone does not live up to your expectations, see it as an opportunity to clarify things for the future.

2) **Intentions**

Intention refers to our purpose when we interact with others. Our intentions explain why we do or say certain things or why we have decided *not* to say or do certain things. When we have an intention, we have given forethought to what we would like to see happen. All too often we get into the content of our message without letting others know why we want to have the conversation.

One way to avoid misunderstanding is to be clear about our intentions. The best drivers share their intentions by using their signal and brake lights. When you are driving, it helps other drivers if you signal before changing lanes. The flashing signal light gives other drivers information about your intention to change lanes before you do it and it gives them time to adjust their speed and leave room for you to make the change. Similarly, tapping the brakes alerts the driver behind you to reduce speed. When you don't use signals it makes people angry because there is no warning.

Telling others our intention when we are communicating is like using our signal lights when we are driving. It alerts the other person about where we are trying to go in the conversation. It helps the receiver of the message understand why we are communicating. It gives them time to get prepared for our message and adjust to receive it. It also gives them better odds of understanding the message in the way we intend. For example, if the lady in the line-up at the beginning of the chapter had said she needed to pay for her items quickly to catch a bus for a volunteer slot — we would easily have understood her and obliged.

A workshop participant, Judy, said one Thursday evening she was sitting at home thinking how much fun it would be to go out on Friday night. Soon her sister-in-law's number appeared on her cell phone on an incoming call. Judy was excited. She thought, "Great, she is phoning to go out tomorrow!"

Her sister in law, Maggie, said, "Hi! How are you?"

Judy responded, "Great!"

Maggie asked, "Hey, are you busy tomorrow night?"

Judy said, "No!"

(Judy was waiting for Maggie to tell her where they would go for Friday night drinks.)

Instead, Maggie said, "Good! Bob and I are going out tomorrow, and since you're not doing anything, we would like you to babysit the kids."

"Oh…" Judy replied, deflated.

Judy agreed to babysit, but she felt she had been set up because Maggie had not been clear about her intention. Judy felt that she had been manipulated into babysitting and it undermined her trust in Maggie.

Judy would have preferred it if the conversation had gone something like this:

Judy's cell phone rings and she sees on her call display that it is her sister-in-law Maggie.

Judy: Hello!

Maggie: Hi, how are you tonight?

Judy: Great!

Maggie: I am phoning because I have a favour to ask. (This is an example of being clear about her intention). Bob and I are going out tomorrow night and we are wondering if you are available to look after the kids for us.

Judy: Oh, so you need a sitter. (She realizes that Maggie isn't calling to arrange for a fun night out together.) Well, I'm not doing anything, so I would be happy to do it this time.

Maggie: Thank you! It's a big help.

By sharing her intention up front, Maggie gave Judy a chance to adjust her thinking and prepare for the request. In this case Judy decided to say yes from an assertive point of view rather than feeling she had been manipulated.

Being clear about our intention gives the receiver of the message a better chance of understanding what we mean. In our quest to communicate effectively, how much better would our interactions go if we were clear about our intentions?

As well, it is fair in situations where someone requests a favour or wants us to perform a task outside our normal role to ask for time to think about the request before we answer. In that case, "Can I think about this and call you back in a half hour or so?" is a reasonable response.

Think about how you communicate with your colleagues. Sharing your intention about why you are communicating with them before you get into the details is comparable to using your signal lights in traffic. Here are some examples of intentions with others at work and how we could express that intention:

Examples:

- **To share information:** I am sharing this information because it will affect how you do your job and it will help you complete your work items more quickly.

- **To train someone:** I have set up this time to take you through a new process that we will be implementing so that you will be able to do it well.

- **To ask for help:** I am stopping by because I would appreciate your help.

- **To get approval:** I am giving you this analysis because I would like to get approval to proceed with this project.

- **To fix problems:** We are all aware that our project did not go according to the plan. My intention in this meeting is not to attribute blame. It is simply to hear your experience and highlight lessons learned so we can avoid situations like this in the future.

Our Intentions When Communicating at Home

With all the demands on us at work and home, we often forget to share our intentions with family members and jump into conversations without letting people know why we are speaking with them. Look at the difference in these exchanges when we don't share our intentions.

> *Situation: A husband and wife, Sharon and Dennis, are having a chat after dinner. At her work, Sharon has been putting in a lot of overtime hours at month-end, and today is the last week of the month.*

Conversation with No Intention:

Dennis: What time will you be home tomorrow night?

Sharon: I don't know. It's month-end and I will probably have to work overtime. (She is thinking he is going to get on her case about working late.) I wish you wouldn't get on my back about that. I have to do my share to keep my job.

Dennis: Hey, I was just asking. No need to get uptight.

Same Situation with use of Intention:

Dennis: I'll be home in good time tomorrow night and can easily make supper. I'm wondering what time you'll be home, as I can either make a later supper, or put a plate away in the fridge for you.

Sharon: I'm not sure what time I'll be home because I may have to work overtime. I should know by noon tomorrow. How about I text you and let you know?

Dennis: That would be great.

Some intentions we might have at home and how we could express them:

- **Sharing information:** I would like to tell you some information about my schedule that will affect my ability to make meals this week.

- **Requesting help:** I would like to talk to you because I need your help.

- **Getting advice:** I would like to talk to you because I have a problem and I would like to get your opinion on what I could do to solve it.

- **Getting support:** I had a big fight with a co-worker today. I want you to listen to me vent without trying to solve it.

- **Sharing some time:** I would like to spend some time with you relaxing and not thinking about responsibilities for a while.

- **Problem solving:** I would like to talk to you about some ideas on what we could do to care for your Mom.

Think about how much clearer some conversations would be if they were opened with a statement of an intention.

Clarifying Intentions:

It is a powerful practice to clarify our intentions so people understand our words and actions in a way that is accurate. In workshops, participants who have to leave early will often say, "Just to let you know, I have to leave fifteen minutes early to pick up my child from day care. I am sorry to disrupt the class and I wanted you to know why I am leaving so you don't think I didn't enjoy the workshop." Other times I have had participants say, "Please excuse me if I don't say much today. It isn't that I don't like the course content, it's because I'm not feeling well." Again, clarifying intentions helps us interpret information and situations more accurately.

I have seen many emails that begin with, *"This is a friendly reminder..."* This line shows the intention that the information is sent simply as a reminder and not to chastise anyone.

Understanding Our Own Intentions

Before you communicate, do some reflecting and ask yourself, "Why am I engaging in this conversation?" As human beings we can do things for positive reasons and sometimes we can do things for negative reasons. In other words, we can have good intentions or bad intentions. Often we share information to help someone or develop a better relationship, but there are times where we do things that are not so helpful. For example, have you ever heard someone say, "I'm going to show them who's boss!" Sometimes we intentionally embarrass people, call them out, insult them or even hurt them. When we have negative intentions, the communication we are about to engage in will lead to difficulties with the other person. Really think about your own intention before you do something that may damage a relationship.

Tips about Intentions:

Ask yourself...

- What is my intention?

- What do I hope will be the result of this interaction?

- How can I express my intention to the other person so he has a good chance of understanding me? A helpful guideline to prepare to share your intention with others is using these key phrases:

- ○ The reason I want to talk to you is ...

- ○ I would like to share some information in order to ...

- ○ I want to spend a couple minutes discussing ... because ...

- ○ I'd like to spend some time ...

- When you are unsure why someone is saying or doing something, consider the following root phrases to invite them to share their thoughts:

    - ○ Can you help me understand your intention?

    - ○ What is your intention in saying/doing this?

    - ○ Can you help me understand why you are taking this approach?

    - ○ Why are you telling me this (or sharing this information)?

3) **Effect**

Has someone ever said something to you that made you mad or caused you to be stressed out? Or maybe what someone said made you feel happy and loved. Effect in communication refers to how we interpret information and the feeling we are left with after an interaction. It describes the impact the meaning we have interpreted has had on us. We experience an effect based on what we have observed and heard and the conclusions we have drawn about the information we have processed.

The interactions we have with people can leave them feeling good or bad, happy, sad, joyous or excited; there are an unlimited number of ways people can be affected. How we feel is up to us. We are the ones processing and interpreting information and we choose how to feel and be affected by a situation. Sometimes our choice of how to interpret information can have a profound impact on others and our relationship with them.

One of our friends, Ben, has two children who share a car. One day, Justin was driving the car and got T-boned at an intersection by a driver running a red light. Justin was fine, but the car needed an extreme makeover. Ben got the car fixed and a couple weeks later his daughter Bethany came out of a store and into the parking lot only to find that someone had backed into the car and seriously damaged it.

Bethany was very reluctant to tell her dad. She thought he would be upset because he had *just* got the car repaired. Their exchange went like this:

Bethany: Dad, I have something I need to tell you that you won't like very much.

Ben: What is it, Beth?

Bethany: I was shopping at the mall and when I came out I noticed someone had hit the car. It looks like they backed right into the front and the bumper, light and fender are damaged. I am so sorry, Dad!

Ben: Well, are you okay?

Bethany: Yes, I am.

Ben: That's all that matters, that you are fine. Cars can be fixed. Don't worry about it.

Bethany: Thanks, Dad!

Bethany was relieved her father wasn't angry. She was worried the news of the car being damaged again would anger him. He interpreted the information with a mindset that cars are easy to fix and kids are not.

How we interpret information will have an impact on the other person and our relationship. Ben's response showed he loved and cared for his children and it increased trust about sharing future information, good or bad.

Keeping Things Hidden

Consider this exchange between a dating couple:

She walks by him and sits down and lets out a big sigh.

He asks, "What's wrong?"

She, sighing again, tersely replies, "Nothing," and rolls her eyes.

He says, "No seriously, what's wrong? Obviously, you're not happy. What can I do?"

She says, "Well if you don't know, I am certainly not going to tell you!"

Reflecting on this scenario, it certainly seems something is wrong, but she is not going to tell him. Hints, innuendo and negative body language signal something is wrong but it only makes things uncomfortable. It is not clear enough to help solve the problem. This is a good example of when it is destructive to keep our hidden thoughts to ourselves. It seems "he" has either done something wrong or neglected to do something she expected. If you have been negatively impacted by another person's actions, don't make them guess. Tell them what is concerning you so they can address it. Blaming someone for not being able to read your mind is not productive.

Here is an exchange where she tries a more direct and productive approach to share her intentions and the effect he has had on her:

She says, "Honey, I am not sure if you are aware of it, but you did something the other day that made me feel very frustrated and I would like to talk to you about it."

He says, "Yikes, what is it?"

She says hesitantly, "I started dieting two weeks ago but every time you come over you bring donuts. You know I like them and it's hard for me to resist them and makes me fail at my diet. I don't know why you do that."

He says, "Oh wow! I only bring them because you like them. I am just trying to do things you like. Now that I know that you don't want them around I won't bring them anymore. Thanks for telling me."

She affirms, "Thanks, that would help a lot."

Considerations about Effects:

- Recognize you are the one putting meaning to what has been said or done by another person.

- If someone's action has negatively affected you, explain to him or her how it affected you. See it as an opportunity to have a discussion about it and improve the relationship. If you do not share how you feel, the other person will not know.

- People may not interpret things the way you intend.

When to Keep the Inner Voice Quiet

There are times when our private thoughts are best kept to ourselves. Unkind or disrespectful remarks such as insults, threats, criticisms or attacks are best left unsaid. We have all heard someone say something inappropriate and then say, "*Oops, did I just say that out loud*?" When we say negative things it undermines our relationships and makes others feel bad.

SUMMARY

- There is a private side and a public side to communicating.

- At times, there is a gap between the private and the public, causing miscommunication.

- Sharing certain private elements such as expectations, intentions and effects, helps others understand us. This fosters trust and strengthens the relationship.

- When in doubt, share your interpretation of what was said with the person who said it. This allows the speaker to clarify his intention. What you interpreted may not be what the speaker intended.

Tips for Applying Ideas to Your Own Perfect World:

- When you are communicating, think about what your intention is and how you will explain it to the person you are talking to *before* you jump into the content of your message.

- When you are on the listening end of a conversation and you are unsure about what someone is saying or why they are saying it, help encourage effective communication by asking, "What is your intention in this conversation?" or "Why are you asking that question?" With this type of approach you can help the sender to be more explicit about their private information.

- Remember you are keeping some information to yourself and so is the other person.

- Check out the meaning with the other person to ensure clarity.

Chapter 8
Conversation Preparation Checklist

If you fail to plan, you plan to fail. — Benjamin Franklin

Sonya, a healthy 94-year-old, made an interesting choice in preparing for old age. When she was 80, she noticed several of her contemporaries were succumbing to the plight of falling and not being able to get up. She did not want to experience this problem, so she began lowering herself to the floor twice a day and then getting up safely. This activity strengthened her muscles, gave her practice and increased her confidence to manage a potential problem. She was investing in preparedness.

If you have ever introduced someone at a meeting, proposed a toast at a wedding or delivered a eulogy at a funeral, chances are you didn't show up unprepared. When a communication is very public and important, most people take some time to plan, prepare and even rehearse what they will say.

Our day-to-day conversations with our bosses or colleagues, clients, spouses, children, family or neighbours can be even more life-altering than a one-off event yet often we "wing it." When we don't take the time to prepare for these situations, things can go wrong. It is important, for instance, to identify the objectives of having the discussion, and the results we expect to flow from the exchange. You may not need to write everything out or type a script before every conversation; however, it can be helpful to be clear about what your intention is in having a conversation, clarify the results you are looking for and assess what you can do to make the conversation as effective as possible.

People often give me an example of a situation in which they don't know how to communicate and ask, "What is the right thing to say?"

I suggest they concentrate not on what the right thing is to say but on the effective way to communicate in the situation.

Considering the following factors will help you to prepare:

- Who are you communicating with?

- What role do you have with them?

- What is your relationship like with them?

- What is their style of communication?

- What result are you striving for?

- Are there cultural considerations that need to be addressed?

- What are the possible consequences — positive and negative — of engaging in the interaction?

Considering these aspects will help determine whether it is even appropriate to have the conversation.

For example, in today's society children live at home later in life than they used to. There is a phenomenon occurring when parents phone their adult child's employer to discuss job issues. If a parent were to go through the considerations above, unless there is a health issue that prohibits the child from communicating with his employer, a parent does not have a role in this scenario and would be best to let their son or daughter handle the matter directly with the employer.

On the following page is a checklist that you can use to help you plan ahead for those important discussions.

Conversation Preparation Checklist

Before you have an important conversation, assess the considerations below to determine which of them apply and how to manage these elements to give you the best odds of having a successful interaction.

1) What is your intention in having the conversation?

☐ share information ☐ get approval ☐ instruct

☐ get information ☐ provide a response ☐ express feelings

☐ ask for help ☐ ask permission ☐ introduce self

☐ solve a problem ☐ persuade ☐ get to know
someone better

If not one of the above, write your own intention.

2) What is the best time and location for this conversation? (Would it be best to make an appointment with the other person or approach him with no set time?)

3) What is your goal? In other words, what outcome, action or result would you expect as a result of this conversation?

4) What is the benefit or significance of the conversation for the other party? (What is in it for them — will they do their work better? Avoid a problem?)

5) What data or information would improve the clarity of the communication?

6) What is your mood like now? How you feel affects your tone and body language. How might that influence your effectiveness? (Do you need to postpone the conversation until you have better self-control?)

7) What kind of tone will help you get your message across and what do you need to avoid so you don't put the other person off?

☐ Volume: quiet — loud

☐ Pauses: Will you need some? Do you need to listen?

☐ Pace: fast — slow

☐ Tonal Variation: How much intonation will you
need to make yourself understood? What parts of
your message do you need to emphasize?

8) Body Language — What do you need to keep in mind about your body
language in this conversation?

☐ Facial expression: smile — or more reserved?

☐ Posture

☐ Sit or stand?

☐ Is a handshake appropriate?

9) What questions would be helpful to pose to the other person to draw
out information or to understand his interpretation of the message or
other hidden information? Are you in a passive, assertive or aggressive
state of mind? Will this mindset help you or hurt you? How can you
shift to assertion?

10) What other considerations do you have for preparing for this particular conversation?

PART THREE
Relationships and Communicating with Others

*The quality of your life depends
on the depth of your relationships
and the authentic moments you have with others.
What you say and what you don't say.
The choice is yours. — PH*

Chapter 9
Relationships: The Gift of Being Present

We live in a society of social networks and Twitter pages
and Facebook. That's fine and stuff, but you know, we have
contact with our work associates, our family, our friends
and it seems like half the time we're more preoccupied with
our phone and other things going on instead of the actual
relationships we have in front of us.[7] — *Brady Quinn*

With Friends Like That

Trevor, a 28 year old man in a workshop, said he was really getting frustrated
with people in his social circle. He explained his friends do very little pre-plan-
ning so most socializing is spur of the moment, when he is informed of an event
by a text message. The text might say: *Meet us at Joe's Bar. We are here now.* Often
he receives these texts when he is just walking into the gym or has just finished
preparing a meal, so he ends up missing many events because he is busy doing
other things. Now his friends are saying he is a jerk for not showing up and they
want to quit including him in activities because he "doesn't care" and he "never
tries to make it" to these impromptu get-togethers. He thinks they are unfair
to expect instant compliance with their last-minute "invitations." He believes it
should be understood if he can make it, great, and if not, no worries. If friends
want to be assured Trevor can attend an event, he needs at least 24 hours' notice.

Listening to Trevor's description of his friends' behaviour reminded me of
the old adage, "With friends like that, who needs enemies?" He asked the workshop participants and me what he should do about this. Most participants said,
"Get new friends!"

I agreed it was an option. I also suggested he have some conversations with his friends to clarify their expectations. Do they really expect him to jump at a moment's notice?

We are at a paradoxical state in our communications. With the Internet, mobile personal devices and software such as Skype, it has never been easier to communicate with anyone, anywhere, at any time in the world. At the same time, because we have so many devices and media competing for our attention, we are at the brink of epic failure when communicating with those closest to us. Why? Because our attention is rarely on those we are with. If we fail to pay attention to those closest to us, we fail to pay attention to our lives and happiness.

Relationships form the essence of our lives. There is little we do that does not depend on our relationships and the support of others. People we live and work with and choose to be our friends form the closest relationships we have. Brady Quinn, an American football quaterback, had a teammate who made the tragic choice to take his own life. As Quinn suggests in the opening quote to this chapter, we are spending so much time communicating electronically with our virtual friends, we neglect those who are closest and most important to us. We miss seeing who and what is right in front of us because we are disengaged and not fully present.

The quality of our relationships rests largely on our ability to communicate effectively on a daily basis. We need to take the time for face-to-face contact with those in our circle.

This primary circle of relationships includes our family and friends, our associates at work and the people in our community. Relationship-building includes building trust with those close to us, spending time with others, listening, understanding and supporting others, resolving differences and doing things that are appropriate and meaningful within our role.

A relationship happens when we are associated with someone and are interdependent. We are in relationships by birth, by choice and by circumstance.

The frequent and intense use of electronic communication has made us lose sight of the importance of interpersonal communication and behaviour. We are substituting electronic contact for the real thing: face-time spent together in each other's company. People text each other even when they are sitting side by side. In the workplace, co-workers who are separated only by a cubicle wall email each other rather than walking around the wall to talk. Electronic media is a wondrous tool for keeping in contact and sharing information, but it is no replacement for looking someone in the eye. Being together strengthens and deepens our relationships.

THE MAGIC RATIO

To maintain healthy relationships we must have more positive interactions than negative ones. The positive interactions are ones that help us experience joy and happiness, increase our self-esteem and our sense of closeness and positivity. Every relationship will have ups and downs. However, if the negative interactions outweigh the positive ones, the relationship will not thrive.

If you have a life partner or spouse, think about how much of your happiness is connected to the interactions you have with that person. You likely eat with them, sleep with them, finance your lives with them, raise children and make life decisions with them. According to the book, *How Full is Your Bucket?*[8] in order to sustain a positive relationship in marriage, we need to have at least five positive interactions to every negative interaction. If the number of negative interactions (*bucket-dipping*) increases in this ratio or surpasses the positive interactions (*bucket-filling*), the chance of divorce is high.

At work, you interact with the same people day after day. Getting results at work depends on working with others and communicating effectively. The magic ratio at work is at least three positive interactions to every negative one. If the number of negative interactions is higher, the relationship will be unhappy and troubled. These ratios confirm we need to be aware of the interactions we have with those around us and we need to cultivate our closest relationships. The health of our relationships depends on creating positive experiences with others.

Taking care of our interpersonal relationships and focusing on those close to us can be challenging. In many ways, taking care of our cyber-friends is easier. We get automated notices giving us updates and statuses. When we have not provided enough information, we get a notification to update or complete information.

Managing our face-to-face interactions can be more challenging. In order to understand what those closest to us need, we must be fully aware when we are with them. Face-to-face interactions with people allow us to get so much more information than by words alone. We can hear their tone, see their facial expressions, and experience their body language and energy. Interpersonal day-to-day relationships take time, attention and effort.

How Many Relationships Can We Handle?

Many people have upwards of 5,000 Facebook friends, or thousands of Twitter followers. But the question remains, how many actual relationships can we maintain on a personal level? Dr Robin Dunbar, a professor of Evolutionary Anthropology at Oxford suggests that 150 is the maximum number of friendships the human mind is capable of handling.[9] This means our capacity to interact with others is limited. We should ensure we use this capacity to maintain those relationships that really count.

For most people, happiness is influenced by our life partner, our circle of friends and the work we do. Are you taking good enough care of your primary relationships? How many people would that include?

The Pareto principle is the law of the vital few. It suggests that 80% of effects comes from 20% of causes. In other words, 80% of a company's revenue typically comes from 20% of its clients. In our relationships we could say that 80% of our interactions and life activity comes from interacting with the 20% of the people who constitute our closest relationships: the vital few. This means our life will centre on our relationships with about 30 key people.

So who are your top 30? The better you get to know them, the more you understand their interests, dreams, motivations, values and preferences. Their happiness will affect your own to some degree. When you understand their perspective, you communicate better with them because you have a better sense of how they will interpret what you have to say, and what their frame of reference is.

We cannot expect any one relationship to give us everything we need in life. Our spouse can interact with us in ways that a sibling or friend cannot. But we should not expect one person to be everything. It takes a village to raise a child, and I think it also takes a village to maintain a full life.

OUR CLOSEST RELATIONSHIPS

A core of five types of close relationships forms our interactions; they are described below. There are questions after each section that can help you decide which people form your list of top thirty relationships. You may also find you are able to identify the relationships that are working well. If they are, keep doing what you are doing or do more to make them even more incredible and fulfilling. You will also identify some relationships that could use special attention.

1) **Family of Origin**

Our lives and relationship-building experience begins with our parents, siblings and extended family, including grandparents, aunts and uncles. The parent-child relationship is one of the longest lasting we may have in our lives. Parents are supposed to provide for our care and growth. This relationship is complex because at some point we need to leave it and separate, to stand on our own as individuals. Later in life, roles may be reversed, where children become the caregivers of the parents who need care, support and advocacy.

Both intentionally and unintentionally, our parents instill values in us. They provide an example and act as role models for marriage, parenting, problem-solving and communicating. Once we reach adulthood, we reflect upon our parents' behaviour as a reference and tend to judge what we liked and did not like about their parenting style.

We learn about relationships from interacting with our siblings. Are you an only child or do you have brothers and sisters? Where are you in birth order? Were you the responsible one who looked after others, or were you the one who was looked after? All of these factors will have an impact on what you think is the right way to handle relationships.

Your Closest, Most Important Relationships
Make a list of those people who are your 20% (the most important relationships).
Nurture and cultivate these relationships.
Give these relationships priority in terms of your time,
attention and effort in communication. — *PH*

Today, many children live with their parents well into adult-hood. Families are learning to live with each other differently, as adult children live under the same roof and pursue an education or a career. Relationships change once children marry and have their own children.

How are you doing with your family relationships right now? Consider the following questions regarding your parents, siblings, grandparents, cousins, aunts and uncles:

How many of these people are part of your vital few relationships?

- Are you paying enough attention to them?

- How much time do you spend with them?

- How often do you communicate with them?

- What do you expect from them?

- What can they expect from you within the relationship?

2) **Friendships**

After family, the next type of relationship that forms is friend-ships. We don't get to choose our family or the people we work with, but we do get to choose our friends. Friends are the gifts we give ourselves. True friends are people who love you, care about you and support you in good times and bad.

Many of us spend a great deal of our lives in the company of friends. They are often the people who know us best.

True friends don't throw you under the bus. They have your back. The miraculous thing about true friends is they are there when many other close relationships aren't. Friends celebrate with us and support us as we encounter the good times in life and the challenges as we go through school and get jobs; experience romantic relationships and family problems; and mark the significant events of life, like marriage, births and deaths.

Friends provide a perspective in our lives and are witnesses to our milestones. How often has a friend that you didn't expect to see shown up at a surprise birthday party, housewarming or even a funeral? You say, "Wow, I didn't expect to see you here!" And they reply, "I wouldn't have missed it!"

How reassuring is it to know you can drop by a friend's house any time and always feel welcome? How satisfying is it to know that you can call a friend for help. Our best friends tell us the truth. They are patient listeners and coaches.

Friends give us the opportunity to give back. To have a friend is to be a friend. All the support we get from our friends fortifies us to do the same for them. The friend relationship gives us an extraordinary chance to practise our interpersonal skills, contribute to another's life and learn about ourselves. We can have lifelong friends, work friends, neighbourhood friends or friends that are activity-specific, like someone we have met through a sport, hobby or volunteer organization.

They do not love, that do not show their
love. — *William Shakespeare*

Questions for Consideration:

- Who are your best friends?

- How do you feel when you interact with each of them?

- How much time do you spend with each of your friends?

- What role and support do you provide in their lives?

- What role and support do they provide in yours?

3) **Spouses/Partners**

When we choose a spouse we choose a life partner. Practically and legally speaking, whatever happens to one of us happens to both of us. Ideally, a spouse has our back and provides a soft place to fall. As a team, partners make a living, maintain a home, raise children and deal with families of origin and extended family.

Of all the relationships we have, this one involves the majority of the communicating we will do. Spouses have so many things to negotiate including money, parenting, housing, holidays and the list goes on.

Relationships work best when couples have similar values and frames of reference. We need at least a 5:1 ratio of positive to negative interactions to make a marriage or partnership happy. We rely on this person to fulfil the role of intimate partner, providing love, sex and support. We have so many expectations when we begin a partnership. It has been said that 90% of our happiness or misery depends on the partner we choose.

Marriage can be a tough gig. Almost half of marriages end in divorce. Partners deal with infidelity, spousal abuse, verbal abuse, addictions, the blending of families and illness.

Once we make the choice to walk through life with someone else, we open ourselves to the possibility of extraordinary experiences. Maintaining this bond takes patience, thought and effort as you go through lows and highs together.

Problem-solving, listening and building a trusting relationship are important steps in creating a thriving partnership. I see many people who got it right when it comes to finding a life partner. They committed to their best friend and maintain a mutual loving kindness with that person. Above all, they truly like and respect their partner. To love and to be loved is a gift like no other.

In his book, *The 5 Love Languages*, Gary Chapman suggests part of the success we will have in intimate relationships depends on how well we know our spouse or partner, and whether or not we understand what behaviours he or she values that show love and affection. If we are to communicate successfully with a partner, we must be able to speak that person's preferred "love language" — that is, to show our affection in ways that he finds meaningful and appreciates. Chapman suggests that there are five main languages of love: words of affirmation, quality time, receiving gifts, acts of service and personal touch.[10]

Questions for Consideration:

- How do you show love and support to your partner? (How does that work for him or her?)

- How do they show you love and support?

- Do you tell your partner what you appreciate about them (accentuate the positives)?

- How are you doing at sharing responsibilities?

- Do you make time to have fun and share new experiences together?

- Are you able to work through your differences and disagreements?

4) **Children**

What is more miraculous than bringing a new life into the world? Parenting gives us an incredible chance to learn about ourselves and life. From the time my son took his first breath, I was hooked. I later became further enamoured with my daughter. My view of parenting is kids get only one chance to grow up. When we decide to have children, we take on the responsibility of raising them to be independent, happy, capable, responsible, balanced adults who can look after themselves and be contributing members of society.

As parents, so much of our role is simply loving children and teaching them to love themselves. As parents, we also teach life skills: cooking, cleaning, money management, interacting with others, showing respect, good manners and kindness. We want to really get to know each of our children as individuals and understand what their interests are so they can pursue their own dreams, not ours.

Parents can help children develop a positive perspective on life that will allow them to get through anything. Children will not respect others if they are not respected themselves.

When my daughter was young she was very outgoing and would talk to anyone. She was extremely aware of the influence she had on others. Even as a five-year-old she would get angry with me if I mentioned manners. She would say, "I know my manners, Mum! You don't need to tell me in front of others!"

I realized when I reminded her about manners in front of others, it embarrassed her. So we agreed when I was observing that her manners could be better, instead of me saying something in front of others, I would use our "manners code" which was a tug on the ear. When I observed her not using manners I would simply make eye contact with her, smile and touch my right earlobe. Then she would smile at me and give me a little nod and use her best manners.

In all of our relationships the challenge is to support people while respecting them. With children especially, they need to know that parental love is not contingent on behaviour. We love them no matter what; we just don't always love their behaviour.

Parenting is not easy. Some situations provide more of a challenge than others. Behavioural issues, illness, disabling conditions and divorce all affect the parenting experience. There are several community resources now to help parents with challenges. Many employers provide Employee Assistance Programs

(EAPs) — access to counsellors and other professionals. Many schools provide counselling for students and will also provide educational assistants for children who need extra support.

Parenthood is a wonderful adventure. Those who enter into it will be presented with the biggest learning opportunity of their lives and the chance to enjoy a lifelong, loving relationship.

Questions for Consideration:

- Are you spending quality time with all of your children?

- How do you show them your love and support?

- How do they show you love and support?

- Do you take time to tell them what they are doing well and give them positive feedback?

- Do you take the time to teach them skills and values and provide coaching that will prepare them for life?

- If you need help with your child, who can help you? Who else can help your child?

5) **Co-workers, Colleagues and Professional Connections**

Whether you are an employee of an organization or a business owner, the people who help you make a living are important in your life.

Cultivating professional relationships is one of the most important things that you can do. Whether it is getting to know your co-workers and developing teamwork, or playing golf with a supplier, the better the relationship, the more trust is built and the easier it is to work together. You spend at least a third of your time from Monday to Friday at your job. If you have bad relationships with co-workers, colleagues, clients, suppliers or bosses, the negativity from this will spill into your personal life. You don't have to be best friends with everyone, but it helps to have a productive working relationship with everyone and contribute to a positive work environment.

Treating others with respect and handling your share at work is the basic minimum requirement to maintaining these relationships. Getting to know others as people and finding common ground can help you work through differences. Do you acknowledge people's contributions? Do you celebrate their successes?

Questions for Consideration:

- Who are your key professional connections (co-workers, colleagues or professional contacts)?

- What is your relationship like with these people?

- What is the benefit of improving the relationship?

- How could you do that?

THREE KEY BEHAVIOURS

For your closest relationships, there are three things you can do to deepen the connection, increase trust and improve communication and understanding:

1) **Offer a loving kindness**

   A mindset of loving-kindness is one we can use in all our relationships. This means showing love, affection and respect to everyone. It is the opposite of treating others with hostility or indifference. With those closest to us, such as family and friends, it means telling them we love them and care about them, and showing affection with hugs, pats on the back, hand-holding and smiles. It means supporting their endeavours and being there when they need someone in their corner. When we wonder about our loved ones and their intentions, we give them the benefit of the doubt, knowing they wouldn't intentionally hurt us.

In professional relationships it means showing others respect, kindness and fairness while living up to the commitments that we have made to them.

2) **Spend time together**

You can spend time with each person in your life in a way that is appropriate for the role you have with that person. With your spouse, you may go away for a romantic weekend or take an evening walk; with your children, you may read to them if they are young, or go cycling or kite-flying with them; with colleagues, you might take the time to have lunch to socialize, or listen to their ideas about a project. Some co-workers will become close friends with whom you will share many experiences.

3) **Create a cycle of giving and receiving**

The best relationships are balanced. In many relationships there is a giver and a taker, and this doesn't always work well. If both parties can see themselves as givers and receivers, balance can happen. A balanced cycle means relationships work best when we give our time, love, attention and material things and are willing to receive these things from others.

Imbalance happens in two ways: by over-giving and by over-taking. When people are constantly giving to others and are unwilling to receive, it creates an imbalance and robs others of the good feeling of giving. All too often I hear complaints when dealing with conflict such as "My mother never lets me pay for anything and it makes me feel like a child" or "I'm worried that if I receive a gift, there will be strings attached" or "I often give a friend a gift and she says, 'You didn't need to do that' rather than just smiling and saying, 'Thank you.'" A healthy mindset for relationships is to see ourselves not as takers, but as receivers, enabling others to have the positive experience of giving. We honour those who give to us and ourselves by receiving gracefully.

The other imbalance happens when we are habitual takers and expect to receive from others with a sense of entitlement and without giving back. There are people who call us only when *they* need something otherwise we don't hear from them. I've been told, "I feel taken advantage of by my friend (or neighbour or child)." Sometimes it seems the relationship is one-sided.

Everyone has different abilities, income levels and talents. Contributing to the cycle as best we can is our opportunity. It does not mean keeping score in a relationship so much as ensuring there is some kind of flow, even if the giving is just to say thank you for what is received or having a pay-it-forward spirit.

Talking about balance in a relationship and how to achieve it is a healthy discussion.

LETTING RELATIONSHIPS GO

Not every relationship we have is good for us. Some are destructive. You will find that by assessing your key relationships and employing effective interpersonal skills you may not want to hang onto every relationship you have. For example, I had a friend who was so negative and blaming, that every time we talked, I felt uncomfortable. She was a person who blamed others for what had happened to her and was the first to take a shot at them to let them know how stupid they were in their own lives. If you had problems, her view was, "You made your own bed, so lie in it." After careful analysis and clear conversations with her, I believed she wasn't ready to change her approach and her constant negativity wasn't what I needed in my life. So I finally quit interacting with her. It was a difficult decision, but in the end I became happier because it eliminated stress and negativity from my life.

I have had a number of people tell me that in some of their key relationships they have had to draw clear boundaries to maintain their own health and energy. For example, some people find interacting with their parents, who may have very different values or beliefs, to be exhausting. They do not wish to cut off the relationship, but they have to create clear boundaries such as "Please don't just drop in to visit; call before you come" or "Please do not discipline my children in my home, that's my job." Other people I know have suffered abuse, violence and neglect in relationships and have made the choice to discontinue them.

It is normal in the course of a lifetime for our primary relationships to change. People will come and people will go. You are encouraged to think about your primary relationships and make deliberate choices in maintaining those that are important to you. It has been said that people come into our lives for a reason, a season or a lifetime.

DEALING WITH THE OTHER 80%

While the key to happiness lies in cultivating our most important relationships, we can't ignore our peripheral relationships and the new people we may meet. There are other folks you associate with regularly in your community: a neighbour, a gas station attendant, a store clerk or someone in your local soccer, golf or hockey league. The interactions you have with the people who are on the periphery of your life also affect your happiness.

I try to be present with people no matter who they are. We are all human and looking for respect and acknowledgement. Sometimes when I am at the checkout in a store and the cashier says, "Did you find everything you were looking for?" I sense a lack of enthusiasm or even sadness. When I experience this, I often say, "Yes, thanks. And how is your day going?"

People usually brighten up at this inquiry. They often smile and say, "Pretty well!" or "Very busy." The act of giving them some attention and basic kindness often changes their mood and the quality of the interaction I have with them. I believe when you give people *your* best, you invite them to give you *their* best.

It is normal not to anticipate being best friends with everyone we meet. We won't click with everyone, although each person we meet has the potential to have an impact on our lives. So whether someone is a passing acquaintance you meet on vacation or your future mother-in-law, there is always potential in connecting with that person. It is exciting to think about what we might learn from others in our interactions with them, even if it is brief.

Meeting New People

When you meet someone for the first time, some basic practices that can help you start to form a relationship include:

- Shaking their hand and introducing yourself.

- Smiling at them and making eye contact.

- Remembering their name so you can use it the next time you see them.

- Taking the opportunity to ask them about themselves, if your interaction is longer.

Questions That Engage Others

- How is your day going?

- How long have you worked here?

- Where are you from?

- What brought you here?

- What's new and exciting?

- Are you familiar with … ? (something that you may have in common)

- Say, do you know … ? (a possible mutual acquaintance)

Things to Say When you Leave

- It was a real pleasure meeting you.

- Have a great day.

- I'll look forward to seeing you the next time.

What Truly Matters

We got the call at 6:09 a.m. The nurse was on the phone saying, "Come as fast as you can, your dad is not doing very well."

"Is he dying?" I asked.

"He is not doing well. It would be a good idea to call your brothers and sisters," she replied.

I woke my kids, grabbed our dog and began the forty-five minute drive to the hospital.

As we drove down the highway the sun shone brilliantly, juxtaposed against the fog from the river that hung like shrouds foreshadowing what lay ahead. My son called my sister in Calgary and asked her to phone the rest of our siblings.

When we walked into the hospital room at 7:12, my brother was already there by Dad's bed. There was a look of disbelief on his face. "He's not going to make it," he said, tears in his eyes. He was holding Dad's hand. Dad's eyes were unfocused, blankly staring at the wall. His breath was a Darth Vader rattle — a moan mixed with rushing, unproductive air. I sensed Dad's fear as I reached for his hand. He was unable to speak.

Once I took Dad's hand, my brother went to the care home to get my mother. "Lillian is coming," I said to him. He grew visibly calmer. His breathing slowed and he seemed to understand.

My children stood looking at their grandpa, horrified by the sounds he was making and the state he was in. I suggested they go out to the car to get Sally, our dog, so she could say goodbye, too. Throughout Dad's last year, Sally had brought him much comfort and unconditional love.

While I was alone with Dad I wanted to crumple up and cry. I realized, though, I had a choice to make. I had an incredible opportunity to be with him and to do the best I could to make his last minutes with us the best they could be. I wanted to comfort him. I told him that he would finally get a chance to see his mom and dad and sister again. I told him that his best friends Perce, Jack and Gordon would be ready and waiting with a great fishing boat and they'd take him to a place where they would catch the most amazing fish ever. I told him that we all loved him. That he was a wonderful father, grandpa, uncle and husband. That he was a good friend and neighbour and those are the things that count in the end. It was okay to go ahead and leave — he would feel better and be able to move and be free from pain.

I felt him give my hand a quick squeeze, which to me was a testament that the people in his life were what had mattered to him the most. He lingered for close to an hour, and in that time I began to come to terms with the loss of one of the key relationships of my life.

Not all of us have a parent or a life-long partner as a key relationship. But there is someone. We need to think about whether or not we are doing our best to nurture the connection we have with that someone while they are here.

Assessing our relationships today and doing our best will ensure we have no regrets when the unexpected happens.

A MINDSET FOR RELATIONSHIPS

- We do not control relationships. We influence and participate in them. We are only half of the equation.

- We have the right to create clear boundaries in relationships and let go of the ones that are not in our own best interests.

- We have opportunities in all relationships to show love, respect and affection.

- Spending time on our most important relationships will enhance our life.

- Relationships benefit from a cycle of giving and receiving.

EXERCISE: Creating Your Own Perfect World

Think about the most important relationships that you have and consider the following:

Your relationship with _____ .

1) How do you currently show love, respect and affection for this person? How do they show the same to you? What else could you do to enhance this relationship?

2) How do you spend time together? What other things could you do together that would enhance the relationship?

3) Reflect on the balance in this relationship. Do you give and receive and share a positive cycle so one person does not feel taken advantage of and you both feel loved and fairly treated?

Chapter 10
Listening: The Skill That
Makes a Difference

When we listen to others, we help them clarify their
own thinking, facilitate problem solving, show respect
and affirm their human experience. — *PH*

The Confession

When I was just out of university, I visited Dachau, a concentration camp near Munich. Touring the camp was like walking through a church. Everyone was quiet and reverent as they struggled with what people had endured behind the fences. I was in a contemplative and sombre mood as I sat at the back of the bus on the return trip to Munich. At a stop, a very old man got on the bus. I gave up my seat for him and ended up standing beside him. He spoke to me in German, which I did not understand. When I said, "Ich spreche kein Deutsch" (I do not speak German), he stopped and looked at me for a long time. He pointed back towards Dachau and then he pointed at me. I interpreted from his gestures that he was asking me if I had been at Dachau. I said, "Yes," and I nodded.

Next he looked into my eyes and then looked at the floor. He remained silent, yet I sensed that he was going to tell me something. I waited. Finally he looked up at me again and pointed violently at himself and said, "SS." Then he lowered his head, and cried. His teardrops splashed on the floor. In that moment I understood his shame, his regret and his sorrow.

Listening is a key skill that helps us understand others. An effective listener doesn't just hear words. An effective listener hears the words, observes the accompanying body language, assesses the tone and assigns meaning to what is said. Effective listeners listen, not for what they want to hear, but for the actual meaning that the speaker is trying to express. They endeavour to understand.

Most people know what makes for good listening skills, yet we don't always use them. Why are we not so fond of listening? Perhaps it is because listening is hard work. It takes concentration and attention to focus on others rather than ourselves.

THE IMPORTANCE OF LISTENING

When people are asked to cite effective communicators, most list names of great orators like John F. Kennedy, Winston Churchill and Steve Jobs. In North America, we have a high regard for those who can deliver a message powerfully and succinctly. In fact, there are several organizations worldwide dedicated to the improvement and development of speaking skills. This penchant for speaking means many people do not care about an interaction once they have spoken. We train people to *speak* in our society, but do not provide much coaching in the skill that really makes a difference to all our relationships: *listening.*

Although expressing our ideas through speaking is an important part of communication, the cycle is not complete unless there is someone who can hear it. So important is the act of listening that in 1979 a group of scholars and interested parties got together at a conference and established the International Listening Association (ILA). The association was formed to study listening in human relations and to facilitate research on the topic.

According to the ILA, "Listening is the process of receiving, constructing meaning from and responding to spoken and/or nonverbal messages."[11] Their efforts remind us listening is an underestimated yet essential tool in our repertoire of interpersonal skills.

RELATIONSHIP BUILDING: THE MAIN REASON TO LISTEN

How often has someone asked you, "Hey, do you have a minute?" or "Can I talk to you about something?" Have you ever asked someone the same question yourself? To be listened to and understood by another person is a gift. When we are preoccupied with problems or worry, or have exciting or happy news to share, there is a real sense of affirmation when someone listens to us *well* and responds in a way that we are hoping for. When others ask us to listen, they are inviting us to share their private realm.

As a mediator helping people resolve issues, I've learned the root of many problems is people have not really heard or understood each other. A husband will say, "My wife really doesn't understand me." Children will say, "My parents are never around to listen to me." Employees will see only their own points of view and not understand or care about the views of their co-workers.

Listening to and understanding others are at the heart of all relationships. When we listen well, trust builds and the relationship grows.

Effective listening skills allow us to:

- Receive information from others

- Learn about people's values, preferences, experiences, points of view, perceptions and goals

- Understand the general expectations others have, and their expectations of us in the relationship

- Receive feedback about how we are doing in the relationship or in our role with the other person

- Get a sense of someone's communication preferences

- Affirm others and validate their feelings and experiences

When we listen to others well, we help them clarify their own thinking, facilitate problem solving, show respect and affirm their human experience. When we listen effectively, the speaker is comfortable and encouraged to share more information.

When we listen poorly, it shuts people down, leaves them feeling disrespected and erodes trust. Our relationships deteriorate.

CONSIDERATIONS WHEN LISTENING

Role: What is your role as listener?

We listen to hear what others have to say because we cannot read their minds. When people approach us to speak, they may have various expectations of what we should do as a listener. Some people simply want to be heard and understood. Other people come to us and want us to take action. Therefore it is important to determine what the speaker wants when he approaches us, so we can determine what type of listening we need to undertake. It is important to realize that effective listening does not mean we agree with the other person; it means we understand what he means.

Does the person want you to just listen to him vent, does he want you to help him solve a problem, give him advice or take action? If you are unsure of your role as a listener, ask the other person, "By sharing this information with me, what are you expecting of me?"

Timing: Is this a good time to have the conversation?

Sometimes people approach us to talk when we do not have the time or energy to listen. For example, we might be in the middle of cooking dinner or at work trying to meet a deadline. If we attempt to engage in listening but continue with our primary task, we miss a lot of the information and alienate the speaker. In that case, let the speaker know that you are not able to listen at the moment and schedule a time to talk later. For example, at home if you are busy, you might say "I would like to talk to you and I am unable to at the moment. Can you give me fifteen minutes to finish making supper and then we'll talk?" or "I would like to talk to you and I can see it is important. Can we talk after supper so that we won't be interrupted?"

At work if someone approaches you and you are busy, you could say, "I would like to talk to you and I am unable to at the moment, as I am in the middle of this project. Can we talk in half an hour?" a caveat being, if it seems that someone has a serious problem or is in crisis, it is best to drop what you are doing and listen.

Location: Which setting will help you have an effective interaction?

It is important to find a place where your conversation won't be interrupted and where you can both be comfortable. At home, it is wise to choose a private place such as a bedroom, office or living room with little traffic. Another option is to take a walk outside to have your discussion.

At work, a conversation can take place in an office rather than in a cubicle where there are people within earshot. Another option is to talk in a place that is very busy, like a cafeteria, or you can leave the building altogether.

Giving Our Attention

You cannot multi-task while communicating. In order to really listen you need to stop the other things you're doing and focus on the person. This means no typing, texting, watching TV, listening to music or talking to others. Give the speaker your full and undivided attention. Be fully present in the moment with the person you are with.

Listening Posture

In European-North American culture, a speaker perceives us to be listening if we make eye contact during the conversation, have a neutral or interested look on our face and sit an appropriate distance from him — not too close and not too far away. It is best to keep an open posture. Recognize that effective body language is culturally specific. As you listen, be aware of the speaker's tone and body language.

Giving a Heads-Up

Often we have multiple deadlines to meet and actions to take each day. If you are listening to someone who may take more time than you have, make him aware as soon as possible you have only 15 minutes before you need to go to a meeting or pick up a child from school. This will alert him to time parameters before you get too deep into the conversation. It also gives him information that allows him to decide if he wants to reschedule the conversation.

Using Active Listening Skills

The basics of active listening are focusing on the speaker and listening for understanding. Some techniques that can help with the listening process include:

- Asking effective questions that elicit more information from the speaker. Effective questions engage the speaker and encourage him to say more. Ineffective questions are off-putting, judgmental or presumptive.

- Paraphrasing to check for meaning, to slow things down and allow the speaker to clarify.

- Summarizing what was heard or discussed.

TYPES OF LISTENING

Listening to Understand

In many situations people seek us out to listen so they can express themselves. People are often happy to share good news with us or express ideas they are excited about or things they've learned. It is a pleasure to listen to someone's happy experience.

Listening becomes more difficult when things are not going well. Sometimes others want to vent anger, share a fear, process a concern, or talk about a problem or an experience that left them off balance. They want to think out loud. We are called upon to listen as parents, friends, siblings, bosses, co-workers, neighbours and in day-to-day business relationships. We even have opportunities to listen and learn from total strangers.

In these moments people don't want to be judged. They don't want someone to solve their problems and they don't want to be interrogated for details. They want to express themselves, have their experiences affirmed and be heard in the presence of another.

The goal in this type of listening is to understand and be willing to let the person express himself. People have a need to share, and if we are able, our role is to be that understanding presence. Effective listeners know that listening for understanding is a distinct process. It is very freeing when all you have to do is listen for understanding and not adjudicate or react. Just listen and understand.

Do:

- Recognize your role as a listener and the fact you do not need to act or have an opinion as a result of the conversation.

- Be silent while the person is speaking.

- Let the person talk as long as necessary, and recognize he will have far more airtime than you.

- Ask questions to help the person express himself as appropriate, *i.e.,* How *did that make you feel? Why did it affect you that way? What wasn't okay?*

- Show your interest and attention by nodding your head and using minimal prompters such as "go on," "m-hmm," etc., to invite them to continue. Keep listening until you think you have it all. Ask the question *"Is there anything else?"*

- Be prepared for emotion. People may express anger, grief, hurt and frustration. The person may even cry, swear or yell. Once people express their emotions and vent their feelings, they are ready to consider action or problem solving, and are more equipped to determine whether a forward strategy is required or if venting was enough to help deal with the issue.

- Offer support and affirmation once the story has been told. "That sounds frustrating, difficult…" etc. (whatever feeling that they are conveying). You could say, "I'm sure you will figure it out." Sometimes people need to hear things will be okay.

- Be empathetic, realizing even though you may not react to the situation the way the speaker did, it is about that person's experience — not about you.

- Keep an open, nonjudgmental and quiet tone.

Don't:

- Judge or criticize someone's experience or interpretation of the situation.

- Make the other person feel stupid or wrong.

- Over-react to or get angry about what someone says, especially children; it is important when they are sharing to let them talk about what they have experienced. Problem solving can come later, if required. Likewise at work, when people share things that may ultimately have an impact on us, we need to separate ourselves from the situation.

- Take over the conversation and talk about your own experience; it is not your time.

- Interrupt the person and disrupt their train of thought.

Listening to Act

Every day we communicate with people to achieve results. We have several roles in our lives: parent, spouse, boss, co-worker and friend, to name a few. People will approach us to talk and they are not looking for understanding alone. They are looking for us to take action within our role. They may want us to make a decision, give permission, approval, or an opinion based on our expertise, or clarify a process. They want us to act by supplying one of these items.

Do:

- Clarify why the person is approaching you to determine the kind of action he is seeking.

- Ask questions to clarify information. (You may want to use the W5 model as a framework for eliciting information to ensure you have as much information as possible before you act. Ask questions concerning: who, what, when, where, why and how). Samples of questions to ask:

  - What has happened so far?

  - What would you like to see happen?

  - Who is involved?

  - What do you need from me?

  - Are there time factors or deadlines involved?

- Process what they are saying.

- Provide a response about what action you are going to take. This can be offering them a decision on the spot: "Yes, you can bring your toddler to work for the half-day when you have no sitter." Or provide them with the tangible item they are asking for: "Yes, you may use the company van to pick up your new living room suite." Or the action might be you needing to do something else to finalize a decision. For example at home, you may decide you cannot release your car to your teenager for the whole weekend without consulting your spouse about setting up a list of expectations.

- Tell the speaker where you are at in the process of taking action.

- Interrupt the speaker with a kind tone if he is going too fast or if you are not sure what it is he wants: "Please excuse my interruption, but before you continue, I want to be sure what it is you need from me." Or, "Excuse my interruption, but I need to clarify this piece of information so I can follow your discussion."

- Use a patient tone. It is extremely difficult to listen to someone you disagree with. Be patient and listen for understanding. When you maintain a mindset of curiosity, patience happens naturally.

Don't:

- Engage with people if you do not have the time and won't give them your attention; if that is the case, reschedule.

- Rush or push them.

- Finish their sentences.

- Hesitate to send someone to another source for action if you are not the right person for the job, or if someone else can provide action more quickly.

When we are aware of our role and the action that is intended, we can listen in a way that meets the goals of the communication interaction.

When Listening is a Chore

Some people share a lot, especially when they experience difficult circumstances. A person in my life was experiencing problems with his spouse. I listened regularly to him vent for many months. It became overwhelming for me to be constantly present in listening, and to repeatedly hear his concerns. I realized I was becoming an unwilling listener and felt resentful about his expectation that I constantly "be there" when he was not willing to change or take action. I found myself feeling uncomfortable when he approached me. I finally said, "I love you and wish only the best for you. I care about you and your situation. I also appreciate you as a friend and would like to have some positive experiences with you instead of always listening. It is difficult for me to hear about your problem repeatedly and it's having a negative effect on me." I asked him who else he could share with. He thought of a couple of other friends and said that he would try them. Also, I suggested that he talk to a counsellor through his employee assistance program, a benefit he had through work. We cannot be all things to all people all of the time.

Listening is an overlooked, but vital part of the communication process. Understanding what is expected of us in a conversation will help us be alert to the type of listener we need to be.

Taking the time and energy to be an effective listener can enhance your relationships.

Chapter 11
Trust: The Invisible Factor

Love all, trust a few, do wrong to none.
— *William Shakespeare*

A Ticket to Vancouver

Have you ever trusted a stranger? What if they asked you for money? A young man named Jeff who works for a charitable organization in Calgary was faced with that choice. One day, a homeless man, Luke, walked in and asked for a bus ticket to return home to his family in Vancouver. Luke had been down on his luck for some time, living on the street, and was desperate to start a new life.

Jeff had not met Luke before. Was Luke really going to go to Vancouver or was he looking for cash? After some thought and influenced by his principles, Jeff took time off from work, drove Luke to the bus station and, with his own money, purchased a ticket for Luke. Satisfied he had done a good deed, Jeff returned to the office, only to be chastised by Julia, one of his employees, who believed Luke was scamming Jeff. She predicted Luke would cash in the bus ticket or sell it.

Jeff said, "Well, you might be right, but if I don't trust him, neither will anybody else and he's going to be stuck on the streets forever."

Jeff faced the age-old question: Do I trust this person or not?

Trust is central to all relationships. It is invisible. We cannot see it or touch it, but we feel trust or mistrust in our hearts. We are forever wondering what people's intentions are towards us and whether they will deliver on their promises. Every day we are bombarded with potential breaches of our trust. Cell phone and Internet scam artists tell us we have won something and all we need to do is give our credit card number to pay for shipping. Once we give them the number, they rob our account.

Internet communication makes it possible for two people to strike up a friendship online or even get engaged without ever seeing each other. It is easy for people who have never had face-to-face communication with you to pretend to be someone they are not. It is easy not to trust *anyone*. However, without trust a healthy relationship can't exist. When we do not trust others, we withhold information because we are uncertain about how they will interpret or use the information. Will they judge us? Will they use it against us? When there is no trust, we cannot be our authentic selves.

TRUST AND OUR CLOSEST RELATIONSHIPS

When we trust others, we share information and our feelings; we depend on others as they depend on us. Trust is like glue that holds our relationships together even when they could come apart.

When trust is high, communication between two people is easy. That is because either a personal or a professional relationship has formed between them. Each has a better understanding of who the other is and what he thinks. In other words, the two people understand each other's frame of reference much better, and so communication is easier. When high trust is established it creates a flowing river of agile communication and understanding between people.

When those we trust do things that are questionable, we put faith in them that we would not extend to others. For example, if someone you trust promised that he would call you at 2:00 and he still hasn't called by 2:15, you do not assume he is ignoring his commitment. You trust that he is doing his best to reach you and that circumstances are preventing him from following through. This faith we have in those we trust and our belief in their positive intentions towards us is also referred to as *giving others the benefit of the doubt*.

We tend to judge ourselves on our own good intentions — our thoughts. Other people judge us on our behaviour — our actions. Because only we know our thoughts, our own role in building trust with others is about communicating effectively with others and following through on our commitments.

If the other person follows through on promises, treats us with respect and communicates, trust will grow. If the person breaks promises, has values we disapprove of and does not communicate with us in a way we expect, trust fades.

Our views and beliefs concerning trust are very personal. Some people find it difficult to trust anyone for any reason and subscribe to a low-trust mindset, trusting only themselves. People who have a high-trust mindset choose to trust others until something or someone proves them wrong.

A productive mindset for trust can be one that is situational, where we assess each situation, what is at stake, and how much we feel we can trust the other person involved. If the risk is high, we may be more cautious. For example, if you are deciding whether to trust a babysitter to look after your children, the risk is high concerning the safety of your children. Going into a business venture with someone you don't know very well can be financially risky. Factors like the duration of the relationship are relevant. For example, meeting a blind date for lunch involves a very short time frame. The risk of association is much lower than making a decision to marry someone, which implies a lifelong commitment.

We also need to assess what skills, abilities and talents the other person possesses, and whether or not he has what it takes to do the job we need him to do. A number of years ago, I needed help with yard maintenance. I looked in the local newspaper and phoned a few companies who could do the work. I selected one that agreed to send someone to my house on a Saturday morning at 9:00. The crew did not arrive until 10:30. Furthermore the two men looked as though they had just rolled out of bed; their eyes were red and bleary and I could smell alcohol on their breath. They said they were ready to work and I said, "No thanks, you can leave." Their late arrival with no phone call, unkempt appearance and obvious hangovers from the night before made me feel that I could not trust them to do the work. They were unhappy, but I insisted that they leave. I did not feel safe having them around.

TRUST BUILDERS

Trust builders are the types of activities and behaviours we can use with others in order to enhance confidence in the relationship.

Be honest and have integrity. We trust people we perceive as being honest and telling the truth. We are constantly assessing others as to whether or not they behave and speak in a way that shows integrity. We look for consistency in what people say and the actions they perform. We also believe people are honest when they can tell the truth about situations and do not sugarcoat or misrepresent the truth, or deliberately mislead us. People trust us when we show integrity.

I had a problem after I purchased a used car with an extended warranty. Legally the contract I had signed showed I could change my mind on the extended warranty and get all my money back within a specified time frame. I had the car for two weeks and found problems with it that made me decide to sell it. I was still within the time period to cash in my warranty. When I called the salesman to advise him, he denied I could do that.

I asked, "Are you sure?"

He said, "I am absolutely sure! I am sorry you cannot get your money back on the warranty."

I said, "Well, maybe you did not get a copy of the sales agreement, but my understanding of Clause 4, Section B clearly states I can cancel the warranty and receive a full refund with no penalty."

He said, "Oh — uh — I have to go now…" And he hung up.

Later on I asked Norman, a salesman at another dealership, why the first salesman would tell me something that was so obviously wrong. Norman speculated that the intention might have been to discourage me from cashing in the policy because the salesman would lose his commission on it.

Keep confidences. Keeping a confidence for another person is an important way to build trust. If you plan to divulge the information someone has confided to you, you must always have that person's permission to do so, unless, of course, there are legal reasons for breaking the confidentiality. Lately, I have heard from many employers who are bewildered and amazed at the imprudence of their employees leaking information about office conflicts or operations on the Internet. Sharing work information with others outside of work, especially in a public forum, shows a lack of discretion. Those in leadership positions, especially, must keep sensitive information private if they are to be trusted. Confidences are also important in our personal relationships. When friends share information that we have entrusted them with, it damages the relationship. We trust people who use discretion and keep confidences.

Be loyal. We trust others when they show us loyalty and support. People show us loyalty when they speak well of us to others, show trust in our abilities by letting us do what we have committed to without micro-managing or directing us and by giving us the benefit of the doubt. People also show us loyalty when they ask our opinion of situations or draw on our expertise.

An acquaintance moved from Australia to Canada and landed a job in a small café. She applied to several companies for a better-paying position. A month into her work at the café she was offered a lucrative job with a large corporation. She chose to stay with the café because they believed in her and had given her a chance. She felt loyal to those who were loyal to her.

Show respect. The golden rule is to treat others the way you want to be treated. The platinum rule is to treat others the way *they* want to be treated. Respect is in the eye of the beholder. People judge what is respectful based on their own ideas and values. What we deem to be respectful may be different from what other people believe.

When we take the time to get to know others, build a relationship and understand their perspective, we get a sense of what others value. To honour others' beliefs is a sign of respect. Thomas Jefferson said, "There is nothing as unequal as the equal treatment of unequals." We are all unequal, as we all have different experiences, backgrounds, beliefs and preferences. People who show us respect communicate with us and treat us in a way that honours and recognizes our uniqueness. Your boss might speak to you in a very polite, soft-spoken and conciliatory manner because he has perceived this is your idea of respect. Your co-worker across the aisle might have a completely different notion of respect, and the boss might approach him or her in a loud, jocular, teasing manner. Just like pantyhose, a "one-size-fits-all" approach to communication does not work for everyone.

Be accountable. We trust those who show accountability. That means they take personal responsibility for their actions and commitments. Following policy or house rules, delivering on the expectations of others, meeting deadlines, and making people aware of our own mistakes and correcting them are all ways to show our accountability. Accountable people make commitments and keep them. They are reliable. However, because they cannot control everything in their lives, situations can arise that make it difficult or impossible to honour every commitment they make. Accountable people recognize when they are not going to be able to fulfil a commitment, and they proactively show respect to others by letting them know they are willing to renegotiate the commitment. Being accountable is about following through on your promises.

Recognize others' efforts and accomplishments. When people give us credit for the positive things we have done and efforts we have made, we feel appreciated and valued. When people are able to give positive acknowledgement it shows they are fair. When people give credit where credit is due and don't operate on their own agenda or self-interest, it builds trust. Trust is strengthened when we recognize other people's accomplishments, say thank you to those who do positive things and celebrate others' successes and milestones.

Cultivate your reputation. People judge us on our track record. When you communicate effectively with others, follow through on your commitments and do as you say you will do, you develop a reputation. A trustworthy reputation helps people who don't know you, to trust you more quickly. When people refer you to others, they are saying they trust you implicitly. When you make a recommendation, you might qualify it by indicating whether it is on a personal or a professional level. For example, a friend referring me to a mechanic said, "You may not like his communication style because he won't tell you much, but he can fix your car at a reasonable price and stand behind any work that he does." When we refer someone, we are really putting our own reputation up as collateral. Rightly or wrongly, people will judge us based on our referral and the experience that they had with the person we referred. Reputation matters.

Take care of your reputation by being aware of your behaviour and what information you are putting out in the public realm. Today employers look at online sources such as Facebook to see what potential employees are posting, what they're saying about others, and what type of pictures of themselves they post.

TRUST KILLERS

There are a number of behaviours that undermine trust. If we do the opposite of anything above, we can kiss trust goodbye.

There are key reasons people might not trust us:

Being dishonest. When someone says something we think is untrue, our reaction is to call him a liar. It is a strong word. When someone lies, it implies he has said something he knows to be false. Lying may include withholding facts, omitting certain information or telling others we did something when we did not, or vice versa.

A place where people commonly stretch the truth is on résumés. They pad their work experience, embellish job titles, say their salary was higher at their last job than it really was and even say they have credentials when they do not. Many of these inaccuracies will be revealed when references are checked.

Trust is a factor in marriage. Infidelity is a common problem in many marriages.

People can be deceitful right under your nose. In my career I worked with a leader who broke my trust. I had been deeply immersed in an initiative for several months. When all was ready, my administrative assistant drafted an announcement about the new program that I intended to send out later that day. When I stepped out for coffee, my boss called my admin into his office and instructed her to send the announcement out immediately under his name before I came back from my break. When I returned, my admin was in tears.

The boss took credit for my accomplishment. Worse, he did not talk to me about it to share his point of view and discuss options. Perhaps we could have sent out a joint release. Instead, he showed a lack of faith in our ability to work together. He made a deliberate move that fractured our relationship and his reputation with others in the company. He also put my admin in a terrible position, threatening her with insubordination if she did not comply.

Whatever justification you have for deceitful behaviours, they will be seen as dishonest and they will undermine your reputation. Regarding lying, Friedrich Nietzsche said, "I'm not upset that you lied to me, I'm upset that from now on I can't believe you."

Blaming others. Some people regularly fail to take responsibility for their actions and missed commitments. What makes a lack of accountability worse is when people blame others for their own lack of follow through. For many, their best defence is a good offence. Rather than being accountable for their own actions, they choose to deflect responsibility from themselves by finger pointing. We tend to avoid people who blame others because they are negative to be around, and it's hard to trust those who won't take responsibility for their own actions.

Trash-talking. When people belittle others and gossip or speak ill of them, it creates an atmosphere of mistrust. If a leader speaks ill of a staff member at a staff meeting, or a father speaks ill of his son in front of his daughter, the question remains, who will be the next target?

In the virtual world people freely share their opinions and information about others. People who say negative things about others or engage in Internet bullying will not be seen as reputable, as worthy of hiring or getting involved with.

Having double standards. We undermine people's trust in us when we criticize others for things we do ourselves. A senior manager in an organization I worked for always condemned co-workers because he believed they were undertaking unnecessary travel for personal interests. But the manager himself took "business trips" to destinations where he happened to have a lot of family. It was the *do as I say, not as I do* approach that undermined his credibility. When we say one thing and do the opposite, it is hard for people to trust us.

When Trust Is Broken

For years, famed Tour de France winner, Lance Armstrong, was accused of using performance-enhancing drugs, accusations he vehemently denied. Finally, in January 2013, he publicly confessed he had used banned substances. His friends and supporters were shocked and betrayed.

Through the natural course of all relationships someone will break our confidence and we will break theirs. Someone may lie to us, steal from us, hurt us or let us down. We will feel shocked by such falsehoods.

Often our first reaction is to blame ourselves for having been taken in and believing in someone who didn't deserve our trust. I am a big advocate of not beating ourselves up over trusting someone. In order to be trusted and develop relationships, we need to give trust. We are all only human and imperfect. We will make mistakes and need to be forgiven. We need the grace of one another to give second chances and rebuild trust and the relationship. We also have the right to make the decision that the breach of trust has been so serious we are not willing to continue a relationship with the other person.

The question is, what was the breach? How big was it and what can be done to rebuild trust? In most cases when someone lets us down, we will have a conversation about it and discuss the terms of forgiveness. We usually say, "I will forgive you, but you can never do this again" or "In the future I would expect that…"

When trust is broken, it gives us an opportunity to talk clearly about our expectations and boundaries and what we expect from the other person in the relationship.

ESTABLISHING ASSERTIVE BOUNDARIES

You are living your life and are entitled to make choices about who you have relationships with and the types of behaviour that you think are fair, respectful and trustworthy. You do not have to trust blindly. You have the ability to draw lines and assert boundaries around trust.

It is normal when you don't know someone well to ask for indicators of his good intentions. For example, if someone wants to buy something from you, typically you ask for cash or a bank draft, so you don't have to worry about a cheque bouncing.

When we are creating contracts with people, they must show their commitment by endorsing the contract with their signatures. When people are reluctant to sign an agreement, it implies there are terms in it they don't like or they don't intend to follow through. Some people are so trustworthy that a handshake or their verbal promise is all it takes to clinch the agreement.

Have you ever heard anyone say, "You trust me, don't you?" When they say this, it implies you should not question their integrity. From an assertive perspective, you have the right and responsibility to look after yourself and decide what boundaries you have with others in the process of trust building. There is no shame in asking for someone to make a show of trust.

A friend of mine explained her "trust rule" for boys dating her daughters. If a boy wants to date one of her girls, he has to come over and have dinner with the family first. If he isn't willing to do that, he fails the integrity test and the daughter can't date him.

Think about your relationships and the level of trust you have with others. Are you being trustworthy? Are they? Are you willing to work at rebuilding trust if something goes wrong?

Vancouver or Bust?

Two days after Jeff sent Luke on his way to Vancouver, he got a phone call from Luke.

Luke: Hey, Jeff, how are you doing?

Jeff: Fine, thanks. How's Vancouver treating you?

Luke: Well, funny thing, I'm not in Vancouver, I'm still in Calgary.

Jeff: What do you mean? I gave you a ticket so you could start a new life.

Luke: Yeah, well that didn't work out. I cashed in the ticket so I could see if things got any better here. I was wondering if you could help me out again.

Jeff: Well, Luke, it seems like you lied to me, so I don't know, man...

Then Luke hung up and the conversation was over.

Later that day over lunch with a colleague, Jeff was blaming himself because Luke had taken him in. The colleague told Jeff not to worry. He said every day we are faced with the decision whether or not to trust someone. He told Jeff, "You erred on the side of compassion, so you must be doing something right."

PRODUCTIVE PRINCIPLES ON TRUST

- High trust is important to maintain healthy relationships.

- Your reputation as a trustworthy person will influence your relationships.

- To get trust you need to give trust.

When Trying to Build Trust

Do:

- Keep your commitments and renegotiate them when you can't keep them.

- Speak about others as if they are in the room with you.

- Communicate with others in a way that shows respect to them from their perspective.

Don't:

- Purposely deceive others.

- Divulge confidential or important information others have shared with you without permission.

- Withhold information from others that affects them or has an impact on an area where they have responsibility.

- Make promises you know you can't keep.

- Throw others under the bus (blame or defame).

- Expect others to do things you are not willing to do, or adhere to values you do not follow yourself.

- Take credit for something you did not do.

EXERCISE: Creating Your Own Perfect World

1) Who do you trust the most? Why?

2) Who do you mistrust? Why?

3) Who do you think mistrusts you?

4) What can you do to close the trust gap with these people? What is the value of doing so?

Chapter 12
The Human Touch: Basic Manners

Manners are a sensitive awareness of the feelings of
others. If you have that awareness, you have good
manners, no matter what fork you use.[12] — *Emily Post*

A Convenience Store Christmas

A friend of mine stopped at a convenience store to buy ice cream en route to
a Christmas celebration in cottage country. While my friend stood in line, a
couple and their kids came into the store. The couple was arguing and the children were crying.

"Mom, I'm hungry," whined one child.

"I *know* you are, honey! If your Aunt Lorna weren't so *mean*, we would be
sitting down right now and eating a nice Christmas meal. Instead we are going
to get some snacks *here* and drive *two hours back home!*" (It seemed this information, delivered in a sniping tone, was given more for the benefit of the husband
rather than the child.)

"I didn't know she would freak out!" said the husband defensively. "I had no
idea she expected us to bring dessert!"

"Well, it's *your* frigging family!" replied the wife. "How was *I* supposed to
know? Now we have to take these kids and drive these roads again and our
Christmas is ruined! Thank you so much!"

What my friend deduced from the exchange is the couple and their kids
had shown up empty-handed at the husband's sister's house for Christmas.
Apparently "Auntie Lorna" was just *waiting* for them to show up to *yet another*
family event without contributing anything. When they arrived bearing no gifts

or food, Lorna told them to hit the road. She told them she was sick and tired of their rude behaviour. She was done cleaning and cooking while they sat around stuffing their faces, contributing nothing.

Although Lorna's approach may seem harsh, she had reached her breaking point at the perceived lack of manners of her brother and sister-in-law. Even if the couple had not known they were to contribute a dish to a shared meal, they could have followed what many consider to be good etiquette by bringing a bottle of wine or other hostess gift. Such a lack of basic manners is a common complaint in today's society.

WHY MANNERS?

Manners are important because they show respect and regard for others. Manners are the human touch — the special way we interact. When you don't use them, it makes others feel disrespected. Whether you are dealing with a family member or a co-worker or you're in a movie theatre, a store or on a bus, manners are important and they go both ways. It is not up to only one person in an interaction to exhibit manners; both parties have the opportunity to be civil.

If we ignore manners, we will find people do not want to deal with us. In fact, when I am asked to intervene through mediation, a lack of manners and courtesy are often cited as an issue between parties.

This chapter covers some basic manners that help create respect and rapport amongst members of a family, a workplace or a community. If you believe you know your manners and use them, but feel others around you don't, you might:

- Let them borrow this book and read the chapter.

- Start a discussion in your family, community group or workplace about the manners and etiquette amongst you.

- Review this chapter to discover whether or not you actually share the same views as others about manners.

It is worth noting what constitutes good manners varies between individuals and cultures. The ones I am describing reflect my view of European-North American manners when we are interacting on a face-to-face level, but other regions of the world or cultures may have very different expectations. For example, a woman in one of my workshops was gracious enough to share some of her experiences acclimatizing to Canadian culture and manners. She said that in her country one is not supposed to blow one's nose in public, especially when in close quarters with others, such as on public transit. Public nose blowing is considered to be impolite, so people deal with their runny noses by sniffling and snorting. Now that she is in North America, she notices people blowing their noses into tissues or hankies all the time. She feels stressed about this, as her challenge is one of overcoming a lifetime of learning to adjust to new social norms. She wants to accept those around her blowing their noses in public, but realizes that it is a process. The bottom line remains, good manners facilitate improved communication and relationships with others.

Good manners start in childhood. If you are a parent, model good manners to your children, and encourage your children to practise good manners. Using etiquette and showing respect to others is a lifelong interpersonal skill.

PROTOCOLS FOR TYPICAL SITUATIONS

In the following pages I offer up some basic manners. You may agree or disagree about what is appropriate, so take the opportunity to discuss manners with those around you with a view to coexisting harmoniously.

Acknowledgement — Being in the Presence of Others

On any given day, people come and go in the space around us. Acknowledging the presence and departure of others shows basic respect. When people are not acknowledged, it makes them feel insulted or not as valued as others who *are* acknowledged. Many people cannot identify exactly what acknowledging the presence and departure of others looks like, but they can easily describe what being slighted looks like.

So how do you acknowledge others? Generally, it means greeting people when they come into your presence or you enter theirs, by saying, "Hello" or "Good morning" or another greeting to reflect the time of day. You may even go so far as to ask the person, "How are you today?" Again, this question reflects a basic regard for and courtesy to the other person. If you are in the service industry, you may even add a question after the greeting: "How may I help you?"

When we encounter another person, whether it's someone you walk by at work or a family member or a guest watching TV in your own home, we may want to say, "Hi" or if we don't want to disturb the person, just make eye contact and smile or nod. Joggers tell me it is an unwritten rule of etiquette to smile, nod or say hello to a fellow runner while on the trail. Motorcyclists give a two-fingered wave as a greeting to other riders.

A common complaint I hear is about a third party interrupting two people conversing, without displaying any courtesy or manners. For example, in many workplaces, when two employees are talking, a third party may come into the conversation and without saying "Hello" or "Excuse me," will announce, "I need you to do this now." This interruption with no acknowledging words creates a sense of disrespect because the underlying message is that you shouldn't be talking, you should be working and you deserve no respect. This type of exchange may also occur in a home environment amongst family members.

How do we politely insert ourselves into an exchange between two people? The third person arriving on the scene could say something like, "Hello, please pardon my interruption" or "Hello, excuse me." These types of basic acknowledgement go a long way to show respect and get the other parties' attention so they are open to hearing what the third party has to say.

Acknowledging others is also important when we arrive at functions such as weddings, conferences, or public meetings and we are looking for a place to sit where others are already seated. It is polite to smile and ask, "May I join you?" In most cases, people will say, "Please do" or if they are saving seats, they let us know, so as to avoid problems when their friends arrive.

Likewise, there are some basic manners associated with taking one's leave. We may get up and say, "Thanks for your time" or "Well, I have to get going, so see you later." These simple words show a regard for the people or person you are leaving.

The right words for leaving a group can be more formal when we are eating. Dining is a shared experience and it is polite to address the host or say something like, "I am going to excuse myself, so thank you for the pleasure of your company." If you are taking your leave from someone who provided or cooked the meal, it is also customary to thank that person for the meal and to say you enjoyed it.

Many of us participate in meetings, another circumstance where we are moving into the presence of others. In most cases, basic manners apply. One big complaint I hear about is people arriving late. It is a common opinion that people showing up late is a sign of disrespect to those who were on time and indicates the late arrivals don't value others enough to bother being on time. I believe that view can be a bit harsh, as we all juggle numerous priorities. Sometimes there is a valid reason for being late. However, the point is, if you are late coming to a meeting, some percentage of the group will think you are rude. Most people will excuse your transgression if you simply apologize and give a brief reason (which is optional). You can also tell another person who is going to the meeting — or if possible, the chairperson — that you are going to be late and ask them to pass this information on to the group, along with your apologies. People will forgive our imperfections when we show regard and courtesy.

Making Introductions

Introducing yourself to someone you don't know is a common courtesy. When you are meeting people for the first time, you don't need to wait to be introduced. Merely extend your hand and say, "Hello, I am…" If you have others with you, it is polite to introduce them as well.

I meet a lot of people and often remember faces, but not always names. Greeting people with a handshake or hello is one thing, but it is also important to acknowledge whether you have met them before. I have found individuals to be very gracious when I confess I've forgotten their names but remember their faces. Half the time, people do not remember my name, either.

Acknowledging Special Events and Accomplishments

Celebrating milestones with others, even in a small way, shows respect for them and for your relationship with them. *How* you as an individual or as part of a group acknowledge events like birthdays, anniversaries, graduations, retirements is up to you to decide. Other events that are huge milestones in people's lives include marriages and births. If you are unsure of what is expected, consider what that person would do for you if it were *you* celebrating. We tend to act in a way that we feel is appropriate. To acknowledge events or milestones you could:

- Send a congratulatory card.

- Send flowers or a gift.

- See the person for a visit or have them over for dinner.

- Call or Skype them.

The Magic Words: Please and Thank You!

Most people I work with say they would appreciate it if people would use more manners in a day. Saying "please" and "thank you" for the things other people do for us is a very basic element of manners. Those words are almost magical in the way that they have the power to quickly convey to others that you have respect for them. All the way from "Would you please pass the salt?" to "Thank you for putting the laundry away" or "Thank you for staying late to finish this project" — these words are essential for acknowledging others' contributions.

One of the biggest complaints I hear is not receiving a verbal thank you or even an acknowledgement from a person to whom a birthday gift or card was sent. Texting or phoning with a thank you lets the sender know you have received the item and gives you a chance to say thanks. As well, if someone has sent an item via the mail or a courier, it is polite to let him know that the item arrived safely.

When I travel to a country where English is not the first language, I make a point of learning the words *please* and *thank you* in that country's language, as it shows a regard for their practices and manners. I have also done this at social gatherings in Canada where the primary language used is one I don't know.

When People Go Out of Their Way for You

For more significant deeds or favours, it is appropriate to say thank you in more tangible ways:

- Send a thank-you note.

- Send a bouquet of flowers.

- Emails are okay, but not as meaningful as a handwritten note.

- A box of chocolates, a bottle of wine or appropriate food can also be a nice thank-you.

- Words like *thank you, I appreciate your time, effort, and thoughtfulness* are all helpful.

People do expect a written thank-you note for baby, shower and wedding gifts.

If you don't say thanks for the big deeds or for a significant gift someone sent you, it can be seen as hurtful or impolite.

Well, Excuse Me!

When we get in others' way or they get in ours, not acknowledging this can be seen as disrespect.

- Say "excuse me" when you pass in between two people (which you should try to avoid when possible).

- Say "excuse me" in a store aisle when you pass between someone and the shelf that they are looking at.

- If you get in someone's way or jostle someone accidentally, it is customary to say "pardon me," "excuse me," or "I'm sorry."

- Opening the door for others can be a kind and helpful gesture, especially if the other party's hands are full.

- Letting other people go ahead of you through a door, into an elevator, down a staircase or onto an escalator are ways of showing regard for others.

- It is also kind to offer a seat to the elderly, to pregnant women, and to people who have an obvious injury.

Mother, May I? — Manners For Using Other People's Stuff

Manners extend to expectations people have regarding their property. For example, it is considered *im*polite by most people to:

- Take or use personal items from their room or home without asking permission first, i.e., "May I use your computer?" This also applies at work. Many people express anger when co-workers take equipment or other personal effects from their desk or workspace without asking. Taking people's lunch or food without having permission is a definite violation. If something is not yours, ask for permission or leave it alone.

- Neglect returning things borrowed from others. Items borrowed should be returned in a timely fashion, and remember to say, "Thanks for letting me use your… "

- To return a borrowed item in damaged condition. Proper etiquette dictates repairing or replacing the item.

When you are requesting something, it is customary to ask, "May I…?" which shows respect while requesting permission. "May I borrow your stapler?" "May I have this dance?"

Handling RSVPs

At some point you will be invited to events where the host requests an RSVP. This stands for *répondez s'il vous plaît, a* French phrase meaning that a reply is requested. Usually there is a *reply by* date. The function of the RSVP is to supply the host with a head count so he can provide enough food, seating and any other items required for the event.

Most hosts who book a venue are responsible to pay for a guaranteed number of guests. It is very impolite not to contact the host by the RSVP date on the invitation, unless the invitation states, "Regrets only." This phrase means that the host expects you to reply only if you *cannot* come.

Once you reply "yes" to an RSVP, you are expected to attend, unless you are ill or there is an emergency.

Dressing for the Occasion

Steve Jobs, the former CEO of Apple, was noted for his black turtleneck sweater and blue jeans. Dressing for him was easy, since he had a self-styled uniform. The question I hear many people ask when they are going to specific events is "What should I wear?" the concern being that they don't want to be over-dressed or underdressed.

What we wear affects what people think of us. Today there is no one standard dress code that applies to everyone in every situation.

For more formal occasions, such as weddings and funerals, people are usually expected to honour the "no jeans" approach. Often men will wear jackets and/ or ties to show respect for the occasion. Invitations to events sometimes specify a dress code, such as "formal," "business casual," "cocktail attire," etc. Many companies have dress codes that explicitly state what type of clothes and accessories are allowed and what are not. For example, some companies prohibit the use of certain body jewellery or will designate the colour of clothing.

Start with being clean and kempt. That means having a clean person — smelling clean, brushing your teeth and wearing clean clothes. Cleanliness shows a respect for yourself and a regard for others. I have mediated more than one workplace dispute where someone's basic hygiene was an issue. Similarly, combing your hair and grooming any facial hair will give others a more favourable impression.

Having manners concerning one's wardrobe comes down to having a regard for others. How might what you're wearing affect how others feel? Will your clothing make someone feel disrespected or uncomfortable? Wearing clothing that reveals underwear is too revealing for most situations. Be mindful of the cut of a blouse or dress, the length of a skirt or how low one's waistband droops. It is an unpleasant experience to see the top of someone's underwear band, or worse, an exposed behind!

When in doubt, ask the host of an event what type of clothing is expected. In a workplace situation, adhere to the dress code.

Making Appointments and Scheduling Time

Dropping in on people used to be a normal way to maintain friendships. Today, with everyone's busy schedules, a way to respect people's time and privacy is to arrange a time with them, as opposed to dropping by unannounced. Those closest to us may not mind the drop-in. But what if they are hosting someone else or are in the middle of a business transaction?

When we drop by someone's home or even a colleague's office, we cannot expect he will always have time for us. In addition, if you have a special request, or if you need someone's time at a school, a government agency or business, your interaction will probably go better when you have an appointment. Appointments allow the other party to prepare and be of better service. Be proactive and make appointments, ensuring you schedule time in your calendar for the people and activities that are important.

Manners in a Group

If you have been at a movie theatre recently, you may have noticed that, along with upcoming movie trailers, theatres show a list of guidelines for how people should conduct themselves during the movie. Guidelines such as: do not talk, no texting, throw your refuse in the garbage — are all hot tips on how to make the theatre experience good for everyone who has paid to enjoy the show. That is because one person's inconsiderate or disruptive behaviour can take way from other people's enjoyment.

Common group settings include the classroom, school events, post-secondary environments, staff meetings, community meetings, presentations, ceremonies and performances.

When we are part of an audience or group it is important to be mindful of listening and conducting ourselves in a way that does not disrupt other people's experience. This at a minimum means:

- Being prepared to sit and be quiet to listen

- Giving the chair, performer or MC the floor

- Taking conversations outside the room rather than disrupting the group

- Using your cell phone for conversations and texting outside the room

I was surprised and dismayed recently that during a graduation ceremony, the audience had to be reminded repeatedly to remain silent so that the graduates could hear their name being called to receive their diploma.

Manners mean being considerate of others. Check with your group to see what guidelines are appropriate.

MANNERS DURING DIFFICULT CIRCUMSTANCES

People often struggle with what is polite and appropriate when others are dealing with illness and death.

Illness

If someone is seriously ill or dealing with a family member who is sick, the main thing is to respect their privacy and not put them in an awkward situation or ask awkward questions that are none of your business. If people choose to share details about the illness, that is up to them. When I was on crutches after surgery, I was shocked by total strangers coming up to me and asking, "What happened to you?" I was very put off by this type of approach. On the other hand, people opening doors for me or carrying things to my car showed basic humanity and courtesy.

Dealing with illness creates stress. We do not want to create more stress by inappropriate behaviour. What is appropriate is a factor of the closeness of the relationship you have with the people involved. If you are not close to someone, but wish to show concern, you may decide to send him a get-well card or a bouquet of flowers. This can be done as an individual, a family or a group at work.

Also when someone is sick, we can help in tangible ways by offering child care, providing meals or gift cards for places that offer prepared food, driving people to appointments or treatments, shovelling walks or mowing lawns.

Death

When a friend, acquaintance or co-worker experiences a death in the family, it is sometimes hard to know what to do. Some considerations:

- Send a sympathy card. You do not necessarily need to write anything in it, other than the names of the people you are addressing it to: "The Smith Family" or "Bob and Joan & Family" — "with sympathy" or "sincerely" and sign it.

- You can send flowers to the home of a family that has encountered a loss, or make arrangements to have flowers sent to the funeral service. (You may want to check on the cultural norms regarding this practice.)

- Some families ask that donations be made to certain charities in the memory of the deceased. As well, when young children are left behind special funds are sometimes set up for their education.

- Attending a funeral service is a sign of respect and support.

- When someone has encountered a loss, a way to share your condolences is to say to the person, "I offer my condolences" or "I am sorry for your loss." It is also appropriate to shake the person's hand or, if your relationship is fairly close, to give them a hug.

We often shy away from these circumstances because the people grieving feel uncomfortable and that can make us feel awkward.

Behaviours That Say, "I Diss You"

Diss is a slang term for *disrespect*. Manners are inherent in the body language and non-verbals we use. You need to be careful of the following behaviours, which may be viewed as impolite by others. If you continue with these types of behaviour, you run the risk of undermining your relationships by:

- Standing with your back turned to others

- Texting while you are with others — particularly in a meeting or a social setting

- Taking a phone call in the presence of others. If you must take it, excuse yourself

- Talking too loudly on the phone when others are around

- Playing music too loud

- Wearing perfume or cologne; many people have allergies or sensitivities to strong smells

Are Manners Passé?

Although people appreciate manners and etiquette these days many are unsure how to approach the topic. It is not about adhering to an etiquette manual but about behaving in a way where our words and actions show a regard for others.

Many people use the concept of "political correctness" as a reason to ignore social decorum. Because we live in such a culturally rich society, people are worried about making mistakes, so they may do little in terms of acknowledging and connecting with others for fear of making a mistake. Given our cultural differences there are times we may need to research what is appropriate. When in doubt, check it out.

It is true we all have our own beliefs about manners and respect. We judge others' propriety based on our own expectations. So there are times when we feel slighted by someone's lack of manners, yet that person may have no idea what we expect.

To treat others with the kind of manners and respect that are appropriate to *them* means taking the time to understand what is important to them. It also means letting people know our intentions in our behaviour — when our goal is to show honour, consideration or respect. Manners are the human touch that shows our regard for others and strengthens relationships.

EXERCISE: Creating Your Own Perfect World

1) Do you feel that you are well mannered?

2) Do you experience a lack of manners in your daily interactions?

3) What is this lack of manners doing to your personal relationships?

4) How could you start a dialogue, at home, at work, or in your community group or team, to create a shared approach to manners?

Chapter 13
What I Like About You: Giving Others Positive Feedback

My feelings will not be repressed. You must allow me to tell
you how ardently I admire and love you. — *Jane Austen*

You Made My Day!

I was facilitating a leadership workshop in a major Canadian city. The participants were from all across the country. One of the vice-presidents of the company popped in unexpectedly. He welcomed everyone and invited us to join him for dinner that night. During the weeklong session he came by a few times. His presence and the hospitality he extended to the employees of his company inspired and engaged them and made them feel valued and connected. I had not asked him to do this yet he did.

After the session I sent him a thank-you note for the dinner and acknowledged each thing he had done — making an effort to be present, greeting staff, putting the session in the context of their work, and asking questions — because he was showing them leadership in action. His behaviour was a model for the best leadership practices and reinforced the learning.

I was surprised to receive a response from him a few days later. He said, "Thank you for your thank-you note! I know it sounds funny, but when I got it, it made my day!"

It was a great reminder to me that even those at the top of an organization benefit from positive feedback and need to know the efforts they undertake are worthwhile.

One of the most challenging aspects of effective communication is being able to share opinions with others in a way that is respectful, appropriate, meaningful and genuine. Making the choice to give others positive feedback elevates our relationships.

POSITIVE FEEDBACK BASICS

Providing positive feedback is simply telling people what we like about them or their behaviour. It also includes acknowledging and appreciating the things they do.

When we have a good experience with another person we have an opportunity to provide positive feedback, which is a requisite for maintaining relationships of any kind. If we are to have healthy relationships with spouses, children, friends and colleagues, ensuring that our positive interactions far outweigh the negative ones will help us with that goal. The habit of affirming others is a good one to get into.

Some people are reluctant to give positive feedback. My grandfather used to say if you give a child too much positive feedback, he might get a "fat head" and develop an arrogant attitude.

Some leaders in organizations also subscribe to this thinking. They wonder why they should bother giving employees positive feedback when they simply do the things they are getting paid to do. The answer is simple. Human beings need acknowledgement and they need to know what they do matters and is noticed. Positive feedback nurtures us, provides affirmation and encourages us to keep on doing things that provide value.

When we are generous and genuine with positive feedback, it provides balance in our communication with others. Chapter 9 introduced the concept that interactions can either fill our buckets (make us feel good) or dip from our buckets (make us feel bad). Think how difficult it is to be in a relationship with someone who only points out your mistakes. It is exhausting and depressing.

Various Types of Positive Feedback

1) **Acknowledgement and Manners**

   When we acknowledge what others have done, it shows we notice and value their efforts and contributions. When others use good manners, people feel respected. So a primary type of positive feedback is saying *thank you*. Phrases such as *"Well done, thanks!" "Nice job!"* or *"Way to go!"* are simple acknowledgements.

Even when we are merely fulfilling our role at work, most people like being acknowledged for the effort made or a job well done. Many parents say they like being thanked by their children. "Thanks for making a good lunch" is an expression of appreciation. Likewise, using manners with our children is a simple way to model positive feedback. "Thank you for cleaning up your room" or "Thank you for texting me when you realized you were going to be late" are examples of acknowledging helpful behaviour. When we acknowledge positive behaviour we boost a person's self-esteem and increase the chances of them repeating the behaviour.

I have seen couples take the time to express acknowledgement to each other, even for everyday events. Comments such as "The lawn sure looks nice after you mowed it" or "It's helpful when you take out the garbage — thanks" acknowledge another person's contribution. The more positives we can find, the more positive behaviours will grow.

Using manners and acknowledging what others have done are forms of positive feedback and a simple and effective approach to enhancing relationships.

2) **Compliments**

Compliments are comments that express our approval, regard or favourable opinion. They are different from acknowledgements in that they are not necessarily tied to performance or fulfilment of a task or role. Giving someone a compliment such as "Your haircut looks great!" or "You look nice" or "You are fun to be with" or "You're great" are all examples of compliments.

While many people are pleased to receive praise, compliments can seem vague. Some people feel suspicious of flattery because they believe it is insincere or someone is setting them up for an "ask." Although it is important to give others as much positive feedback as possible, it has to be genuine. People can tell when we are being insincere and saying things just to "butter them up."

3) **Specific Positive Feedback**

While compliments can be helpful, many people appreciate specific positive feedback. They want to know exactly what they did so they can verify it and replicate it. Being specific about what we value helps the receiver of the information understand and validate it.

The most effective positive feedback includes three elements:

1. What was done to generate the praise?

2. What impact did it have on the person who is giving the feedback?

3. Why was it significant (the "so what?" factor)?

For example, we went on a holiday, leaving our nineteen-year-old son home alone. When we came home we were delighted everything in the house was in as good shape or better than we left it. I said to my son, "Matt, you did a great job managing things while we were away. Thanks!"

A more specific approach to the feedback would have been:

1. What specifically was done to generate the praise? (*You brought in the mail and the newspaper; you put the dishes in the dishwasher; you cleaned up the kitchen well, including the stovetop.*)

2. What impact did it have on the giver of the feedback? (*It was so nice to come home and have a clean house so I could get on with my work.*)

3. Why it was significant (or the "so what?" factor)? (*You've shown us once again that we can trust you, that you are capable and you care about our home.*)

Too often, the feedback process is a one-way conversation. You can enhance the positive feedback experience by inviting the receiver of the feedback into the conversation. I asked Matt, "You really did so well. What was your secret this time?" He happily replied, "I just felt it was important to do my part and I really made an effort with everything because I'm not a kid any more." The interaction seemed to make him feel good and his behaviour was certainly appreciated.

Inviting the other person into the conversation allows you to understand more about him and his perspective on his accomplishments and gives you the opportunity to learn new information you wouldn't have if you hadn't invited him to participate.

Invitational questions can be anything that is effective. Consider the context of the situation in order to formulate an appropriate question. Some examples include:

- What is your secret for doing so well?

- How do you feel about what you did?

- What motivated you to do it?

- Did you try anything special that helped you do this?

- What do you think about this?

- What did you learn from this?

- What are you grateful for in this situation?

- How did accomplishing this make you feel?

You will want to consider the subtleties of word choice in phrasing your questions so you can effectively engage the particular person you are communicating with.

As well, there are times when people accomplish things with the help of others. When we invite the receiver of positive feedback to share a response, it gives that person an opportunity to note other people who were involved in the achievement, giving us a chance to share more positive feedback with others.

4) **Sentiments**

Another type of positive feedback that helps maintain relationships is when we express our sentiments. This gets into a "touchy-feely" area that may be difficult for some people to express, yet is powerful in creating engaging and positive relationships.

Expressing positive sentiments like "I love you," "I am proud of you," "I care about you" are expressions that help people understand how they are valued. These types of sentiment are often expressed in relationships with our close friends, an intimate partner, our children and extended family. When talking to her friends and family, a friend always ends a telephone or a face-to-face conversation with a simple, "Love you! 'Bye!"

A friend of mine, Della, said her mother never told her she loved her. Della accepted the fact her mom probably did love her, but didn't like saying it. Then on Della's fortieth birthday, Della was surprised and delighted when her mother told her she loved her. It was a special turning point in their relationship.

Della said she has freely told her own children from the day they were born that they are well loved. She never wanted her children to wonder about it as Della did growing up.

Expressing sentiments in our closest relationships is a real opportunity to cultivate love, respect and security.

5) **Encouragement**

Encouraging others is a form of feedback that gives people comfort and support. When people are in the middle of difficult or challenging circumstances, encouragement from others can help. When we cheer others on it helps them maintain a positive self-view even when they are unhappy with their own performance or situation. Encouragement fortifies us.

A friend of mine who was going through a divorce was talking with her brother about her difficulties and what she would have to do to move forward. Rather than offering encouragement, her brother said, "Well, everyone thought you were making a mistake when you married him, but you just wouldn't listen. I hate to say I told you so, but I did, and now you're paying for it just like I predicted!" Discouraging things can slip out of our mouths without us thinking about it. We end up belittling others and undermining our relationship with them. These types of behaviour are bucket-dipping events.

Words of encouragement are phrases like:

- "I know it's tough now, but you'll figure it out."

- "You are a hard worker and you'll get where you need to go."

- "You always do your best and you don't give up."

- "Things will be okay."

- "I know you can do it."

- "Whatever happens, you will learn something from it and it'll all be good."

- "Don't beat yourself up, you did what you thought was best at the time."

Encouragement gives others the confidence to accept the ups and downs of life with grace and to see challenges and mistakes as a natural learning process. Having an encouraging mindset means having faith in the capacity of others and respecting their right to live their own lives, make their own choices and experience the consequences.

6) **Tangible Rewards**

Most parents have used the strategy of giving treats to their children as rewards for doing things that they wanted them to do such as "Put your toys away and you'll get a candy."

Some companies give out awards for years of service and provide bonuses or trips for employees who have hit performance targets. At schools, students with high grades receive academic awards and scholarships. Special interest groups and volunteer organizations give out certificates and awards. The point is that positive feedback may be expressed in some situations by giving people something tangible. This type of positive feedback is less available and more exclusive. It usually means people have to achieve extreme outcomes to get recognition.

If we rely only on the formal, tangible or monetary ways of giving feedback, we are missing out on the opportunities to give feedback to others every day.

Some people find it hard to give others positive feedback. What's stopping you? You are missing a great opportunity to enhance your relationships. — *PH*

LEARN TO TAKE A COMPLIMENT

Giving someone a compliment or positive feedback is a gesture that takes time, thought and effort. Too often when given a compliment or positive feedback, people will say, "Oh, it wasn't that big a deal!" or "I was just doing my job!" or "You didn't have to say that!" This type of reaction, while good in intention because people don't want to come across as arrogant, has a negative effective on the giver. The giver has put some effort into giving the positive feedback. The comments above minimize the gesture. It is as if someone has offered you a gift and you have pushed it away.

Accepting positive feedback with grace encourages the giver of feedback to keep it up. The best way to accept a compliment is with a simple thank you and a smile.

Feedback — A Cycle of Giving and Receiving

In order to create a culture of feedback, it is helpful for people in an organization, family or community to view feedback as a cycle of giving and receiving. Because of the benefits of feedback, it is a gift that enhances our performance and lives in many ways. If everyone can be part of the cycle, it supports people giving feedback. When people receive feedback with graciousness, it encourages the cycle to continue.

SUMMARY

Being able to give all types of positive feedback enhances relationships. Caution: separate positive feedback from negative feedback. Comments such as "Wow, you did a great job, but you could even do better next time" are a mixed message. Are you really saying that I did a good job or are you just not telling me what you didn't like? In workshops, I make a point of getting people to separate positive and negative feedback. I insist people start feedback by sharing what they liked or appreciated about something. Only once they have identified those things that are valuable to continue can they get into opportunities for improvement.

Giving Positive Feedback at Home
Do:

- Find as many opportunities as possible to give your spouse, children or roommates positive feedback.

- Give positive feedback to others about the behaviours you want them to continue, i.e., "Steven, thanks for remembering to shut off the TV."

- Give compliments: "Bob your new golf shirt looks great!"

- Remember: positive feedback helps people feel good and enhances relationships.

Don't:

- Say it if you don't mean it.

- Lavish praise on one person in the household and ignore others.

- Be afraid to try it even if you are unaccustomed to it.

Giving Positive Feedback at Work
Do:

- Connect with the person privately, one-on-one.

- Be specific about what you appreciate and how what they did is relevant or significant to you.

- Include them in the conversation; ask questions to invite their comments.

- Find opportunities to give positive feedback to others (colleagues, co-workers and even your boss).

- Try to give all people who contributed to an outcome positive feedback.

- Be mindful that delivering positive feedback to an individual in a group may embarrass some people who do not like public accolades.

Don't:

- Be discouraged if someone is not receptive to your feedback; many people do not enjoy receiving positive feedback or feel it is only appropriate for exceptional results.

- Let the fact you can't give monetary rewards stop you from giving positive verbal reinforcement.

EXERCISE: Creating Your Own Perfect World

1) Make an effort to give positive feedback to those with whom you have close relationships.

2) As a start, try to give out positive feedback at least three times a day to three different individuals. (These could be people at home, at work or in your community.) Try this for two weeks.

3) At the end of two weeks, consider how your relationships with others have changed. How have those people changed? How have you changed?

PART FOUR
The Challenges and Hurdles of Interacting

*We all have our own preferences around communicating.
Sometimes people's styles or the medium
they use make it difficult for us to understand each other.
Dealing with negative emotions and opinions takes some heavy lifting.
Working through it helps us break through. — PH*

Chapter 14
Why Can't People Be More Like Me? Adapting Communication to Connect with Styles

---

When you adapt your communication to reflect someone else's preferences — communication can flow more easily and you get better results. — PH

When you go to social gatherings you may have noticed the different types of personality: the persuasive salesman types who like to chat with everybody; the quiet, intelligent types in the corner of the room who figure things out by watching others interact; the domineering types who share their opinions and tell others what to do; and the nurturing, supportive types who advocate cooperation and teamwork.

William Marston, a psychologist, noticed that people exhibit different preferences, styles and reactions to everyday events. He conducted extensive research to explore and explain these differences in behavioural patterns and published his findings in *The Emotions of Normal People*. In this book he identified four main behavioural patterns that typify styles and preferences of communication: Dominance, Inducement, Submission and Compliance.[13]

His work led to the development of several personality style assessments. All four patterns are present in people, but to varying degrees. We have a preferred style and tend to communicate more easily with people who share our style.

IMPLICATIONS OF STYLES

When we interact with people who have a style different from ours, it can be challenging to understand them. We tend to see our style and way of communicating as being the best and see other people's style as wrong. Differences in style can create a barrier to communication.

We often misinterpret the intentions of people because of their different mannerisms, and take offence when none was intended. For example, the *compliant* style tends to be quiet and unassuming and may find someone who is an *inducer* to be loud and obnoxious or disturbing, while other inducers would think he is fun. We can use knowledge about styles and preferences to help us be more effective communicators. In order to make use of this knowledge about styles, we can:

1. Observe a person's behaviour and notice their word choice, body language and facial expressions, and assess what the style is.

2. Shift from our style and adapt to use the elements of communication that are preferential to the other style.

3. Mirror the other person.

In truth, no one style is good or bad. Each style and behavioural pattern has strengths and weaknesses. We can improve the efficacy of our communication by applying knowledge of these styles. Our first opportunity is to identify another person's style and then to adapt our own to match. When we match styles, we mirror elements of communication such as word choice, tone, body language, volume and tempo. Matching the other person's style makes him feel more comfortable and will typically lead to a more effective exchange.

THE FOUR STYLES

1) **THE DOMINANT**

Descriptors: direct, prevailing, über-assertive, in charge

Mindset:

- Likes to exercise control over others and the situation

- Task-focused

- Prefers to prevail over others

Characteristics:

- Assertive and often seen as aggressive, promoting his own thoughts and agendas

- Strong-willed

- Talks mainly about getting things done

- Does not like to talk about feelings and emotions and personal issues

- Says what is on his mind and remains silent on matters that don't interest him

- Focuses on completing the mission

- A competitive risk-taker

- Self-reliant

- Motivated by achieving goals and the satisfaction of getting things done

- Appreciates monetary rewards and status associated with accomplishments

- Enjoys power and autonomy

Communication Tendencies:

- Self-confident and direct

- Does not wait to be spoken to, shares what is on his mind whether asked to or not

- Dominates conversations

- Holds others' attention

- Might use tentative or exploratory terminology, but maintains a focused and direct tone that makes everything he says sound like an order or a fact

- Tone is authoritarian and commanding

- Facial expressions are intense and focused

- Tends to ignore the emotional impact of situations in favour of results

- Is an impatient listener who may speak in incomplete sentences

- Often perceived by others as being terse, bossy, controlling, aggressive and angry

When confronted with a style that is characterized by a passive body language and tone, dominants can become frustrated, as they just like to get on with the task and want others to speak up. They do not like small talk and tend not to acknowledge others unless they need something from them. They are decisive, stubborn and have an inclination towards competitiveness. Other styles can be intimidated by the dominant style.

Adapting your Style to the Dominant:
Do:

- Use confident body language (stand up straight and make eye contact).

- Clearly explain your intention for having the interaction.

- Speak loudly and confidently.

- Be succinct and brief.

- Be ready to explain what you want or what you are providing.

- Be respectful of their time.

Don't:

- Push them for a decision when there is not enough information or background, because they will make a decision and then stick to it.

- Take their lack of focus on you as a person as an affront.

- Make small talk unless they initiate it.

- Get into pleasantries.

- Talk about personal matters — theirs or yours.

- Send thank-you emails to them.

Each style has its strengths. Dominants are especially valued when decision-making and the ability to take risks are called for. You don't want a wishy-washy doctor who doesn't know whether or not he should remove your appendix or an explosives expert who can't decide whether to cut the blue wire or the red one to deactivate the bomb. Dominants tend to be direct and sure.

2) THE INDUCER

Descriptors: friendly, people-person, optimist, schmoozer

Mindset:

- Looks for the positive in every situation

- Achieves goals by engaging, cajoling and inspiring others

- Likes to be liked and wants others to feel good

Characteristics:

- Assertive, animated, not afraid of being in the spotlight

- Tends to be enthusiastic and optimistic

- Laughs a lot and is a loud talker

- Is recognized as being a good storyteller

- A source of fun and creativity

- Seen by other styles as too flamboyant and over the top at times

- Likes to talk about experiences, feelings and self before tasks

- Engaging and generally empathetic

Communication Tendencies:

- Friendly, open and approachable

- Shares opinions but considers the audience

- Varies pitch, emphasis and volume

- Tends to use hand gestures

- Noted for using animated facial expressions

- May be seen as a "sweet talker" or having the "gift of the gab"

- Appreciates and uses humour

- Moderately good listener

Inducers are viewed as the life of the party. They enjoy engaging others and talking about fun and interesting things. They are dynamic, interesting to listen to, and like to tug on the heartstrings. They use hand gestures and words that are associated with feelings and energy, while speaking at a brisk pace and using pauses expertly for emphasis. They like compliments.

Adapting your Style to the Inducer:
Do:

- Provide positive feedback and recognition when possible.

- Smile and be upbeat.

- Engage in some personal exchange before you get down to business.

- Follow up with written ideas, as they don't always take notes.

- Ask questions to extract details or provide details to them; because they prefer big picture thinking they may not always think about the finer points.

- Speak at their volume and vary your pitch of voice for interest and emphasis.

- Match their intensity.

- Use feeling words — *love, enthusiasm, fun.*

Don't:

- Be negative.

- Blame or criticize them.

- Talk about what cannot be done.

- Speak in a monotone.

Inducers are chameleons. They can usually talk to anyone about anything. Others may think that inducers are too busy having fun to get any work done or to make a difference. But inducers are the ultimate connectors. They invite creativity and a can-do outlook. If you need to build bridges with others, if you need to be inspired or entertained, ask the inducer.

3) **THE SUBMISSIVE**

Descriptors: supportive, stable, team player, caregiver

Mindset:

- Yields to the will and needs of others

- Focuses on feelings

- Tends to work and behave within the guidelines of a given role while including and respecting others

Characteristics:

- Seen as having a passive style

- Has a tendency to respond to others, as opposed to initiating conversations

- Has a caring nature and is motivated by acknowledgement

- Quick to support others and to speak up when a colleague or loved one is overlooked, but does not usually speak up for himself

- Tends to be humble and self-effacing

- Accomplished at getting the job done, yet always has time to listen to others

- Appreciates good manners and positive feedback

- Uses variations in tone and often touches or hugs those who are dear to him

- A great supporter of others, extremely patient and loyal

- Can be indecisive and indirect

Communication Tendencies:

- Sensitive to the needs of others and the impact of actions on others

- Supportive and a great listener

- Speaks at a low volume

- Does not easily share negative feelings about himself (i.e., wouldn't reveal feeling stressed or being over-worked)

- May come across as a martyr for all he does for others while being selfless

- May say he doesn't need help or attention, even if he needs it

Submissive types will share information when they are invited to and only if they truly trust the person they are speaking with. They are quiet in their communications, speaking in low tones, with a slower pace and with more pauses than either the dominant or inducer styles. They care about others and their feelings and believe people should work together and be considerate of each other. They tend to say yes to everything and sometimes feel stressed and overwhelmed with all they have to do. They do not like to say no to people and prefer to be accommodating. Their body language can be hard to read sometimes because, even when they are overwhelmed, they put on a brave front.

Adapting your Style to the Submissive:
Do:

- Use a calm and quiet tone.

- Ask how they are and show interest in them as people.

- Use manners and show respect (excuse me, please/thank you).

- Express gratitude often and sincerely, sending a thank-you note or email.

- Take time to build a trusting relationship.

- Highlight their strengths (tell them what you value about them).

- Ask them questions about their opinions.

Don't:

- Speak too fast or intensely.

- Take them for granted.

- Overload them with expectations or responsibilities.

- Be loud and overly talkative.

- Use phrases such as "Can you handle it?" because they will find even the slightest inference of an inability insulting.

Submissives are, in many ways, caretakers, thriving on looking after and supporting others and being of service. They want to cultivate community and be inclusive of others and in return do not want to be accused of not doing their part on a work team or in a family. This style prefers peace to conflict. They are good at creating harmony and will accommodate others, sometimes at their own expense.

4) **THE COMPLIANT**

Descriptors: thorough, meticulous, thinker, rule follower

Mindset:

- Focuses on following established processes, guidelines and rules

- Detail-oriented — likes to create outcomes that are accurate and correct

- Believes that for things to be right, a comprehensive process or framework needs to be followed

Characteristics:

- Seen as passive in behaviour

- Requires time to assess and think as he works or sorts through options

- Quiet, does not speak up unless he has something very important to say; is unlikely to initiate conversation

- Task-focused

- Tends to avoid sharing his emotions

- Does not like surprises

- Will not share information or an opinion unless he has had a chance to research and think about it

- Typically prefers to work alone and keeps to himself

- Strives for accuracy and thoroughness

- Will over-analyse if there are not clear parameters in a scenario

Compliants are motivated when they have the opportunity to follow clear processes and can identify clear goals and guidelines. They believe others rely on the information they provide, and strive for perfection and accuracy so they will not negatively impact others. They thoroughly analyse situations, weighing pros and cons.

Communication Tendencies:

- Requires details and specifics

- Uses little vocal variation

- Speaks quietly

- Avoids conflict

- Even when a compliant has something to say, the information needs to be drawn out

- Will be very quiet as they work, think and process

- Needs downtime to rejuvenate

- Will share information when asked directly (does not respond to a general "Does anyone have anything to say?")

Adapting your Style to the Compliant:
Do:

- Be focused and specific.

- Be prepared to share details.

- Listen to them and their details.

- In order to draw them out, ask what they think is important.

- Give them lots of lead-time to do things and think about decisions, because they will not enjoy being put on the spot or being required to think on their feet.

Don't:

- Engage them in small talk.

- Be loud and in their face and space.

- Share your feelings with them unless they ask.

Compliants are quiet by nature. They often speak quietly and in a monotone and can be hard to hear, making it difficult to decipher whether or not something is important to them. They do not emphasize things in the same way other styles would and they do not like to speak in front of others. As well, if you ask them for input and they have not had a chance to analyse or think about it ahead of time, they will not say anything because they are not prepared. Compliants have a way of understanding the big picture and the small details all at the same time. If you want things done right or to know what steps have to be followed or wonder how one thing impacts another, ask a compliant.

ADAPTING TO OTHERS' STYLES

The intention, when we identify styles, is *not* to put people into boxes. Observing other people's behaviour allows us to get a read on their preferences in order to communicate better with them, not to stereotype them.

Also be aware that everyone exhibits the behaviours of all styles at one time or another. While we all typically have a predominant style, our secondary style can have a big impact on our behaviour. The most effective communicators are ones who can shift their style and adapt to whomever they are with and the situation they are in.

Many people get distressed and angry at the thought of shifting their own style to adapt to another. In workshops, people bluntly ask the question, "Why should *I* have to be the one to change my style? Why don't other people do it for *me*?"

My response is you cannot control another person's behaviour; you can only influence it. You can control your own. So, if you make the choice to mirror the other person's style, you will communicate more effectively with him, which means your message will be understood and you have a better chance of achieving the results you are looking for. This shift will give you improved relationships and less stress.

The other thing to remember is that you are not changing your style. You are momentarily modifying it in order to be a strategic and effective communicator. It is like being able to speak more than one language. If you speak French when you are in France, you will be more easily understood than if you speak English. You will benefit by getting better directions and have less stress trying to navigate the country. That doesn't mean you give up English and never speak it again. Shifting and adapting your style is like being multi-lingual. It opens up the world, helps you connect with others, reduces conflict and misunderstanding, and improves results.

SUMMARY

- Be conscious of other people's styles.

- Remember you can adapt your style for better
  results and richer relationships.

EXERCISE: Creating Your Own Perfect World

1. Think about the people you interact with on a daily basis who are
   challenging to communicate with.

2. What do you think their main style is? What is their second most
   preferred style?

3. How could you adapt your approach to communicate effectively
   with them?

Chapter 15
Dealing with Anger and Emotion

It is easy to have healthy relationships when everyone
around you is pleasant and you are not facing any
significant issues. Relationships are much more
challenging when we get angry and emotional. — *PH*

The Hockey Game

When my son played hockey, I went to many of his games and often sat with the
other parents from our team. One day we were seated across the rink from the
parents of the opposing team. Previous games between the two teams had not
gone well. They were filled with bad penalties and rivalry.

Early on in the game one of our boys body-checked a player on the other
team and that player went down with an injury. Although there was no penalty
called, the parents on the other side started yelling. They called our player an
idiot and swore at him. They also yelled and swore at the referees. Their anger
triggered anger in the parents on our side of the ice. Our parents retaliated with
name-calling, heckling and other bad behaviour.

We were seated directly behind our team's bench. The head coach of our team
turned around, looked directly at us parents, and yelled for us to be quiet. Once
we were quiet and he had our attention, he said in a calm and firm voice, "Look,
guys — you are the adults here. Just because the other team's parents behaved
badly and got angry doesn't mean you should, too. Your sons are only 12 and
they're watching you, and right now you're *not* setting a very good example. As
the coach, I am asking you to hold your temper and be quiet despite what the
other team or parents say. If you can't do that, please leave the stands now. I

don't want you yelling or swearing or starting a fight. Let's set a good example for these boys and let them play the game."

We all listened to him and agreed to stop reacting to the other parents. Eventually their jeers subsided when we did not feed it with negative energy.

DEALING WITH ANGER

What makes you mad? When someone steals the parking space you were clearly signalling to get into? When your friend owes you money and doesn't pay you back and doesn't mention it? When you realize your children did not do the chores you had asked them to do? At work, do you get angry when co-workers come in late or don't do their work, leaving more for you to do? How about when, in front of your peers, a co-worker calls you out for not doing your job? There is a limitless array of behaviours that annoy us and make us ready to retaliate.

It is easy to have healthy relationships and communicate well when everyone around you is pleasant and you are not facing any significant issues. However, relationships are much more challenging when we get angry.

Learning to manage our emotions, such as anger, is referred to as emotional intelligence. Having this ability means we can recognize and manage our feelings. Emotional intelligence also allows us to recognize feelings in others, empathize and navigate emotions that arise in our relationships. When we can't manage our emotions they can highjack our behaviour and get us into trouble with others.

In this chapter, particular attention is dedicated to anger because it is one of the most difficult emotions to control. Anger is a state triggered by a perceived life-threatening event and is meant to give us energy to save our own lives. Most of our experiences are not life threatening, but our brain can't tell the difference. A trigger can be a frustrating conversation, an unpleasant email, negative feedback or even dealing with someone we do not like. The trigger makes us feel fearful or threatened.

When you feel this threat, a physiological process called *fight-or-flight* takes over to prepare you to defend yourself. Adrenaline is one of the hormones that pumps into your bloodstream to heighten your senses and physical ability. Your heart rate accelerates to feed blood into the large muscle groups to aid in your physical confrontation. You start to take shallow and frequent breaths to increase the intake of oxygen, so you literally "get huffy." This surge of physical ability turns you into the Incredible Hulk. You are now full of adrenaline and strength because your body has prepared you to fight or flee. Unfortunately, just like the Hulk, in this state you react instead of think, and can inflict physical and emotional damage to others until you can get a grip and turn back into yourself.

If you choose to fight, you might "flip someone the bird," call names, make threats, throw a punch, send a scathing email or make some ugly remark or accusation. Some people take their anger to the Internet with rants and negative posts. If you flee, you may remove yourself from the situation or be like a deer in the headlights, unable to speak or think.

The upside of the anger state is that it stimulates our physical ability to protect ourselves. The downside is that the blood drains from the frontal lobe — the thinking part of our brain. We bypass the executive functions such as strategic thinking, manners and self-control and instead rely on the primitive, reflexive part of our brain. This state of not thinking properly literally makes us *mad*. The danger is that the stronger we get, the dumber we get as we act in blind rage.

It is not *if* we are going to get angry, it is just a matter of *when*, and then *how* we are going to deal with it. We get angry when we feel we have been threatened, disrespected or unfairly treated.

When we are angry and let the fight-or-flight autopilot take over, we forget our effective communication skills. When we let anger take charge we are more likely to say things that hurt or antagonize others. This will erode our relationships and often needlessly escalate otherwise benign events. So managing our anger is the key to maintaining healthy relationships.

It is not that anger is a totally bad thing. We feel emotions as we process our environment, our interactions with others and our relationships. When we feel anger or other compelling emotions, it is our conscience telling us it is time to evaluate some relationships or behaviours and decide how to address them.

The key to dealing with anger is preparation. There are two sides to dealing with anger: one is dealing with our own, and the other side is dealing with someone else's. Both these points of view are important, as we will face each in our day-to-day communications.

Taking a Break from Anger

In a meeting several years ago, one of my employees, Eddie, started yelling at me and accusing me of not following protocol on a project. While he raged, he was unaware of the uncomfortable stares and the confusion of the other six team members. I became angry about his behaviour. I stopped the meeting and managed to speak in a calm voice, even though I wasn't feeling calm. I said, "I think we have probably gotten as far as we can today. Thanks for your participation. I will send out an agenda for our next meeting so that we can follow up."

I felt embarrassed and unfairly treated. I had never dealt with Eddie or any of my staff in such a manner. After people had dispersed from the meeting, I told Eddie I was unhappy with how the meeting had gone. I could have really laced into him and ranted, given my inner voice. However, I knew from past experience that venting my anger in an undirected way would just create more problems. It was at the end of the day and I thought we could both benefit from a cool-down period, so we agreed to schedule a meeting two days later to talk about the situation.

We literally took a break from the anger. What I did to help manage my own anger in the meeting was a technique that I call, "stop, drop and control." When we feel the flicker of anger catching hold of us, we can stop the escalation of anger and the flood of adrenaline, drop our angry thoughts for productive ones and control our behaviour. Managing our anger is a choice.

Tips for Managing Our Anger:

It is best to *avoid* some behaviour when we are in a state of anger.

Do:

- Prepare for situations where people will confront you or circumstances that could anger you, and think about ways you could handle being triggered.

- Recognize when you are getting angry and calm down with self-talk.

- Remove yourself from the situation (take a break) if you cannot get your anger under control.

Don't:

- Try to address the other person with your concerns while you are incensed; it will most likely make the situation worse.

- Yell at others and make people uncomfortable.

- Blame others, swear or name-call.

- Get physical with others.

- Threaten others physically or verbally.

Other Considerations:

What you choose to do may depend on the situation and the person you are with. Here are some options:

- Use the twenty-four-hour rule, a guideline that suggests when you are angry with someone, choose not to confront him with your anger until you have had time to cool down and reflect on the situation, taking a break of at least twenty-four hours between the time you were angered and the time that you confront the other person.

- Take a walk to reduce the physical side effects of anger.

- Take deep breaths to slow down your body's reaction.

- Make a list of what concerned you or made you angry. Write it down on paper, in a journal or in a secure data file. What was not okay about what happened, and what would you like to see happen in the future? This writing process will help dissipate your anger and form productive thoughts to help you develop an approach to discussing the situation and preventing it from happening again.

- Reconnect with the person by setting up a time when you can discuss the situation in private. It also helps to let the other person know it is your intention to talk about what triggered your anger so new behaviours can be discussed and agreed to. If the other person knows what is going to be discussed, he can also prepare to discuss productive strategies for the future.

- Remember that managing your anger is a choice.

The upside of anger is, when people get mad, it is a signal that something is not right. Expressing anger and identifying the cause of it allows discussion and problem-solving to take place.

An Enlightening Exchange with Eddie

When Eddie and I met to discuss what had happened, we did so away from the office so we would have some privacy and a neutral environment. My assumption was that Eddie was mad about something. I believed in order for us to restore respect and trust, we needed to really understand each other. I invited Eddie to tell me what his concerns were. I said to him, "The other day in the meeting, you acted in a very angry way, a way in which I have not seen you act before. Can you tell me what was going on for you?" (Even though I did not like how he behaved in the meeting and I wanted to let him know what I thought, I believed starting with *me* would not help the situation. I wanted to open our meeting with listening to understand his perspective. Just because we listen well, does not mean that we agree.) When we model good skills to others they are more likely to reciprocate the behaviours.

Eddie revealed he felt that I had not followed process on the project. He also felt I was passing him over on some interesting projects he would have liked to do.

Once I was sure he had said all he had to say I paraphrased what he said back to ensure my understanding was accurate. He said I had it. Then I explained how I had complied with our process, and he was not aware of some of the steps I had taken. I also explained the reason I was keeping some assignments from him was to reduce his workload, in response to his complaint that he had too much work to do.

Although the conversation was not the most fun I'd ever had, it was enlightening to learn his point of view and expectations. The positive result of the conversation and his anger was that we agreed we would avoid having similar disagreements in front of other people. We agreed that disagreeing was normal and that we could solve issues between us. We also agreed if either of us had an issue with the other, we would book a meeting time to discuss it calmly, not raising it in an ambushing way. We also talked about the danger of making assumptions.

Eddie started to think about the impact his behaviour had had on the rest of the team. In hindsight, he felt a little embarrassed about his outburst. He decided he wanted to apologize to the group. At our next meeting, he said, "I wanted to take a minute to apologize for my comments at the last meeting. They were not helpful and I should have discussed them offline. I'm sorry I took the meeting off track, and I want to let you know if I have an issue with any of you, I will raise it with you in a private and calm way. I had an off day."

I thanked him for sharing his comments. I told the team I had also learned from the experience and reiterated where the team could find information about the project and processes, and emphasized if anyone had a question, they could ask it in the meeting or see me in private. I committed to sharing information as much as possible. I did not want Eddie to lose face, because nothing happens in a vacuum.

His comments did a lot to help the team put his behaviour behind them and rebuild trust.

Dealing with Other People's Anger

I worked for a leader who got angry quickly and intensely. I remember sitting in his office and experiencing his wrath when he did not like something my team had done. He would usually stand over me and yell. He would often swear and he would shake. I could tell that the tirade was almost over when little puddles of spittle would bubble at the corners of his mouth.

I would sit calmly and listen. He would usually end his rant with a blaming: "*Why* did *you* guys *do* that?" I would keep my voice quiet and calm and respond. Often his anger stemmed from assumptions he had made. Once I clarified them, we were good. He would typically phone me an hour or so later to apologize for his outburst.

When someone else is angry, the best approach is to choose to defuse him, rather than fuel his anger.

It is easy to blame and dismiss someone who is really angry, because most people would agree that over-the-top outbursts are inappropriate. However, if we judge others and blame them for their angry reactions, we might miss the important part about what made them angry. For me, when confronted with someone else's anger, I try to get curious, not furious. When I realize that people are responsible for their own anger, it puts me in a better place to be patient with them, because we do not *make* other people angry; anger is how they choose to respond to the circumstances around them.

When someone is having a temper tantrum, it might seem he does not deserve your ear and heart. However, this may be when he needs you to be an effective listener the most. If we can listen to the other person and understand what made him angry, we can help him be more aware of dealing with his own anger, allowing him to find strategies to deal with issues in a productive way.

We can choose to defuse another person's anger in a number of ways:

- Let him vent, acknowledge the anger and provide him with a chance to communicate what the anger is about.

- Remove ourselves from the situation and let it cool down or suggest everyone takes a break to cool down and then reconvene.

- Tell the person that if he wants to continue to talk with us, he needs to take it down a notch or we'll walk away.

- As our hockey coach did, we can match the other person's intensity to get his attention, and then take our volume and tone down to a calm level.

Often when we provide an effective way of communicating, other people will mirror us.

When you are confronted with another person's anger,

Do:

- Stay calm yourself.

- Let the person vent if you feel safe to do so.

- Try to understand what made the other person feel angry.

- Change space, with or without the other person. Moving and walking can dissipate the physical effects of anger.

Don't:

- Yell back or name-call.

- Stay with him if you feel that you are in danger.

- Escalate the situation by getting angry back or saying things to trigger more animosity.

- Don't get furious with the other person. Get curious about how to solve the situation.

The goal in dealing with someone else's anger is to keep yourself safe, maintain the relationship and defuse the situation. If we react to his anger, we often either intentionally or unintentionally do things that escalate anger.

Venting

There are times when we get frustrated or angry by a person or a situation. We are left upset, stressed or confused and keep it to ourselves because we don't know what to do.

When you boil a pot of potatoes, you need to take the lid off and let the steam out otherwise they boil over and make a mess. Similarly when you keep a lid on your frustrations and don't vent, you may find that your anger spills over and makes a mess with your relationships. When you need to process your feelings — vent. Venting is sharing your less pleasant, personal thoughts with another trusted person. When you vent:

- Find a person who will keep the information confidential (friend, co-worker, clergy, counsellor).

- Let him know you are venting and may say things that you don't actually mean.

- Let him know that you just want to vent and be heard and don't require feedback.

Do it in a place where others cannot hear you.

Triggering Anger in Others

There are times when we spark other people's anger. Making choices about how to respond to someone is the key. For example, listening to someone and then saying, "Yes, but…" is like a verbal eraser that can anger others. Consider the effect of each possible approach when you are interacting with someone.

Demanding:

Sometimes we can be seen as bossing others around. This can trigger or escalate their anger. Imagine the impact of some unhelpful phases like:

- "What I want you to do right now…" or "What you should do is…"

- "What you need to do right now is…"

- "You shouldn't feel that way!"

More helpful phrases:

- "Will you please…?"

- "An option is…"

- "One way to approach this is…"

- "From my point of view it would be more preferable to _____, because…"

Attacking and Arguing:

Taking an aggressive stance with others can trigger anger. This includes name-calling, judging and threatening. It often plays out between two people where they get into an argument about who is right and who is wrong. People say things such as "What is your problem?" or "You are such a bitch" or "No — you are wrong!" Rather than rant at someone it is more helpful to hear their side and use questions such as "Can you tell me about your situation? Or can you explain your view to me?"

Find out what the person's concerns are, rather than attacking him and making the situation and relationship worse.

Blaming:

Another frustration is the act of blaming. We blame when we fail to take responsibility. Blaming is infuriating and exhausting. I have worked with employees who are frustrated and unhappy because when they ask a colleague for help, the response is a blaming comment and no help is provided. Such unhelpful blaming phrases include:

- "You didn't do this right."

- "You're wrong."

- "You're confusing me."

- "You should have done it this way. Why didn't you?"

- "It was your fault that this happened… If you hadn't…"

Helpful responses instead include:

- "One good way to do this is…"

- "I can see there has been a miscommunication."

- "I am confused; can you help me understand what has happened so far…?"

- "It is helpful to take this approach when solving this type of problem…"

PASSIVE-AGGRESSIVE BEHAVIOUR

Expressing discontent or anger in indirect ways is referred to as passive-aggressive behaviour. Some people get back at others without expressing concerns directly.

Passive-aggressive behaviours include:

- Sarcasm — making rude or hurtful remarks and then brushing it off as humour

- The silent treatment — refusing to communicate or speak with someone

- Sulking or withdrawing — being with people but staying by oneself, perhaps even crying excessively

- Gossiping and complaining — talking to everyone else about an issue except the person with whom you have the issue

- Procrastinating or forgetting — making promises to do something and then forgetting or indulging in delaying tactics

These behaviours are indirect ways of showing anger. Chapter 19 provides some tips in assertively asking for changes in behaviour. If you are confronted by someone's passive-aggressive behaviour, ask questions such as:

- "Is there anything you want to ask/tell me?"

- "Do you have any concerns or issues with this?"

- "Is there a problem with _____ you would like to discuss?"

- "I am open if you would like to discuss something."

All you can do is inquire. Many passive-aggressive people will say, "No, everything is good," and will continue with the destructive behaviours. I was trying to work out a problem with someone in a productive way and they tried to put me off with, "Hey I don't have time for this drama!" I replied, "I am not trying to be dramatic. I am trying to find out what your issue is so that we can solve it and stop the drama." That assertive comment invited a discussion that solved the problem. Sometimes all you can do is ask someone to work things out and then try to avoid the negative behaviours if they will not participate.

Realize that uncontrolled anger can be a damaging force in relationships. If you are in a relationship with someone who is angry and has outbursts on a daily basis, recognize that person may have an anger problem. Passive-aggressive behaviours are equally debilitating to a relationship as full-blown tantrums. People who have anger issues or associate with those who do can get help by contacting their physician, a community mental health association or an employee assistance program.

It is not normal or healthy to be angry all of the time and it is important for you to protect your own safety and the safety of others.

DEALING WITH OTHER EMOTIONS

There are other common emotions to deal with in communication that can be as unsettling as anger. Many of us dread dealing with people who are sad, hurt or upset, especially if they swear or cry, because it makes us feel uncomfortable. We even say when people cry that they "broke down." When we cry, we are simply emoting and releasing feelings. It is a normal human process.

Being prepared for strong behaviour is part of listening to understand. When others express hurt or sadness or are upset:

Do:

- Ask them if they would like some time alone.

- Be prepared to sit with them in silence, if that's what they prefer, until they have had some time to settle down.

- Offer them a drink of water and tissues.

- Give them physical space until they calm down.

- Tell them to take their time.

- Ask them what they need.

- Ask them if there is someone else you could call if it seems they need more support.

Don't:

- Say they shouldn't feel that way — it just undermines their feelings and experience.

- Tell them not to cry or be upset.

- React by telling them that they are acting inappropriately.

- Send them out of the room and tell them to pull themselves together.

- Overreact to swearing, since most people, after venting for a few minutes, remove expletives from their vocabulary.

SUMMARY

Dealing with anger and other negative emotions is not something most people want to do. It can feel overwhelming. We prefer to be comfortable and not have to take care of unpleasant things. Allow yourself to get comfortable with the discomfort of negative emotions, with the goal of understanding others and creating solutions. Working through these challenging emotions with others can build understanding, trust and health in our relationships.

Chapter 16
Choosing How to Communicate

I admire machinery as much as any man.
But, it will never be a substitute for the face of a
man, with his soul in it, encouraging another man
to be brave and true. — *Charles Dickens*

Too Much Texting?

On a bus, a woman I'll call Suzy, told me how worried she was about her daughter, Amber. Suzy was concerned because Amber, a first-year university student, regularly sits at the dinner table and texts throughout the meal. When Suzy tries to ask Amber questions or wants to talk about her day, Amber often ignores her and focuses on her cell phone. Suzy said the situation came to a critical point for her when she received Amber's cell phone bill. Amber had far exceeded her daily texting limit. She was sending over 900 texts a day. Given that Amber slept about eight hours a day, she was sending about 60 texts per hour. Suzy wondered, "How does Amber concentrate in class when she is texting that much?" And "How come she thinks it's okay to ignore me when we are together?" How does our choice of medium impact our relationships with others?

THE EFFECT OF MEDIUM

In 1964, Marshall McLuhan coined the phrase: *the medium is the message.*[14] In his book, *Understanding Media*, he explains that there is a "message" inherent in the type of medium or technology we choose to use. The medium itself introduces a change in the pace or pattern of human affairs. The advent of the telegraph meant people no longer had to wait for letters to be delivered overseas via ships. Telegraphs were almost immediate. Radio changed the news because it meant people could hear inflection and emotion in the human voice instead of reading the words in a newspaper. Sometimes the transformations in human interactions precipitated by technological changes are not foreseen and turn out to be unfavourable.

McLuhan predicted the Internet 30 years before its inception. Now it's here and the presence of the electronic medium is driving habitual reliance on word-only electronic communication. I call this use of the word-only communication "electronic talking." Many people have a mindset that electronic talking is the best and *only* way to maintain *all* relationships.

The benefit of electronic talking is that it is available, convenient and instan-taneous for senders. We text, email, post on Facebook or Instagram, and Tweet one-way comments. Electronic communication has changed the way we com-municate in relationships and it creates complexity because each person has his own idea about what is proper. On the upside, it is an easy and inexpensive way to keep connected to everyone, no matter where they are.

The downside is when we rely too much on electronic communication to take the place of personal communication. This lack of face-to-face time under-mines relationships. How many people say things in a text or post comments to a site they would not dare say to someone's face? How much understanding is lost between people when they break up a romantic relationship through a text rather than taking the time to have a conversation? How much time is wasted and problems created by individuals not communicating with one another face-to-face? An email or text-*only* interaction can lead to several word-only exchanges that escalate and complicate the message because of the lack of tone and clarity. At least a phone call provides the benefit of tone.

The Medium as the Message

The medium we choose can convey much meaning, and influence how others interpret the message and feel about the relationship. For example, what says "I love you" better than 12 long-stemmed red roses? Big brand companies choose the medium of celebrity spokespersons whose reputations epitomize their brand. Think about film stars who represent cosmetic lines, or sports figures who do ads for running shoes. Before any words are transferred, the medium speaks to us.

When we are trying to maintain our most important relationships, the question is: What does each *medium* we are choosing convey in itself? What impact does that medium have on the quality of the communication and how might it impact the relationship?

Face-to-Face

In 1953, when my parents shared with my dad's only sister and her husband the news they were pregnant, they chose to do it at Christmas. They put a wrapped present under the tree with a tag on it that said, "to *Aunt* Nina and *Uncle* Ivan." When Nina opened the gift, she found a teddy bear with a beautiful ribbon on its paw that said, "Merry Christmas, with love from Baby Hirst." My parents chose a face-to-face interaction and created a very special, memorable moment for the family that enriched their relationship and invited others to share their joy.

Contrast that with an experience a colleague of mine had with her son. He texted her to tell her he and his wife were expecting a baby. This choice of medium disappointed her, as she would have liked to share that moment with her son and daughter-in-law, to give them a hug and congratulate them. She could have better understood their choice if they lived far away, but they didn't. She felt them having their first child was an exciting event and wondered why they didn't at least make a phone call to share the news.

I have already highlighted the benefits of face-to-face interaction in Chapter 6, "The Trinity of Talk." My bias is that face-to-face contact or phone calls and Skype-type platforms are the most robust methods to support your most important relationships. Face-to-face says, I care about you and I am making time for you. Face-to-face or the phone says, I want to hear you and have time to connect with you.

Skype and FaceTime are amazing platforms when we are separated by distance. Through these formats we can hear each other, see each other's facial expressions, and even show each other things we can't over the phone.

When a video feed is not possible the next richest option is voice-only communication. Skype with no picture feed, or a phone, are good ways to share. Although voice-only communication means we miss seeing facial expressions or body language, we do get the benefit of tone that we cannot observe through the written word alone.

Electronic methods that are words only, such as email or texting, certainly send out a message, but they tend to be one-way. They do not promote relationship building or allow the receiver to respond, clarify or process on the spot in the way a conversation does. Fuller meaning can be conveyed through the exchange of tone of voice and body language.

Why do some people leave voice messages rather than sending a text or email? For most people it's because they want to convey something that may be too complex, lengthy or important to put into an email or text, or the sender may realize that tone will play an important part in the message. Without tone, it is totally up to the receiver of the written word to interpret a message.

CHOOSING THE MEDIUM FOR COMMUNICATION

We have a variety of ways to communicate. No medium is necessarily good or bad. The primary consideration in choosing a medium is to select the one that is the most effective to transmit your message in a way it is most likely to be understood by the receiver.

One medium can simply not do it all. Take the opportunity to strategically assess and choose the medium that best conveys the message you are trying to impart and provides the type of interaction to support the relationship you have with the receiver.

Consider some common methods and how they impact the message and the relationship.

Emailing

For logistical or detailed information, an email is effective and efficient. When we are dealing with complex, non-personal issues, we need to keep track of details anyway, so supplying an email message with a list of what we need helps the receiver understand. It also forces us to be specific and clear in our own minds.

For example, here is a detailed type of email I send when I am arranging logistics for a training session:

```
To: Ashley Morgan
From: Pat Hirst
Re: Logistics for Workshop — May 4
Good Morning Ashley,
Can you please confirm the following logistics for the
session on May 4?
```

```
Location: Room 6 — Building 12
Time: 8:30—4:30
Number of Participants — 15
Thanks for taking the time to review and advise.
Best, Pat
```

Her reply:

```
To: Pat Hirst
From: Ashley Morgan
Re: Logistics for Workshop — May 4
Good Morning Pat,
```
Please see my replies bracketed by each point:
```
Location: Room 6 — Building 12 (correct)
Time: 8:30—4:30 (yes)
Number of Participants — 15 (currently 17 may go up to
20)
Please do not hesitate to contact me if you have any
questions.
Best, Ashley
```

I highly recommend this type of approach for answering questions and documenting specifics.

Email and texts are helpful when we are sharing factual information and requesting or providing low-risk messages, and are most effectively understood when two people have an existing relationship.

All too often I have seen people misunderstand a text or email because there was no tone to accompany it. This causes a lot of problems.

For example in one mediation case I was involved in, two co-workers, Bob and Ted, did not get along very well. When Ted won an award at work, Bob thought it was a good opportunity to say something positive to Ted to give their working relationship a positive boost, so he sent Ted an email:

```
To: Ted Smith
From: Bob Brown
Re: Congratulations!
```

```
Congratulations Ted on your award
and for a job well done!
```

When Ted saw the message from Bob, he did not pick up on the warmth and good spirit Bob had intended. Ted read it with a sarcastic spin, because he did not believe that Bob could ever do anything kindly towards him. So, Ted sent a rocket email back to Bob, saying:

```
To: Bob Brown
From: Ted Smith
Re: Congratulations!
If I wanted your opinion I would have asked for
it. Keep your comments to yourself, jerk!
```

Bob had truly meant to congratulate Ted and had not meant his note to be sarcastic, but now the discomfort in their relationship was worse. Ted had read a tone into the message where none was intended. A face-to-face interaction or phone exchange may have given better odds of this message being understood the way it was intended.

One crucial factor in communication is the *intention* we have when sending a message. If we are sharing simple information that is at low risk of being misunderstood, using email or text can be a useful tool. However, if we are giving complex information or a message that can be easily misinterpreted or might surprise or upset the person, a face-to-face communication or phone call can head off problems and save time in the long run by providing context before the reader reacts to the email.

Considerations for Using Email

- Clarify what you want from the other person. Do you need them to reply by a certain date? Make it easy for them to understand why you are sending the email and what they are supposed to do with it.

- Sending a string of old emails that include many pages is confusing. Explain why you are sending the history. What is it that you want the receiver to notice or do? What is your understanding or view of the material?

- Before you send an email, consider whether your message would be better understood face-to-face, or through a phone call. If so, consider using a richer medium.

- Minimize the number of people you copy the email to. Why are you copying anyone? If it is for information purposes, is there a shared file where you can copy it to instead of sending it to many people and making many people read it or delete it?

- If you are sending email information that can be complex, open by giving the reader a sense of why you are sending it and what impact it will have on them.

- If the email is necessary but may be upsetting or confusing, supplement it with a quick face-to-face or phone conversation. The sound of your voice and the accompanying tone can help people understand things in the way they were intended, when the email alone may be misinterpreted and cause problems.

- If you are using email to reply to someone who has made you angry, simply type the email, save it as a draft and leave it for an hour or two. After some cooling down time, re-read it and edit it to ensure you are not saying things that will make the situation worse. Even better, you could decide to phone or meet with the other person to discuss the issue.

- Consider the use of greetings such as "Good morning" or "Hello" or "Dear Mr. Jones" and closings such as "With thanks" "Best regards" "Kind regards" "With thanks in advance." Greetings and closings make the email seem friendlier. If the person you are sending an email to is a dominant type of person who likes to stick to the facts, one-liners with no greeting will work.

- If you have something that needs to be taken care of urgently, email may be the wrong medium. Not everyone checks emails regularly. Try face-to-face or phone or text. If you still need to send an email to supply complex data, send the email as well, but supplement it with a more immediate medium to ensure you have the other person's attention.

- When receiving emails, let people know the status of their request. For example, if I read emails on my phone, I let people know I have read it and that I will follow up: i.e., "So noted." When someone sends me an email that requires action, I let him know I will follow up on it and get back to him by a certain date.

- Do not send emails to rant and complain to someone about their behaviour or to discipline or criticize. If you have a serious concern with someone, that message should be given in person or, if that's not possible, on the phone. Discussing serious issues provides an opportunity for understanding to occur and for problem solving to happen.

- If there is a significant change in arrangements you have with someone even in a personal situation, a phone call or face-to-face conversation is the best way to help clarify and explain the new approach.

Considerations on When to Avoid Email

- Do not use email to break up with or fire someone. People deserve a chance to ask questions in situations where they are being dismissed from an important role.

- Consider personal ways to share important news about milestone events, such as getting engaged, having a baby or a critical illness.

- At work when you are right next door to someone, why not share a quick comment with him face-to-face rather than emailing it? If you must have documentation, have the conversation first and then send the email to document it. When you use email only to save time, and a conflict arises because of it, you have not saved any time; you have created problems with the issue and with the relationship with the other party. This will result in much more wasted time than communicating effectively in the first place.

- Don't be frustrated when people don't respond to your email or text immediately. They may be in a meeting, in class, concentrating on work or otherwise occupied. They will reply when they get a chance. A delay is not a personal slight.

- Many people resent receiving jokes, stories or the dreaded chain letter via email. It's best not to send these types of emails to people unless you are sure they like them.

- When you *read* emails, don't judge others on what they haven't said. Try to take some time to digest it and consider that the way the message sounds to you may not be what the sender intended.

- Remember, too, that emails and other written forms of electronic messages can easily be forwarded or posted in places that you may not want them to be used.

SOCIAL MEDIA

An exhaustive analysis of social media is outside the scope of this book but still worth mentioning. Facebook, Twitter, websites, blogs, Wikipedia, Tumblr, webcasts, Pinterest, chatrooms are a few examples of social media tools available to help us communicate. These powerful instruments are incredible in their ability to reach millions of people instantaneously. Such sites facilitate communication with a mass of people as well as the ability to drill down and communicate one-on-one. When choosing which social media tool to use, a thorough analysis must be done to consider the message you are trying to convey and the audience you are trying to reach.

In most cases social media is superb at connecting with a large audience. When it comes to maintaining interpersonal relationships, social media is a supplement when we can't be there.

Facebook Funerals

Many people are choosing to close their Facebook account because of the amount of time they are spending on it. One interviewee said that he would save four to ten hours a week by giving it up.

A Facebook funeral is a party or gathering that people have to let others know that they are closing their Facebook account and how to contact them by other means.

Some people are just tired of too much information being shared by too many and the amount of time and energy required to maintain their account.

Texting

Texting is a fantastic mode of communication. I use it in my life as I would a sticky note. I use it most with family and friends by leaving text notes instead of the note I would have left on the fridge or bulletin board.

What is great about texting is people can read your message immediately. It saves someone the time of having to pick up a voice-mail message and listen to it.

I have begun to enjoy text conversations with busy people. For example, my friend runs a business that relies on walk-in customers. If we talk on the phone, she has to put me on hold when someone comes in. With a text we can have an easy conversation of words, with lots of pauses if necessary.

Texting is a great way to supplement communication in relationships and share information quickly.

Secret Handshake: Gatherings that Create Community

A couple of creative freelancers in Winnipeg, Canada, realized that, although the electronic medium was fantastic to support communication with their clients and to accomplish their goals, working online all day made them feel lonesome for a friendly face. They were missing out on the opportunity to meet other awesome people in similar professions.

In 2010, Leanne Schmidt and Christopher Lobay started the Secret Handshake, or SH, a group formed to promote social interaction among those who work alone or in small shops.[15] Members meet once a month "to get out of their shells … to share ideas, collaborate, drink a beer, and return home to continue Tweeting each other as per usual." Leanne found in her research most members of a group, such as bird-watchers, dog-lovers or knitters, have something in common. The common thread with the SH group is creativity. To Leanne, being creative is not about how you make your living, it is about a mindset — how you think about your career, relationships and life in general. As Einstein said, facts will get you from point A to point B; creativity will get you everywhere else. SH is a welcoming place that connects people with other people to form a community. It fills a void that electronic talking cannot bridge. Looking someone in the eye, telling a joke, bending an ear, sharing an idea — all these things are more satisfying when done face-to-face.

This group fills a void for so many creative professionals. The main benefits are that people get to meet *in person*. They have conversations, a chance to exchange ideas, prototype quickly and interact. Although SH is not intended to be a networking club, much business is done within the group. The personal relationships that have been established have created a high-trust environment, where referrals are happily made and great work is produced. Leanne says the group has changed her life. She finds herself not only enjoying her work, but also interacting with people she really likes, and that makes for a satisfying life. She claims SH, in a word, *inspires* everyone associated with it. She feels positive and optimistic when she is in the midst of such intelligence, professionalism and humanity.

Since SH's inception in 2010, over 1,070 people have joined and the number continues to rise. SH illustrates the power of interpersonal connections and communing with others, face-to-face.

RELATIONSHIPS AND COMMUNICATION CHOICES

When I heard about Secret Handshake, I initially connected with Leanne via email. After several exchanges, we finally had a very enjoyable telephone conversation. Leanne's view of medium choice and relationships is they tend to go through a progression. We usually begin with a one-way electronic connection. As relationships progress we move to the telephone and ultimately meet face-to-face. She believes closing the deal on a new relationship is two people wanting to hang out together. I concur. Our most important relationships are best cultivated by the use of face-to-face and phone with other methods as a supplement.

EXERCISE: Creating Your Own Perfect World

Using this checklist can help you determine what medium is optimum for your message.

Checklist for Applying Skills:
Choosing the Medium for Communicating

1) Determine your intention in communicating.

2) What is your message?

3) Think about your audience. Who do you want to communicate with?

4) What are the possible ways to communicate your message to this person or group?

5) Consider each medium and their pros and cons:

   For example:

   • In person

   • Telephone or Skype

   • Text

   • Web/Internet — LinkedIn, Facebook, Pinterest, a blog, etc.

   • Email

6) Once you choose the medium, be as clear and explicit as possible in your communication. What specifics and considerations will you want to be mindful of during this communication?

7) How can you invite the other person to engage in a two-way dialogue to get feedback on what you have communicated?

Chapter 17
Giving Others Negative Feedback:
From Detrimental to Developmental

He has a right to criticize, who has a heart
to help. — *Abraham Lincoln*

The Critic

I ran into a relentless critic in elementary school. Our teacher's approach to developing young minds was to constantly correct and punish us for wrong answers. While Mrs. Brown liberally applied blame and heartless critiques to the entire class to help us "learn," the kid who got the worst of it was Deidre. Deidre came from a low-income family.

Most mornings started with Mrs. Brown yelling at Deidre, with comments such as "Go and wash your dirty hands! Don't you know any better?" (I suspect Deidre's home did not have running water.) After reading or math lessons, Deidre received a constant stream of negative feedback. "Deidre, why can't you ever learn that word?" or "Deidre, you are hopeless; smarten up for heaven's sake!"

It was upsetting to hear Mrs. Brown speak to Deidre that way. I felt sorry for how Deidre was demoralized by the harsh criticism. I believe Mrs. Brown missed a great opportunity to teach Deidre and show her kindness. When we choose to judge others with no view to help, we are criticizing.

THE MANY FACES OF NEGATIVE FEEDBACK

When we believe others could do something better or we don't like something they did, we may provide negative feedback or criticism.

Feedback can be a gift that gives us insight into how others perceive us and how they are affected by our words and actions. If we are doing things within a relationship or role that are not working, how will we know that others would like us to change if they don't tell us?

Receiving important feedback from others can also help you make life decisions. You might quit a job and find a better one when you realize your boss believes you will never be promotable, or you might leave a relationship where your partner constantly criticizes your weight and what you eat.

Feedback helps us to learn new skills and how to do things better. It can inspire us to reach our peak performance. The challenge is to be able to tell others we would like them to improve or do things differently in a way that is effective and maintains or even enhances our relationships.

Considerations about Negative Feedback:

- Feedback about others is *our* opinion — our subjective point of view based on our own perspective. People do not have to like, accept or agree with us.

- We can give feedback for good or for evil. That means our intention for giving feedback can be from a place of caring, to build and strengthen our relationships, or to help the person we are giving feedback to (for good); or we can use feedback as a control tool to play games with, put down or manipulate others (for evil). Just because we have an opinion doesn't mean we have to share it.

- Not everyone responds well to feedback, even when it is positive.

- When we give feedback about the methods someone is using to reach a goal, be aware there is often more than one way to accomplish things; another person's approach may be just as valid as ours. As long as the same quality result occurs, we need to be cautious about correcting someone else's methods.

- If we don't tell others we don't like something — they can assume we are in agreement with their performance or behaviour. Silence is acquiescence.

- People do not do the things they do because they think they are wrong; they do the things they do because they think they are right. This is important to keep in mind when you give feedback.

- People accept feedback more readily from someone they respect and view as knowledgeable on the subject.

- Negative feedback is accepted more readily when positive feedback is regularly shared.

- The best feedback is given in a two-way conversation. We only understand our side and benefit from inviting the receiver of feedback into the conversation.

From Criticism to Caring

We often put up with bad behaviour or poor performance because we are afraid the receiver may get defensive and not be receptive to what we have to say. He may even retaliate. How can we give feedback to others without being critical and eroding relationships?

A place to start is to become aware of our own mindset on criticism. A general definition for criticism is to find fault. When we have this mindset of criticism, our objective is to point out weaknesses. We become the critic dictating behaviour rather than one person in an interdependent relationship.

Criticism is often expressed in damaging ways. Phrases such as "Can't you do anything right?" or "Why can't you be more like your brother?" or "I told you this once already" or "How could you be so stupid?" are attacks. They hurt and alienate others. These types of comments do not provide specific information that allows the receiver to understand how behaviours or performance could be improved.

A better mindset for giving others negative feedback embraces the concept of development or improvement. If we think in terms of developing others, we see feedback regarding the things they could do better as an opportunity for *improvement* or a chance to develop skills, instead of seeing ourselves as the authority who judges others or puts them in their place.

When we criticize, our demeanour, tone and body language usually convey anger and judgment, because with this mindset, we are taking an aggressive stance against someone else and expecting him to submit to our view. When we give developmental or improvement feedback, it comes from a view of caring about the success of others and respecting them, helping them see opportunities on how to be their best. It also comes from an assertive viewpoint, where we take responsibility for communicating clearly to share our point of view. With an assertive view, we recognize the other person's free choice to accept or reject the feedback. So when our mindset is one of helping, of improvement or development, our tone and body language will automatically be more positive and engaging. Criticism comes from a place of anger. Developmental feedback comes from a place of caring.

Feedback the Wrong Way

I have worked for years with others in feedback workshops. Participants have noted that the worst feedback comes in the following forms of criticism:

1) **Making sweeping judgments**

   The tricky part of developmental feedback is that humans are very "judgy." We feel that being honest is acceptable because we're just telling people the way we see it. Comments such as "You are lazy," "You are unprofessional," "You are doing it wrong" may be your opinion, but it does no good to say things that will alienate the receiver of the message.

   In giving developmental feedback we need to separate the person from the behaviour. The person isn't bad, but we may prefer the person adjust his behaviour. That means when we give feedback, we must express our basic observations about a certain behaviour or result, not our judgment of the person.

From Judgment to Objectivity

Our first challenge is to describe our observation rather than our judgment about it. Notice the difference in word choice and the effect each would have in the following examples:

Imagine your spouse is fifteen minutes late to pick you up from a meeting. He did not call or text you to let you know he would be late. Your judgment may be to say, "You are a jerk" or "You don't care" or "You are so inconsiderate." A more effective way to share this information to provide feedback is to name what you saw without interpreting it. In this case you could say, "You arrived fifteen minutes after the agreed time and didn't let me know." This allows the person to reflect on facts and not our judgment.

Another example could occur if your child has not cleaned up his room as requested. You might want to say judgmentally, "You are lazy" or "You are a disgrace" or "You are irresponsible." A way to provide feedback objectively would be to say "You did not clean up your room today as we agreed." This is fact-based and could start a discussion to solve the problem.

Looking at the examples above, you can see making judgmental comments is an ineffective way to provide meaningful feedback. Such comments will make the receiver unreceptive, preventing them from hearing the message or engaging in problem solving. Even more concerning is when we make judgmental comments, it does not give the receiver an idea about the behaviour that needs to change or what was noticed in the first place.

When we express our disapproval of how something is done we tend to tell people, "*Don't* do this." We don't explain our point of view and how we came to it. We also don't explain what people *could* do instead.

Do not judge and name call. Assertively name the observable behaviour in a neutral way. This is an effective way to invite problem solving.

2) **Complaining**

Attending a recent family picnic, a friend of mine was the recipient of some very public complaints. His sister said accusingly in front of everyone, "Joe, I am so tired of not being able to see pictures of your kids on Facebook. Why don't you get into this century and post some pictures? How am I supposed to be a proud aunt if you don't let me have some pictures?" This embarrassed my friend because it was not the first time his sister had raised this issue with him. She criticized him without ever asking why he and his wife do not want pictures of their children on Facebook. My friend also believes it was inappropriate of her to bring it up in a public venue.

A complaint is really a wish for a change we are not articulating. When we complain, we are being passive-aggressive and are in victim mode, rather than assertively asking for an adjustment. If you have an issue, give the feedback and ask for change. Talking negatively and complaining is an undermining behaviour.

3) **Silent Treatment**

Some people provide negative feedback by refusing to talk to those who have displeased them. It is an inferred type of feedback. A friend of mine says that part of their family culture is to give people The Silent Treatment. That means if you have offended one of the family members, you will only know it because he will not phone you, answer your calls or even talk to you at public events.

"How do you know what you did wrong?" I asked my friend.

"You don't," my friend replied. "You have to guess or start asking others if they know what's wrong. It is quite destructive. I quit playing the game because I would prefer that someone just tell me what they would like me to change, then it allows me to address the problem rather than being shut out. If they can't bother to explain things to me, I guess they feel the relationship isn't worth it."

Others cannot read our minds. If we want to give feedback, we need to be clear, patient and willing to engage the other person in a conversation.

The silent treatment creates some good drama, but will not create good results.

4) **Sarcasm**

Many people believe it is best to give others "hints" instead of direct feedback, so they use sarcasm. Sarcasm comes from the Greek word, *sarkasmos,* which means to tear flesh. While for some people sarcasm is humorous, the joke is made at someone else's expense, making him a target and embarrassing him.

I was at a meeting once where the leader asked if anyone had any ideas. When an employee offered one, the leader said, "Way to go, Sherlock. Did you think about that for a long time? We already tried that last year."

Sarcasm provides feedback to others, but not in a way that motivates them to change. It is an alienating behaviour. Rather than using sarcasm, approach the other person with assertive, objective information.

GIVING EFFECTIVE DEVELOPMENTAL FEEDBACK

In order to give effective developmental or improvement feedback, it is important to follow some basic steps and communicate calmly and effectively. Here are the four areas that will help you give feedback effectively and engage the other person in a robust conversation:

1) Intention — share why you are giving the other person developmental feedback.

2) Specific Behaviour — explain what you have noticed or observed. Use objective and neutral language to describe what you noticed rather than judging or name-calling.

3) Impact — express how the behaviour has affected you, either practically or emotionally. For example, if someone used up all the milk, *practically* speaking, there was no milk to put on your cereal in the morning, and *emotionally*, you may have been frustrated or angry.

4) Solution — name the change you would appreciate in behaviour or performance, or invite the receiver to suggest a solution concerning the situation, or develop a solution jointly.

Here is an example of two different feedback mindsets...
Situation: Mom is in the kitchen in the morning and her daughter, Samantha, walks in. Samantha is on her way to school wearing a revealing top.

Mom: Oh my god, Sam! What are you wearing?

Sam: Clothes, mother.

Mom: Well, go upstairs right now and take that off and put something decent on!

Sam: All the kids at school wear tops like this! In fact, it's hard to buy anything different in the stores. Mass marketing, Mom!

Mom: I don't care; get yourself upstairs and into something decent!

Let's look at this same situation again, and see what happens when the objective approach is used:

Mom: Good morning Sam, how are you doing?

Sam: Fine.

Mom (intention): I'd like to give you some feedback about what you're wearing because I'm concerned. I am your mom and it's my job to give you feedback sometimes to help you think about good choices.

Sam: What? All the kids at school wear tops like this. In fact, it's hard to buy anything different in the stores. Mass marketing, Mom!

Mom (specific behaviour): Well, when I look at your top, I can see bra and bra straps. (impact) I cannot help but think that some of your teachers might feel embarrassed to see that, and how uncomfortable it might make them feel. Also, fairly or unfairly, people will make judgments and unkind comments about you based on what you wear. I don't want you to be embarrassed or harassed. I would prefer that your bra straps didn't show and that you don't wear revealing clothes, especially to school.

Sam: What do you want me to do?

Mom (inviting solutions): What options do you have?

Sam: Well, I could change my shirt or I could wear a camisole and a light sweater.

Mom: Either option works for me. It's your choice. All I ask is that the bra and cleavage are not visible.

Sam: Okay.

Mom: Thanks for working that through with me.

Sam: You're welcome, Mom.

Here is another example, in the scenario with spouses:

Jim arrives twenty minutes late to pick up Susan, his wife, from an exercise class. Jim did not call or text Susan to let her know he would be late.

Judgmental Approach:

Susan opens the door and gets into the car.

Susan: Where the hell were you?

Jim: Hi, sorry I was late. I was watching the hockey game and time got away from me.

Susan: I can't believe you are so inconsiderate! I stood there wondering what was wrong and you couldn't even bother to phone!

Jim: Hey, I already said I was sorry! It was an honest mistake. What else do you want from me?

Susan: I wish you would quit being such a selfish jerk!

They ride home in angry silence. Susan is especially angry because this is the fifth time Jim has been late to pick her up from her exercise class.

Objective Approach:

Susan opens the door and gets into the car.

Jim: Hi, sorry I was late. I was watching the hockey game and time got away from me.

Susan: (intention): I would like to talk about the arrangements we have made for transportation for this exercise class, because it is affecting my enjoyment of it.

Jim: Sure, go ahead.

Susan (specific behaviour): When you pick me up late and don't call to let me know when you will be coming, (impact): I feel frustrated and worried. I am starting to feel a little stressed in my exercise class worrying about whether you will come, because I don't know if you realize it, but this was the fifth class in a row that you have been late to pick me up. I understand things can get away from you, but when you don't call or text, it makes me feel you don't think my safety or time is important.

Jim: Gee, I didn't know it was that often, and Honey, of course your safety is important.

Susan (inviting solutions): What do you suggest we can do differently to solve this?

Jim: Well, maybe on hockey game nights, you could take the car. Other nights I will be on time or I will text you to let you know I'm on my way if I get held up.

Susan: Thanks, those sound like good options. I will try taking the car next week because there is a hockey game.

Consider the benefits of this approach:

- The conversation is more productive.

- It has a problem-solving tone.

- It is said in a calm way.

- Information is shared by both parties and it is not one-sided.

Consider the scenario in a workplace:

Situation: Susan and Courtney are colleagues at work. Courtney plays her radio in her cubicle so loudly Susan cannot think. Today Susan decides to do something about it.

Judgmental Approach:

Susan (walking into Courtney's cubicle): Shut that fricking thing off! You are so inconsiderate!

Courtney: What is your problem?

Susan: Well, it's about time you started realizing you are not the only one who has to work in this department!

(Susan walks out and Courtney is left in stunned silence.)

This type of approach to feedback leaves bad feelings between the parties and may make things awkward among people within the department who may have overheard the confrontation.

Effective Approach:

> **Susan** (intention): Hi, Courtney. We're co-workers and sometimes we affect each other. We've always worked well together and I would like to talk to you about something that would help me concentrate better. Would you be willing to talk about it?
>
> **Courtney:** Sure, go ahead.
>
> **Susan:** Is it okay to talk here or would you like to go for a coffee later or use the spare office?
>
> **Courtney:** Wow, are you going to make me cry or what?
>
> **Susan**: No, I just wondered if you wanted us to have a bit of privacy, because who knows who can hear us?
>
> **Courtney:** No, it's okay — go ahead.
>
> **Susan** (specific behaviour): There are times when I am working at my desk and I notice that your radio is loud. (impact): When it is loud I can't hear the person I'm talking to on the phone or I just can't concentrate when I'm working. I don't know if anyone has given you feedback like that before.
>
> **Courtney:** Yeah, a couple times people have told me to turn it down.
>
> **Susan** (inviting solutions): What ideas have you used to deal with it?
>
> **Courtney:** If it's too loud, just tell me and I'll turn it down.
>
> **Susan:** I would appreciate that. Have you ever considered headphones?
>
> **Courtney:** Yeah, but sometimes it is awkward if I have to use the phone.
>
> **Susan:** Okay, well it sounds as though if I find it to be too loud, I can just tell you.
>
> **Courtney:** Yes, that works for me.
>
> **Susan:** Thanks for listening and finding a solution!
>
> **Courtney:** No problem!

Do We Need To Give Feedback — Or Teach?

While it can be uncomfortable to give developmental feedback, there are times we are not fulfilling the roles we have committed to if we do not give others information. For example, as parents, if we do not give our children feedback about their behaviour, how will they learn?

How will employees deliver the outcomes and the requirements of the job role if we — as leaders, managers, supervisors and colleagues in an organization — do not let them know what they are doing well and what they need to improve?

One of the main reasons people fail in our eyes is they do not live up to our expectations. The problem is we often give others negative feedback when we have never discussed our expectations with them before. Sometimes instead of giving people feedback about what they could do better, we have an opportunity to teach or coach them about skills, targets or processes they may know nothing about. Others cannot be successful when they do not have the right information in the first place.

Maybe we need to demonstrate how to complete a task. Maybe we need to observe the person doing something and give them feedback. For example, in a manufacturing company where I was working, a supervisor kept telling a welder to improve his work. When the supervisor finally observed the employee welding, he found that he could correct some of his work on the spot and demonstrate a different way to do the work that resulted in better welds.

Another approach is to ask coaching questions to let the person come up with his own solutions as opposed to telling him what to do. For example, we could ask him how he thinks things are going and what he thinks he could do to improve. Many people have their own answers when someone takes the time to listen.

Finally, sometimes people just need us to provide things they don't have in order to do better. People may need better tools or a computer program they are missing or more time to accomplish a task.

Tips on Giving Developmental Feedback:
Do:

- Provide concrete examples of performance or behaviour.

- Give developmental feedback when you are in a calm mood yourself. If you feel rushed or stressed, postpone the feedback.

- Give feedback in a private place away from others.

- Give people time to think about your feedback.

- Be aware of your tone and body language. Use positive, non-threatening gestures.

- Talk about behaviour or performance, not the person.

- Give timely feedback — don't let it age.

- Review and follow up on expectations or suggested solutions.

- Make it a two-way conversation.

Don't:

- Call your children, spouse or colleagues names, or use judgmental phrases.

- Do all the talking — invite the person to whom you are giving the feedback to respond, share information and ask questions.

- Give all the solutions. Invite the other person to provide ideas to resolve the situation.

Prepare for Giving Effective Feedback

When you prepare to give someone developmental feedback you usually think about what he did and what you want him to change. It can help to have a couple of questions ready to invite a two-way conversation. The first question should invite the other person to share his thoughts on the situation. Then you will do some listening. You can always ask, "Is there anything else?"

Then, once you have both shared your views, it is good to ask a problem-solving question such as "What ideas do you have to look after this?"

Examples of questions for the recipient of the feedback to get their view:

- What do you think about this situation?

- How do you feel about the work you are doing?

- How do you see this situation?

- What is your view?

- Can you help me understand why you are doing it this way?

- Can you share the specifics of what's going on?

- What have you tried so far?

- What is preventing you from…?

- Why do you think this is happening?

Once you understand the view of the person you are giving feedback to — here are some examples of invitational questions that will encourage him to develop a solution:

- What ideas do you have to make this better?

- What ideas do you have to improve the situation?

- What can I /we do to help you with this situation?

- What could help you do this differently?

- How have you handled something like this before?

- What's your opinion on how to handle this?

Dealing with Sensitive Issues

There has been more than one workplace, school or family where someone has needed to give feedback about sensitive topics that can create discomfort for everyone. Body odour is one that comes up regularly. At some workplaces, people just tape a stick of deodorant on someone's locker or leave it on the desk. Someone may just blurt out — "God, you stink! Get with the program." These approaches are not usually effective. Here is an approach using the objective model.

Intention:

I would like to give you some feedback that might make you feel uncomfortable. It is not my intention to make you feel uncomfortable. I am talking to you because I want to share some feedback that can help you be more successful here. I care about you and how you are doing and that is why I am saying something.

Specific Behaviour:

There are times when the odour of your body is too noticeable.

Impact:
When people notice a strong smell, they may be less likely to spend time with you and it will affect how you work with others.

Invitation to Get Their View:
What do you think about this?

Invitation to Problem Solve:
What ideas do you have to take care of this?

Receiving Developmental Feedback

It can be challenging to listen to others when they are telling you how to improve. Here are some tips to help you listen to and assess developmental feedback:

- Be attentive and open to hearing the feedback.

- Be an active listener by paraphrasing and asking questions. It will help you learn more about the other person's perspective.

- Don't take it personally.

- See the feedback as a learning opportunity.

- Say thank you.

- If need be, take time to reflect, and respond later in another discussion at another time.

- You get to choose whether to act on the feedback or not.

Getting Comfortable with Feedback

Feedback is important to our development and to our relationships, yet many people are uncomfortable with it. One of the things we can do to create comfort around feedback is to invite others to give it to us.

My colleague Brad McRae suggests a very effective exercise, which he calls the 3 x 3 Feedback Form. Here is one example of how Brad has used this to solicit feedback from his daughter:

"Once or twice a year when I am feeling somewhat confident as a father, I ask my children: *What is one thing I am doing well as a father and what is one target for improvement?* In her last year of high school, my daughter Katie said I am a great provider. This made me feel very good because otherwise I would not have known she notices. When I asked her what one target for improvement could be, she said she noticed that I tended to save everything in old empty ice-cream containers. She suggested one target for improvement was to do a better job of labelling things in the freezer."[16]

EXERCISE: Creating Your Own Perfect World

Try using the 3 x 3 Feedback Form with your family, friends or co-workers.

Inviting Feedback (3 x 3 Feedback Form — Dr. Brad McRae)

1) What are three things that I am doing well as a _____?
    (spouse, supervisor, coach, etc.)

(Listen and ask questions.)

2) What are three opportunities for improvement?

PART FIVE
Now This is Awkward!
Dealing with Differences and Conflict

Chapter 18 – Understanding and Assessing Conflict
Chapter 19 – Resolving Differences: Asking for a Change in Behaviour
Chapter 20 – What Were you Thinking? Checking Out Perspectives
Chapter 21 – Apologies and Making Things Right
Chapter 22 – Problem-Solving: From Me to We
Chapter 23 – Enough is Enough: Exploring Other Methods to Solve Problems

Conflict is inevitable.
How we talk about and resolve our differences
is what separates our most genuine
and durable relationships from the rest.
Conflict can be a productive or
destructive force in our lives. — PH

Chapter 18
Understanding and Assessing Conflict

Getting comfortable with discomfort allows
us to talk through our differences and come to
understanding and resolution. — *PH*

Relationships are not perfect and people are not perfect. We are human and make mistakes. Communicating respectfully and effectively is a constructive strategy for building and sustaining healthy relationships and for preventing problems. However, things will not be happy and collegial all of the time. It doesn't matter which family, which workplace or which community you live in, sooner or later someone is going to annoy you, hurt you, disagree with you, stop you from doing what you want and tick you off. You'll have clashes with neighbours. You will disagree and fall out with your friends. If you get married and have children, your spouse, in-laws and offspring will provide countless opportunities to fight. If you get divorced you may have even more conflict with former spouses, stepchildren, lawyers and family. Conflict in workplaces is endless. The list goes on.

We all face disagreement and conflict at some point. How we handle it is the difference between being productive or destructive in our own lives and relationships. It is easy for people to get along when everyone is happy and cooperative. The real test of the strength and health of our relationships is how we manoeuvre through the rough spots.

As a mediator I have spent thousands of hours with people in conflict. What amazes me is how the most competent, logical and fair people can turn into monsters when faced with disagreement. Instead of thinking about their loved ones or colleagues and trying to clear things up caringly, people retaliate. They sabotage and hurt each other. Often the war goes on for so long the initial issue that created the problem is forgotten and overshadowed by the bad behaviour that follows. Just look at some people's Facebook posts and notice the negative and hurtful comments about others who have crossed them. There are approaches to deal with conflict constructively. The first step is recognizing when you are in a conflict and then assessing what to do instead of being destructive. Handle your relationships with love and care.

What is Conflict Anyway?

A sign of a conflict is when we feel discomfort and negative emotions. For me personally, I know there's a problem when I get a bad feeling in the pit of my stomach. I find I can't sleep and my mind is constantly going over an issue. The emotions that erupt during conflict are uncomfortable. The impact of conflict on our daily lives is apparent. People experiencing conflict report they often:

- Feel upset, unhappy, victimized, grief-stricken or depressed

- Are anxious and worried (including sore stomach, headaches)

- Feel deeply hurt or offended by the actions of others

- Don't have the will or concentration to give their best at work or in their lives because they are preoccupied with the problem

Given these negative consequences, it is easy to understand our aversion to conflict and why we try to avoid or ignore it; we hope we won't open a can of worms and make it worse.

Now, This Is Awkward!

The problem with conflict is it stirs up all kinds of uncomfortable feelings, which take time and effort to work through. We do not like discomfort. It is awkward. We don't want to hurt people's feelings, so we let a lot of things go. We do not know how others will react to us. We do not know if other people will take our concerns seriously or blame us for situations and the unknown is frightening. Will Mom be mad at me? Will my spouse understand me, or prefer to be with someone else? Will my boss fire me? Will I get "un-friended"? We avoid conflict because we are uncomfortable with discomfort and fear the unknown.

REACTING TO DISAGREEMENT

When we become fearful, our flight-or-fight reaction kicks in. We tend to be reactive instead of strategic and will behave in one of two ways:

Shut Up: Flee and Avoid

For many of us, facing conflict is frightening and uncomfortable, so we avoid it and hide it. Keeping a lid on our conflict means when someone asks, "Is everything okay?" we say "Sure, it is" even when it's not. When we avoid, we suffer in silence. We get resentful and sick. We lose time and ground in our lives. We shut up to avoid confrontation and we experience more grief. This is a passive approach to conflict.

Blow Up: Fight and Compete

Other people handle conflict by trying to overpower the person they are facing. They go into full-combat, GI-Joe mode and battle others, regardless of the cost. They believe there has to be a winner and a loser. They want to be the winners. In this aggressive approach the person blows up — letting out an explosion of thoughts and feelings in inappropriate ways that make a mess and hurt other people and relationships. Spouses, co-workers, children and neighbours are no longer viewed as people who are important, but as the enemy who must be overtaken. Maintaining loving relationships goes by the wayside. The need to be right and to win prevails.

Step Up: Assess and Choose

Rather than shut up or blow up, we can choose a third course of action: *to step up*. This means to *assess* our conflicts and make a deliberate choice about how to approach them. An active and wise choice may include deciding to overlook the disagreement and put it aside because, upon reflection, we realize it really doesn't matter. Conversely, after assessment we may choose to pursue resolution directly with the other person or with the help of others.

CHECKING OUR OWN THINKING

In my two decades as a mediator, I have worked with many people immersed in a struggle. I have observed how people experience disagreement as a result of their own views, beliefs and what they think is the correct approach. Individuals have a lot of power in terms of how they define conflict, how they think about it and how they choose to navigate through it.

As Henry Ford said, "Whether you think you can, or you can't, you're usually right." This view of the power of our thoughts on predicting outcomes in our lives is especially accurate when it comes to conflict. That's because our views and beliefs form the basis of our decisions about what we say and what we do, and what we refuse to say or do and they become a self-fulfilling prophecy.

The challenge for many of us is we have had little or no education in dealing with disputes in our relationships. As well, our family role models may have handled it poorly. Popular media promote violent, positional approaches and a win-lose outcome.

Unhelpful Thinking Keeps Us Stuck

Many of us have deeply held negative beliefs about conflict that keep us in a rut and prevent us from trying to resolve our differences. Some typical negative views regarding conflict are:

- It is bad and should be avoided at all costs.

- Nothing good can come from it.

- There has to be a winner and a loser.

- Because we do not believe in our own skills or conduct and certainly don't believe in the potential of others to resolve differences productively, most conflicts can't be fixed.

- If you can't say anything nice, don't say anything at all.

- It's a waste of time to deal with conflict.

- If you are going to deal with conflict you must do it on the spot.

- There is a statute of limitations on conflict.

This negative mindset keeps us from seizing opportunities to resolve our differences.

Productive Thinking That Can Help Us Deal with Conflict

A perspective on conflict is to accept the world has good things and bad things in it. It can be helpful to get real about conflict and accept certain truths and realities such as:

- Some people treat us well and others don't.

- Some situations are good and others seem unfair or bad.

- Some people are easy to get along with and others are not.

- Sometimes people do things that we do not like.

- Sometimes we can change things and sometimes we can't.

- Not everyone has to like us.

I read on a baby's bib, "Spit happens!" which is a reminder to not take everything too seriously, to decide which conflicts are significant issues that need to be dealt with, and which ones we can let go because they just aren't that big a deal.

Productive Thoughts for Conflict Resolution

- Some conflicts can be minimized if not solved. Sometimes when we deal with a dispute, the result may not be world peace, but the situation will settle down and the two sides will simply agree to disagree.

- Some conflicts can be resolved, many in a productive way, and relationships can be restored and improved.

- Some conflicts are unavoidable. If you are a leader in a workplace, the authority figure at school or in the community, or a parent, you are responsible for getting involved in others' conflicts by supporting resolution and providing process.

- We all contribute to conflict intentionally or unintentionally. When someone is being bullied or harassed and we say and do nothing, our silence is acquiescence.

- Win-win resolutions are possible. We are so bombarded with the idea of win-lose in our society that it rarely occurs to us that win-win is possible. When working through most conflicts, we believe negotiation is complete when one party has won and the other has lost. Win-win happens when we work towards a solution where both parties' interests are met.

- Resolution takes time, energy and deliberate strategic action. There is no such thing as a *conflict resolution fairy*. We must get involved to resolve.

- Conflict resolution skills can be learned. In fact, we already have the skills: communicating, expressing and listening with respect, and participating in creative problem solving.

- We can be part of the solution or part of the problem. When we gossip or disengage from taking responsibility, take sides or complain, we perpetuate conflict. When we listen, encourage, support and coach, we are a productive resource for resolving differences.

THE POSITIVE SIDE OF CONFLICT

It is hard to imagine that conflict can be positive. However, when we raise our concerns and work through our differences, positive outcomes are possible.

- **Change** — Conflict acts as a catalyst for change so that we can improve our relationships, circumstances and life.

- **Resolution** — Problems can actually be solved and bad feelings and relationships can heal.

- **Growth and Learning** — Working through a conflict creates understanding. We learn how to communicate more effectively and learn about ourselves and others.

- **Opportunities** — Possibilities that were closed to us in terms of work or life are opened up.

- **Empowerment** — When we address conflict, we find our own voice and assert our own views, taking responsibility for ourselves. Most people experience a sense of empowerment when they engage in conflict resolution.

- **Movement** — When we stay stuck and avoid, we deteriorate. When we face conflict, we give ourselves and others the chance to heal, grow and move forward.

Causes of Conflict

When your car makes a noise, it is difficult to know what it will take to fix it if you don't know what is making the noise. Once you can determine the root cause of the problem, you can start to understand how to make repairs. Similarly, when you are in conflict, it is helpful to try to articulate the issue that is of concern to you. Defining the problem is the first step in assessment. Here are some typical issues that are at the heart of many conflicts:

Behaviour — You find a person's behaviour troublesome, irritating or disrespectful.

Process — The way something is being done is of concern to you.

Resources — Problems arise out of a lack of resources or how they are allocated or divided.

Roles — When roles are not clearly defined or people are not acting in ways expected of their roles, it creates problems.

Expectations — When people have different expectations conflict can occur.

Values — Differences in what we value or think is proper creates problems.

Communication Flow — People disagree about how information is shared or withheld.

Communication Style — Differences in communication style and preferences can create conflict.

Power — Who has power and control in a situation?

Defining the issue helps to lead us to resolution. The more issues involved in the situation, the more meetings or conversations it may take to find a resolution.

When preparing to discuss a conflict with another person, it is worthwhile noting that it took you some time and a number of interactions to get into conflict, so logically it will take you a number of conversations to resolve it. Too often we give up after only one short, unsuccessful conversation saying, "Oh well, we tried." Give resolution a chance. Try at least three conversations before you give up or involve others, unless your safety is at stake. In that case, get assistance immediately.

ASSESSING CONFLICT

We can deal with conflict in a number of ways. We usually don't analyse it — we just react. When we react in anger, we often make mistakes. The first step in dealing with conflict is to analyse it. It may take us some time to deal with our negative emotions and get calm before we can think clearly. When we assess the situation we can see whether we need to take action to resolve it, or let it go because it is not a big deal. (See the assessment questions at the end of this chapter.)

Not all conflict is the same. Some conflicts are minor and irritating, but not life altering. Some conflicts are huge and create a big impact. Assessing the significance of an issue will help us determine how to proceed.

Application: Tips to Consider in Conflict
Do:

- Stay calm and think.

- Be optimistic: "I can get through this, we'll figure it out."

- Listen carefully, in order to be aware of other parties and what they are experiencing.

- Assess the conflict, clarify your goal in the conflict and determine steps you could take to get you there.

- Expect to have multiple discussions to resolve a conflict and process both sides. It took a while for the situation to develop and it's going to take a while to resolve it.

Don't:

- Lash out at others or react when you are in the heat of the moment.

- Name-call or threaten.

- Make assumptions.

- View your loved ones as your enemies. Remember you can show loving kindness and patience while working things out.

Being a Third Party to a Conflict

When someone comes to us with a conflict involving another person, our reaction is to pick sides. When someone approaches you about a conflict he is having with someone else, how do **you** respond? Do you just agree and say, "Yeah the boss is a real jerk" or "Your wife seems to be a nag." How you respond to others' conflicts influences their behaviour. Rather than agreeing with an upset person, you might just listen and be empathetic. Comments such as "I can see how that could be difficult to deal with" or "I can see how you would feel that way" shows active listening. You can also ask him questions with an intention to support him in resolving the problem rather than siding with him or slagging the other person.

Ask: What would you like to see happen to resolve this? What have you tried so far? What do you think their intention was? Is it possible that there might be a miscommunication? Who else could help?

Conflict does not have to result in violence or destruction. Analysing conflict and figuring out what issues need to be resolved is a good first step in dealing with it.

EXERCISE: Creating Your Own Perfect World

Assessment Worksheet

Think about a conflict that is concerning you, and work through the following questions in order to assess it:

1. Why do I think there is a problem or conflict? (What are the issues?)

2. How do I feel and why do I feel that way?

3. What isn't okay for me about this situation?

4. Is it possible the other person isn't even aware I may feel this way and how the problem is affecting me?

5. Do I think the other person did this to me intentionally?

6. What did I do intentionally or unintentionally that could be affecting the situation?

Follow-Up:

Now that you have reviewed the situation, consider your next step(s) such as:

- I am okay! I assessed this and I do not need to pursue this. It's no big deal.

- I am still not sure. I think I need to talk to an unbiased third party to get perspective and some coaching. (At work, that could be a boss or colleague or the human resources department; it could be a teacher at school, a parent, spouse, friend or professional, such as a lawyer or counsellor.)

- I am ready to approach the other person and try to work it out.

Resolution:

Resolving conflict can mean different things to different people. In most cases, it means that the bad feelings go away. That can be accomplished by:

1. You deciding you are not going to let the conflict bother you any more because you have assessed it and it doesn't matter

2. Working it out with the other person

3. Turning the conflict over to an authority figure or using a process that involves support from a third party

4. Changing your circumstances (i.e. terminate a relationship or find a new job)

In the next few chapters, we will look at how to pursue these options and ways you can communicate with others in order to resolve differences.

Chapter 19
Resolving Differences: Asking for a Change in Behaviour

Jesus loves you — but everyone else thinks
you're a jerk! — *Anonymous*

Not Martha Stewart

When I was in university I shared an apartment with a roommate, Nicki. We moved into the apartment in late August. Neither of us was Martha Stewart, but I tried to do basic housekeeping. I often felt frustrated with Nicki because she frequently left a mess in the kitchen. She would cook and leave dirty dishes, food and garbage on the counters and table. When I came home from class, I had to clean up and wash dishes in order to have enough utensils to cook for myself. I put up with this behaviour because I needed a roommate to share the cost of the apartment and utilities. So I avoided the conflict, cleaned up after her and didn't make waves. This was okay for me during September and October, but by November I was tired of it. Furthermore, I was frustrated because of all the hours I spent cleaning when I could have been studying or having fun. I was done putting up with it. I decided to confront her one evening.

She usually came home around six p.m. from class. I was ready for her. Six o'clock came and went and Nicki did not arrive. I was really annoyed because I was ready to talk. I was even angrier at seven when she had not arrived, and was furious when she finally came in at eight. I was so worked up by the time she arrived that I started the conversation quite aggressively and indignantly:

Me: Can I talk to you?

Nicki: Sure.

Me (in an angry tone): You are a pig!

Nicki: What!

Me: You leave the kitchen in a mess every day. I am not your mother, I am not your maid, pick up your crap!

Nicki: Okay...

She then walked into her bedroom and I did not see much of her after that because she avoided me. She moved out at the end of the term and I had to find another roommate. My approach left a relationship destroyed where there could have been problem solving and cooperation.

BEHAVIOURS THAT FRUSTRATE

The way people behave can create conflict. Think about people in your life who annoy you. What things do others do that drive you crazy? As you think of these people and their behaviours right now, you are probably feeling negative emotions such as anger and frustration.

How often has a friend or colleague shared these types of complaints with you about the behaviour of others?

- My co-worker is a like a Debbie-Downer. He is constantly complaining about everyone and the company. It's uncomfortable to be around him.

- My son is 20 years old and he still lives at home. He doesn't pay rent because he's supposed to mow the lawn and do his own laundry. He hasn't done either all summer.

- My boss is such a gossip. She tells stories about the private lives of employees in our department. I often wonder who she gossips to about me.

- My co-workers talk outside my cubicle and laugh so loudly no one can concentrate.

- My mother-in-law is constantly telling us how to parent our new baby. She's forever giving us advice and telling us what to do. The baby is our baby! We are the parents!

- My co-worker is always late and that means I have to do some of her work.

One of the best things we can do when we feel annoyed and want a change in behaviour is to *ask for it*. Many of us hesitate to let others know when they are doing things that annoy us or have a negative impact on us. It's the "live and let live" attitude, meaning we are all different and we need to be tolerant of others if we expect them to be tolerant of us.

ASKING IS NOT EASY

Do you want to win the lottery? If so, you need to buy a ticket. Purchasing a ticket does not guarantee a win — but at least it makes it possible.

Similarly, if you want someone to change his behaviour, simply wishing for it doesn't help. You need to increase your odds of success by asking for a change. Asking does not guarantee success either, but it is a start. As well, the more times you ask, the more likely you are to get the person's attention. Suffering is optional. Ask for a change!

Yet, if we say nothing about the things people do that bother us, we teach them it is okay to do what they are doing. Our silence is agreement. When we *shut up,* we have to *put up* with others' undesirable conduct.

However, just because we experience the behaviour of others negatively at times, it does not mean their intention is to bother us. People are not psychic. They cannot read our minds. If their behaviour is bothering you, they may truly be unaware of it unless you tell them. Similarly, if your behaviour is bothering others, how would you know it if they did not tell you?

Most of us don't ask others to change their conduct for our benefit. We put up with repeated annoyances over an extended period of time. After months or even years of suffering in silence, we make a vow we will not put up with it any more, and the next time it happens, we are going to let the culprit have it! This is an example of avoiding conflict (shutting up) and trying to hold it in, and then exploding because we can't contain it any longer. We go from being silent to blowing up without any productive action in between.

When someone's behaviour is creating conflict for you, the question is, how do you deal with it? There are some simple ways to discourage unwanted behaviour:

- Ignore it, don't reward it with a response and sometimes people will stop it.

- Make simple, clear statements such as "Can you knock it off?" "Stop that, please." "That is unnecessary, please don't do it again." "I would prefer you not to do that."

In many situations a simple request can stop behaviours.

ASKING ASSERTIVELY FOR CHANGE

I often regret my poor skills and lack of finesse in dealing with the situation with my roommate Nicki. It was disrespectful and rude. I did not give Nicki enough information for her to understand my perspective and concerns. Nor did I invite her to contribute her views about a solution to a shared situation. It was a poor attempt at solving the problem.

I wish I had used the assertive technique called the I-Message to express my views. The basic formula for an I-Message includes three elements:

1. When you… invites you to describe the specific behaviour you are referring to that you would like the other person to stop or modify.

2. I feel… is intended to have you describe the emotion you experience when confronted with the behaviour.

3. Because… invites you to describe the impact that behaviour has on you or what I like to call the "So What Factor."

As with all effective communication, it is prudent to start the conversation by sharing your intention and getting the other party's consent, permission or buy-in to have the conversation. You can always reschedule if the time you have selected is not convenient for the other person. Imagine if I had followed this approach with my roommate:

Me (intention): Hi, Nicki. I would like to discuss some guidelines for how to take care of the apartment together. We never had an opportunity to share ideas. Would you be okay to talk about it now or do you want to do it another time?

Nicki: Sure — go for it.

Me (specific behaviour): When I go to make a meal in the kitchen and you have left out food and dirty dishes (emotion) I feel frustrated (effect) because I have to clean things up so I can have cookware to make my meal, and it cuts into my study time.

How much clearer and more effective is this request for change than being angry and name-calling? Once this part of the message gets shared, we can go one of two ways to continue the conversation:

I can either:

A) Share my solution for the situation that will help the other person understand my view,

or

B) I can invite the other person to share their views by asking a question that encourages a conversation. This allows you to hear the other person's perspective and get him to share ideas about how to solve the problem.

In my case if I had gone the A route, to share my solution I could have said:
What I would appreciate is if you would clean up after yourself when you use the kitchen, and I will do the same.

If I had gone the B route and asked Nicki to share her views I could have inquired:
Nicki, I know we haven't talked about this before. What is your reaction to this idea? What ideas do you have for dealing with the kitchen?

Imagine how much more effective your requests for change could be if you slowed down and used this approach. The benefits are:

- You are more prepared and able to express yourself respectfully.

- You will be calmer when you have assessed these elements.

- You will share more information that is specific and objective, which will help the other person understand what you really mean and how the situation affects you.

- It is easier for a person to respond positively to you when you are not ordering, threatening, name-calling or demanding.

- It is a two-way conversation, not an attack.

Examples

Compare these approaches:

If the behaviour is that your co-worker, Marge, always complains about others, an aggressive approach would be to say, "Marge — quit complaining" or "I can't take your complaining any more."

An assertive approach would be:

"Marge, I would like to talk to you about something that is affecting our working relationship. Can I tell you about it? When you complain about our co-workers, I feel uncomfortable because they may hear your comments and it may make them mad and make it hard to work with them. I would appreciate it if you would not share these comments with me."

Another example may be that your son has not mowed the lawn as he promised. An attacking way to raise the issue would be to say, "Quit being lazy and mow the lawn!" Or you could threaten with, "Since you did not mow the lawn today I am tired of your attitude and I am going to charge you rent from now on."

Using the assertive approach, would look more like:

Son, I'd like to talk to you about something that affects the agreement we made when you started living here rent-free. Is now a good time?

In the last two months, you have not mown the lawn once. I feel very frustrated because I have had to do it and I also feel taken advantage of because you're not living up to your end of the arrangement.

What are your views on the situation?

Considerations When Using this Model

- There is no right or wrong way to approach how you use this model. You need to decide what will be most effective with the person you are dealing with. By that, I mean decide if the communication would go better if you shared your solution as a way to open the topic — or if it would be better to hear their view first before you share any solutions.

- This assertive approach invites dialogue from the other party and provides a way to problem-solve.

- Some people will be uncooperative and tell you to get lost. Other people will be happy to have been told what kind of impact they are having on you because they didn't know.

- Most people don't want to disturb others or be thought of as troublesome.

- Sharing information gives the other party a chance to change his behaviour.

- When you have finished the conversation, it makes sense to thank the person for listening and for his help in addressing the problem. It is also helpful to summarize whatever you have agreed to as a result of your discussion. For example, "Mary, thanks for taking the time to discuss this with me, and next time your music is a bit loud, I will just let you know by giving you a wave over the cubicle."

- We may need to share information more than once to support the person in changing his behaviour because it takes time to change habits.

- Be prepared for a turnabout. When you engage in requesting a change from others, they often approach you with ideas about what they would like you to change as well.

- When you approach someone, be prepared to let him think about the situation before you come to an agreement. For example, if someone isn't responding, you might say, "It seems I have shared a lot of information. Maybe it would be helpful if we both had time to think about this. When could we have a follow-up conversation?"

DOESN'T HE KNOW HE'S DRIVING ME CRAZY?

Sometimes we can't believe that the people whose negative behaviours create conflict are unaware of their impact on others. However, many of us are oblivious to our own behaviour and are not aware of how we may unintentionally hurt or annoy others. Many people in our workplaces, families and communities who drive us crazy don't really have a clue. These people have what is referred to as a *blind spot*. They do not see the behaviour in themselves that others around them readily observe. If they cannot see it and acknowledge it, they certainly won't change it. When we give others feedback or ask for a change we may help them see one of their own blind spots.

DEALING WITH TOUGH BEHAVIOUR

If we have a hard time with minor annoyances, it is even more intimidating to approach someone who is intentionally behaving badly. These actions include:

- Bullying

- Telling offensive jokes

- Name-calling or making disrespectful, derogatory remarks

Most agencies that handle human rights issues suggest that people who are experiencing unwelcome behaviour make the person who is displaying the behaviour aware of it. That means we need to tell someone when we don't like his behaviour.

Here are a few scenarios:

Eye-rolling
Situation: A supervisor in a workplace is responsible for answering questions and coaching employees about procedures and problem solving. When employees approach this person for help, she usually rolls her eyes and sighs. The supervisor does this so much that most employees see it as harassment or bullying.

An employee could approach the supervisor to provide information about the behaviour and request a change in the situation.

An Approach Using an I-Message
I would like to share something with you that I experience when I talk to you. I would appreciate it if we could discuss it.

When you roll your eyes and sigh when I come to ask you a question, I feel uncomfortable and concerned, because I need to check in with you so that I can do my job. Your response makes me wonder if there's some kind of issue.

What I would appreciate is if you would not roll your eyes or sigh. Instead, just look at me with a neutral expression and answer my question. If I am approaching you at a bad time, it would help for you to let me know that and let me know a better time to come back.

Is that something you would be willing to do?

Or the employee could ask:

Can you help me understand what is going on for you when I approach you, and you sigh and roll your eyes?

Making Offensive Jokes

Situation: When neighbours get together for social occasions, one person has a habit of telling offensive jokes about cultural groups. At one of the get-togethers, the person cracks one of his distasteful jokes. A neighbour approaches him privately later, away from the other guests, and assertively confronts him.

An Approach Using an I-Message

I just want to give you a heads-up about some of the things you say.

When you make jokes about people from specific cultures, it makes me feel uncomfortable, because I have several friends who are of that culture and it is not cool for me to hear this.

I would appreciate it if you would not tell these jokes around me or anyone.

Asking others to change their behaviour is not easy. Using any of these assertive approaches is only part of the process. Once we share the assertive message, we must also be prepared to listen to the other party, to be open to hearing his side and intention in the situation and to be open to brainstorming other solutions or approaches to the problem.

Name-Calling

Situation: A former manager at a past workplace regularly called me bitch. He would say things like, "Hey, bitch — how's it going?" He thought it was funny. I certainly did not. When I did something well, he called me a smart bitch.

Using the assertive model, I approached him:

I would like to talk to you about comments that are impacting our working relationship. Can I share this with you?

When you call me by the term you just used, I feel offended, as it is a derogatory term and it shows me disrespect, especially when it is used in front of my colleagues.

I am asking that you stop using that term whether we are alone or with others.

I used this approach at least five times with that person. He did not stop calling me the name. It left me with the choice of whether or not to escalate the issue.

I did pursue the matter and made a complaint to the human resources department. They talked to him. He apologized and stopped using the term. While the behaviour stopped, our relationship did not get any better. The positive side of asking for a change is it can create a "nothing to lose" attitude about being honest. And when people are really honest with you, you can more easily make a choice as to whether it makes sense to stay in a relationship with them. In this case, I could clearly see that our relationship would not improve, so I looked for an opportunity to change the situation and find a position where I didn't work with him.

SUMMARY

Asking for a Change in Behaviour
It is not easy to ask people to change because everyone prefers the habits and patterns they're used to. Keep in mind it is normal to have to remind people a few times before the changes start to happen. If they do not, you may want to consider stronger interventions. Stronger interventions would include enlisting a third party or involving some kind of authority or decision-making body or even using a legal process. We are not always the right instrument to solve our own problems. We will explore other ways to deal with these differences in the chapter entitled, "Enough is Enough."

EXERCISE: Creating Your Own Perfect World

Asking for a Change in Behaviour
1) Which behaviour of the other person is irritating or concerning you?

2) How does the behaviour make you feel? (uncomfortable, frustrated, concerned, etc.)

3) How is the behaviour affecting you personally?

4) If you were to approach this person, how would you express your intention?

5) Think about which of the following approaches would be best to start the problem-solving process:

Let the person know what you would appreciate: "I would like you to…"
Or
Ask them to share their point of view before you come to solutions.

6) What considerations do you have about a good time and place for this discussion?

Chapter 20
What Were You Thinking?
Checking Out Perspectives

There are two sides to every story... sometimes more. — *PH*

Well, Good Morning to You, Too!

One Monday morning, Alex walked into the office around 6:45 a.m. His colleague, Debra, was already seated at her desk working. As Alex walked past her, he said, "Good morning," and to his surprise, Debra did not reply. In fact, she did not even look up from her work. Alex felt ignored and went into his office.

As Alex worked through the day, his thoughts went back to his morning encounter with Debra. He couldn't figure it out. In their three-year working relationship they had always been collegial. The more he thought about how rude she was, the angrier he got. How dare she ignore him! She had no right to be so rude. He had always been nice to her and here she was, totally dissing him!

As Alex lay awake later that night, his mind continued to review his interaction with Debra. He still could not believe her behaviour. It was totally inappropriate. He decided if she thought that she could treat him like that, she had another thing coming. He would show her. After all, he had recently been promoted to manager. Maybe Debra was jealous.

The next morning Alex was in the office at 6:30 a.m., ready for Debra. When she came in at seven, she smiled at Alex and said, "Good morning!" Alex looked up at her from his seat in his office and without a word got up and slammed the door in her face. "That will teach her," he thought. "I'll see how she likes being ignored."

Debra stood on the other side of the door that had just been slammed. She was stunned and confused. Why would one of the company's managers treat her like this, she wondered? Was her job in jeopardy? She was worried. The week had already started badly. She had been up all night on Sunday with her father in the ER because he had had a heart attack. That is why she was at work so early on Monday. She had come straight there from the hospital with no sleep. In fact, all day Monday she had had a hard time keeping her eyes open. Only Debra's immediate boss knew her dad was sick. Now she would also need to tell her boss that Alex was angry with her and she didn't know why. "Wow! What a horrible week this is turning out to be," she thought.

Debra and Alex were in the middle of an escalated conflict.

This type of situation happens to all of us. My observation as a mediator is we are the architects of many of our worst personal conflicts. As we interact with others daily, we encounter situations that annoy or upset us. Then in our inner voice we narrate a story about how we are *right* and the other person is *wrong*. We think how inconsiderate, thoughtless, unfair or selfish other people are and how *they* should fix the problem.

Our inner dialogue is so powerful that we end up making assumptions and coming to conclusions about a situation without ever talking to the person we are in conflict with, to check out their side of the story. We assume we know why the person did and said what he did.

The worst conflicts happen when we behave vindictively instead of talking to those who are closest to us to try and resolve our issues with a calm and loving kindness. This is the mistake Alex made. He escalated the conflict by retaliating against the perceived snub from Debra. He did this while acting on assumptions rather than checking out what was going on with Debra.

Alex is not alone. It is easy to misunderstand the intentions of others or misjudge how they have been affected by shared events or communications. Our thoughts quickly spin out of control. Once we form an opinion and take action we are reluctant to change our minds, because we still feel the negative emotions that were created by our own thinking.

It is estimated that 80% of our conflicts stem from *perceived* conflict and misunderstandings, and most problems could be resolved by having a conversation to clarify the situation. This practice is called a *perspective-check*.

THE SOLUTION: PERSPECTIVE-CHECKING

In order to deal with conflict and maintain relationships, we need to talk to the others who are involved in the situation to get their side of the story, their perspective.

We only have *part* of the information involved in a situation. The other person provides the rest of the information we need to understand it. Only the other person knows his own intention, why he did or did not do something. If we did something someone else has reacted to, he is the one who knows how he was affected by the situation, and we are the ones who know our own intentions.

Many conflicts are perceptual or perceived in our own minds and the person we are in conflict with may not only be unaware of the conflict, but may not have had any negative intention.

As mentioned in Chapter 7, there is the private realm of communication, which goes on in our own heads (the inside), and there is the public realm, which is information that is shared between people or in a public way (the outside).

During every interaction there is the dynamic of intent, action and effect. That means the sender says or does something in the public realm and the receiver interprets what they observe, and is affected by it in terms of how they interpret the action and how it leaves them feeling. The sender and the receiver often keep the intention and effect private and this gap in information sharing creates many misunderstandings.

Intent - Action - Effect Model:

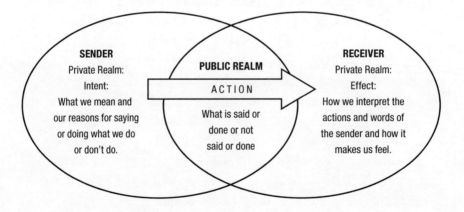

If we keep information to ourselves and don't share it, the other person cannot truly understand our thoughts and feelings and won't have accurate information about the conflict.

Some Considerations about Communication:

- We believe if we have a positive intention, the person we are interacting with will be affected positively. This is not always true.

- We assume if we feel bad about what someone said or did to us, they intended to make us feel bad. This also is not always true.

- When we do not know what the other person is thinking we often act on assumptions rather than checking things out with them and getting the right information.

When to Perspective-Check

Conflicts arise when we experience negative emotions while having an interaction with someone or just by observing his behaviour. The problem is we act as though our assumptions are fact. When I start to feel negatively affected by someone else's words or actions, I realize I have a chance to perspective-check. Although talking to someone about what made us feel bad can be challenging, I see it as a great opportunity to find out "where the gold is buried" or in other words, get the facts and the other side of the story. Getting information from others allows us to act on fact, not assumptions, and allows us to make better choices.

Perspective-checking is a way of acquiring information to help you decide whether or not a substantive conflict is occurring. Perspective-checking is the act of initiating a conversation with the other party to make sure you have the full picture. The benefits of perspective-checking are that it:

- Allows for a better understanding of both sides of the conversation

- Provides a process for clearing up misunderstandings

- Provides an opportunity to raise issues of concern

- Allows you to act on the realization that your interpretation of the situation is not the only one, and the other party may see things quite differently

- Allows you to clarify your part in the situation because the other person may have been misreading you

The perspective-checking process allows each party to speak to the part of the communication he is responsible for.

PROCESS A: If you are not sure of the other person's intention

Sometimes you have an interaction where you are unsure of the other person's intentions. In other words, you do not know why they behaved the way they did or why they did something. Perspective-checking allows you to open a conversation and be an information gatherer so you can decide later what you want to do in regards to the issue.

Prepare by:

- Suspending your judgment of the other person and his intentions

- Beginning the conversation only once you are calm and ready to listen without fighting

- Recognizing the possibility you have misinterpreted the situation

- Shifting from anger and judgment to curiosity

- Keeping in mind when you perspective-check with someone else he may take the opportunity to raise issues he has with you

How to proceed:

1) Explain to the other party the *action* you observed (what was said or done or not said or done) and ask, "Can you help me understand your intention?" or "What was going on for you when that happened?"

2) Be a good listener while he responds. Don't interject with your own opinion — just let him talk. Your goal is to understand.

3) Ask other probing and clarifying questions to ensure understanding, be curious and seek clarification:

   - "What did you mean by...?"

   - "Can you help me understand why...?"

   - "Are you saying that...?"

   - "Do you mean to say that...?"

4) You may decide whether or not to tell him the effect his action had on you.

5) Thank him for his time and energy.

Example: Alex and Debra

Instead of retaliating, Alex could have perspective-checked, asking Debra if she had a moment to talk, and could have invited her into his office so they had privacy.

Alex: Debra, do you have a minute to talk about something that happened yesterday?

Debra: Sure.

Alex: Please have a seat.

Debra: Thanks, what's up?

Alex: Yesterday morning when I came to work, I said good morning to you and you didn't reply. You didn't even look up. That's unusual because we have always had a good working relationship. I am wondering whether I have done something to offend you.

Debra: Oh, Alex — no, you did not do anything to offend me. Yesterday morning I was in early because I was in the ER with my dad all night. He had a heart attack. I came to work straight from the hospital. I had been up all night and, honestly, I did not even know you said good morning. I was in my own world yesterday. I certainly did not mean to offend you.

Alex: Oh, I didn't know your dad was ill. Sorry to hear that.

Debra: No, I didn't mention it to anyone except Roy [her boss].

Alex: Well, I will keep that to myself. Thanks for taking the time to talk to me and please let me know if I can do anything to help.

Debra: Thanks for letting me know I totally missed what you said. I'm glad we cleared that up.

This method of checking things out allows both parties to share information and clarify the situation. There are times when we assume a problem exists when one really doesn't.

Example: Susie and the Principal

An elementary school principal, Mrs. Smith, had been having a lot of problems with the behaviour of a grade six girl named Susie. Susie was often late for school. In class she seemed disengaged. Susie did not have friends at school and was sometimes defiant with teachers. Many teachers disliked having Susie in their class. Mrs. Smith met with Susie several times and felt that Susie needed some support. When Susie had started to change some of her behaviour for the better, Mrs. Smith decided to reward her by sending her to an activity day at another school.

After the activity day, Mrs. Smith heard from some of the teachers who had been in attendance that Susie was back to her old self, standoffish with other kids and refusing to participate in team-building activities. Mrs. Rocher, a teacher from Susie's school (who had attended the activity day), said to Mrs. Smith, "See? Leopards don't change their spots. You're wasting your time with Susie. She'll never change."

Mrs. Smith decided to perspective-check with Susie.

Mrs. Smith: Hi, Susie — I just wanted to ask you how the day went. How did you like it?

Susie: It was okay, I guess.

Mrs. Smith: I heard from Mrs. Rocher that she had a few chats with you about participation during the day.

Susie: Yeah, she did.

Mrs. Smith: I understand you didn't talk to many kids?

(Susie shakes her head no.)

Mrs. Smith: Why was that?

Susie: Because there were quite a few girls there from the old school I went to. They were laughing at me and calling me fat, so I just stayed away from them so I wouldn't get in a fight.

Mrs. Smith: Oh. Well, you did a good job controlling your anger and not getting into a fight. Can you help me understand why you did not participate in some of the activities?

Susie: Well, we started the day running relays and stuff. I got sweaty and I kinda smelled because I don't have any deodorant. I participated in all the activities except one.

Mrs. Smith: Which one was that?

Susie: A relay where we had to hold hands with other kids. I didn't want to do it because I thought some kids would call me fat again. And I also didn't want them making fun of me because I was sweaty.

Mrs. Smith: Well, that makes sense. I can understand why you chose to do what you did.

Their conversation continued and Mrs. Smith learned through this perspective-check that the teachers at the workshop were assuming Susie's intentions rather than understanding them.

Perspective-checking allows us to clear up misunderstandings instead of escalating them.

Perspective-Checking and Handling Conflict

When we use a perspective-checking approach to gather information about a potential conflict, we slow down the conversation and make a point of understanding the other party's view. We share our own views and decide where to go from there, rather than getting into an argument. What you may find when you perspective-check is that there is a major point of difference. You may find that the person you are talking to:

- Does not care about your point of view, may not like you and doesn't want to have anything to do with you

- Has lied to you or others, or has manipulated information in the situation

- Is argumentative and close-minded

- Is engaging in unethical, mean or dishonest behaviour

- Is being unreasonable and nothing you can say or do will change that

The good news about finding out such information is you can decide how you want to deal with it. The succeeding chapters highlight other approaches in dealing with conflict.

Perspective-checking takes patience. We must learn to control our emotions in order to become high-level communicators and have respect for the other person and their perspective.

Curiosity and Patience

When you focus on being curious and really understand what the other party is trying to say, instead of being angry or retaliatory, you naturally become more patient. Your tone and body language become more welcoming and more open, which encourages communication and elicits information from the other party. — *PH*

PROCESS B: If you are not sure how your action affected another person

There have been times in my busy day when I have whisked from one activity to the other, unmindful and not fully present with everyone I have been speaking to. At these times I have thought that I may have made a faux pas that could have hurt or angered someone even when that was not my intention.

If you become aware of a situation in which you said or did something that could have affected the other person in a negative way, it is never too late to have a conversation with that person to perspective-check — to explain your intention and to find out how you have affected him. You follow this process by:

1) Explaining the action (what you said or did or what you did not say or do) and why you did it (your own intention). You might also say, "I realize you may have been affected in a way I did not intend" (e.g., "If I offended you it was not my intention…").

2) Ask them how the action affected them (e.g., "How did you feel when I…?" or "How were you affected by my actions?").

3) Listen to them with curiosity to hear their views.

4) Thank them for their views.

5) If you offended or hurt them intentionally or unintentionally, apologize.

Example:

During a workshop, a participant got up and left during the session. He did not return. I did not get alarmed because people lead complex lives and juggle many responsibilities. The next morning the participant came in and we had a conversation where he initiated a perspective-check with me, because he wanted to clarify his intention and check out the impact his action had on me. It went like this:

Sam: Good morning, Pat!

Me: Good morning, Sam!

Sam: I hope you're not mad at me.

Me: No. Why would I be?

Sam: I left class early yesterday because I got a phone call telling me my daughter was sick in day care and I had to go get her right away. I didn't stop to tell you because you were in the middle of a lecture and I thought it was rude to interrupt, especially when I was going to see you this morning. It wasn't my intention to disrupt things and I hope that you didn't think my leaving early had anything to do with the workshop, because I really enjoyed it.

Me: Thanks for letting me know, Sam. I did assume that you had another priority and I didn't assume there was an issue with the workshop. I hope your daughter is well and you enjoy the rest of the day.

Sam did a great job of perspective-checking his intentions with me and checking in on how I was affected by the situation.

So often we create problems where none exist by acting as if our assumptions are true. When we perspective-check, we get correct information.

How often do we get into an issue with co-workers or neighbours when we don't perspective-check? With our spouses, how often have we escalated a situation because we think they should be able to read our minds? In schools, how often do we attribute blame to a teacher or student without knowing the full story? With our children, are there times we make assumptions about their intentions without ever checking with them? Our first thought is, "Boy, are they in trouble!" rather than, "Wow, that seems strange, I wonder what happened?"

Perspective-checking at the first sign of misunderstanding clarifies situations, reduces conflict and develops effective communication and trust in relationships.

INTERPRETING A MESSAGE — THE RECEIVING END OF COMMUNICATION

The Slighted Sister

A friend of mine, Steven, said he and his wife went into the hospital at four o'clock one morning because their baby was arriving two weeks early. They welcomed their baby girl by six a.m. Because Steve had been scheduled to work, he called into the office to share the news and to advise his colleagues that he would not be in for a few days.

Coincidently, Steve's sister, Megan, called Steve's work to talk to him. The receptionist answered and congratulated Megan on becoming an aunt. "What are you talking about?" asked Megan.

"Well, Steve and Barb had a baby girl this morning," the receptionist said.

"I can't believe I found out this way," Megan said as she hung up.

Megan then phoned Steve on his cell phone and proceeded to yell at him for being so thoughtless in letting someone else tell her she was an aunt.

Steve was surprised. He had never intended for Megan to find out that way. He had never thought to advise the receptionist not to tell anyone. He said their whole communication plan went up in flames when the baby arrived so early.

Steve apologized to Megan for the situation and assured her it wasn't his intention. However, to this day, Megan raises the issue. When we attribute negative meaning to a situation where none was intended, we continue to escalate a perceptual conflict.

What people mean and what we understand can be quite different. Some things to keep in mind when we are receiving and interpreting information:

- We are the ones who are putting meaning on a message.

- Just because we feel unhappy or offended by a message does not mean it was the person's intention.

- When we feel unsettled with a communication, we have the opportunity to check with the sender of the message to clarify what they actually meant.

- Just because we don't believe someone, doesn't mean he isn't telling the truth.

- Check out other people's intentions to make sure you understand the message they were trying to send.

EXERCISE: Creating Your Own Perfect World

1) Is there a situation that made you feel angry, confused or uncomfortable?

2) Have you been treating the other person differently as a result of it?

3) How could perspective-checking with the other person impact your relationship or your understanding of the event?

Chapter 21
Apologies and Making Things Right

An apology is the superglue of life. It can repair
just about anything.[17] — *Lynn Johnston*

Thanks for Noticing!

When I worked with a shipping firm, we had overseas agents in eight countries. Our agent in Japan was Mr. Yamada. At that time, the fax machine was the primary method of communicating with our agents. When I sent Yamada-san a fax, I would sign off, *Mrs.* Pat Hirst. When he replied to me the next day, he opened with *Mr.* Pat Hirst. I did not know whether he thought I was a man, or whether he just used Mr. and Mrs. interchangeably. I did not worry about it.

Eventually, we invited all the overseas agents to our offices for an orientation. We met them for the first time in our boardroom on a Monday morning. The agents were seated along one side of the table and our staff was on the other side. We began with introductions of the agents. One by one, each of us at the company introduced ourselves. I was the last one and I stood up and said, "Good morning, I am Pat Hirst."

Yamada-san stood up abruptly, slapped his forehead and said, "Oh no! You are a woman!" I just smiled, realizing he felt embarrassed and wanting to make light of it, I said, "Thank you for noticing."

Poor Yamada was uncomfortable and embarrassed for the rest of the morning. When we broke for lunch I was called to the receptionist's desk. She presented me with the largest, most elaborate bouquet I had ever seen. It was about three feet wide and four feet tall! It must have cost a small fortune. With it was a note: *Dear Pat, I apologize for calling you Mr. — Sincerely, Yamada-san.*

I felt I owed *him* an apology, because I had had no idea how much he would be embarrassed by this faux pas. However, you have to admit, the man knew how to make an apology!

ADMITTING YOU'RE WRONG

In 2010 a story broke in the media that famed golfer Tiger Woods had engaged in extramarital affairs, betraying his wife and tarnishing his image as the golden boy of golf. Who can forget his contrite look as he stood in front of the microphone at a news conference apologizing for his behaviour? He took responsibility for the injury and embarrassment he'd caused his friends. He also admitted his disregard for his wife and family. His words had all the elements of an effective apology.

In our lifetime, all of us will injure and hurt others in intentional and unintentional ways. At times we are angry and rude when we should be patient and kind. Many times the injuries we inflict are through hurtful words, prolonged thoughtlessness or even indifference.

We will offend our neighbours, co-workers and family at some point. When we behave inappropriately, we cause pain, suffering and upset, and we undermine trust with others, damaging our most important relationships. Some people even engage in violence and cause physical harm. The question is not *if* we will hurt someone; it is *when*. And when it happens, the best way to start to repair our relationships and trust with others is by taking responsibility for our part.

The Value of Apologies

Apologies begin the process of healing and change. When we feel someone has wronged us, we feel angry, hurt, unfairly treated and sometimes victimized. We will often repeat our story of betrayal to whoever will listen. We suffer with the pain and engage in whatever activities it takes to make sense out of what happened to us. If we feel we were unfairly treated, we take steps to try to prevent the same thing from happening to others.

When someone apologizes, it shows the person is conscious of the act and willing to take responsibility for it. It can also help them deal with the guilt and remorse they feel. The apology implies a promise the offending behaviour will not occur in the future. In this way, it rebuilds trust.

Apologies can also:

- Help reduce litigation and create early resolutions to problems at low cost

- Encourage people to engage in open dialogue after problems occur, which can reduce upset, restore relationships and re-establish trust and a feeling of safety for those who were harmed

- Encourage people to take responsibility for their actions

Apologies and Legislation

The value of apologies has been acknowledged in legislation. In 2007 the Province of Manitoba enacted the **Apology Act.** It allows individuals to make an apology without it constituting an admission of legal liability.

This type of law grew from the issue of liability in the medical field. Doctors and other practitioners involved in incidents where patients were harmed were unwilling to apologize to patients and families because they didn't want an apology to be construed as an admission of guilt. When professionals refused to apologize it made patients and families angry and increased the incidence of litigation.

There are approximately eight Canadian provinces, one Territory and 36 states in the U.S. that have apology acts or laws. This type of legislation acknowledges the power an apology can have in settling disputes and restoring relationships.

There are two sides to an apology, the giving and the receiving.

MAKING AN EFFECTIVE APOLOGY

An apology is an important communication. The right words have to be given at the right time to the right person. The apology has to be genuine as well. If the giver of an apology is insincere, tone and body language communicate that, and the apology will only serve to insult the injured party even further.

For example, several years ago, I was experiencing a particularly difficult relationship with a co-worker. He was constantly doing things many people thought were inappropriate. One day, to my surprise, he dropped off an apology card. It literally said, "I APOLOGIZE." It did not say anything about what he was apologizing for. So, while the gesture was a good step, it did little to address any concerns or ensure the unhelpful behaviours would not happen in the future.

Even worse is when someone gives an insult veiled as an apology. Comments such as "I am sorry you feel that way" or "I am sorry that you just don't get it" are unhelpful. They are not true apologies.

What we say during an apology is crucial. The elements of an effective apology include:

- A comment about what you are apologizing for

- A genuine expression of regret

- Acceptance of responsibility for your own behaviour or the impact of what was done, with no "buts" or excuses

- Keeping it brief and to the point

Examples:

- I am sorry I yelled at you. That was unnecessary and inappropriate and I am sorry that I made you feel embarrassed and hurt.

- I am sorry I complained to our team about how you do your job and made you feel uncomfortable. I was out of line and I won't comment to others again how you should do your job.

- I am sorry I called you a name. I hope that you can forgive me. I'd like another chance to be your friend.

Steps to Avoid the Behaviour in the Future

If it is possible in your particular situation that your transgression, whether intentional or unintentional, could be repeated in the future, you can also outline what steps or commitment you are willing to make to avoid repeating it.

Examples:

- I am sorry for damaging your property and I will assure you I will not park on your side of the driveway in the future.

- I am sorry I complained to our team about how you do your job and made you feel uncomfortable. In the future I will come and talk to you directly if I have a concern.

Checking in with the Injured Party

It takes time and energy and some careful thinking to provide an effective apology. Delivering an apology is only one part of the interaction. It can be helpful to check with the injured party to see what he thinks and to invite dialogue. You may want to check in with the receiver by asking:

- Do you accept my apology?

- Can you forgive me please?

Asking these types of questions gives you a sense of how the other party is responding to the apology and what, if any, additional steps are required to get the relationship and trust back on the right track.

RECEIVING AN APOLOGY

Sometimes it is not easy to *accept* an apology. We feel we need an apology when someone has hurt, injured or offended us. As the injured party, we often have long and detailed stories that describe what happened and how the situation affected us.

In some situations the injured party may have experienced much pain, anguish, embarrassment or discomfort. In other situations, he may have experienced inconvenience, additional expenses, a loss of income, or even physical injuries.

Most people are not willing to accept an apology until they have had an opportunity to express their concerns to the offending party. Those who have been slighted are looking for some sense the person who did the deed really understands what they did and won't do it again.

If the receiver of an apology doesn't say anything, it leaves the relationship in confusion. It can be helpful for the receiver to say something that indicates where the situation stands. Helpful comments include:

- Thank you for your apology.

- I accept (or appreciate) your apology.

- I forgive you.

- Apology accepted.

Sometimes we are not ready to accept an apology. It can be helpful for a receiver to let the giver know if he's not ready to accept it and that he needs time to think about it.

MAKING AMENDS

When you have wronged someone it is important to make amends. Making amends is more than taking responsibility and a verbal apology. It means doing something tangible to make up for the wrong you caused. It involves making a gesture that creates comfort and helps trust return to the relationship, gestures like giving someone flowers or cleaning up a mess. It may include giving others compensation.

The Morning After

Making amends and re-establishing trust in a relationship is a process. Such was the case with Janice's daughter, Marie. Marie went to a party at the Brown home. Alcohol was served because kids there were of drinking age. Marie ended up drinking too much. She was sick all over the Browns' carpet and furniture. Joey Brown, who had thrown the party, and his dad took Marie home. Poor Marie was already suffering from her mistake, as she was sick and weak, but on top of that, she hit her head on the mailbox and suffered a bruise to her head at two a.m.

The next morning, Janice checked on Marie. Marie did not remember much about the night before, but did feel horribly embarrassed at the thought of what had happened and how terrible it was that the Browns had to clean up after her. She thought she would never be able to face them again.

Because the incident had created discomfort for everyone, Janice phoned the Browns to thank them for seeing Marie got home safely and to apologize for the actions and the trouble that was caused. They were very understanding, reminding Janice that "we've all been there," and asking Janice not to be too hard on Marie.

Janice suggested to Marie that she call the Browns herself and also apologize. Marie, however, didn't want to do that, so she decided to write an apology note instead. The "note" looked more like a letter, but Janice didn't ask to read it. Janice offered to drive Marie to the Browns' home. Marie asked her mother if it would be a nice gesture to take them some flowers to show respect and make amends. Janice supported the idea. They picked up flowers on the way to the Browns'.

In the final act, Marie climbed the steps to the front door alone. Her mom had asked her if she wanted her to go with her, but Marie said no, because "it's my mess to clean up."

Knowing how understanding the other family was made the whole thing a lot easier for everyone. Marie learned a life lesson: one can recover from mistakes only by making amends, doing one's best to take responsibility and moving forward to repair relationships. Doing something tangible can help a person come to terms with an incident they wish hadn't occurred.

In mediation sessions, people often make amends to the people they have injured. Not only are apologies powerful, but often people pay for damaged property or vehicles, broken eyeglasses, dental work or ripped clothing. When making amends the question one can ask is, "What do you need from me to feel okay?" or "What can I do to make this right?" The truth is, saying you are sorry is not always enough to address the harm caused.

The Opportunity for Forgiveness

In some cases, making amends includes not only the verbal apology for your own wrong actions, but also relieving others of any guilt they may have felt. Such was the case for two young friends, Tammy and Ray. Police arrested Ray after he took a laptop and television from Tammy's house while her parents were away. Tammy felt guilty about calling the police but did so because Ray would not return the items. During a mediation session, Tammy expressed her desire to maintain a friendship with Ray. She also said she felt bad about calling the police, but felt it was necessary to protect her home and get her things back.

Ray made amends by telling Tammy that she had no reason to feel bad, because she had not done anything wrong. It was a powerful moment between them, as Ray hugged Tammy, and took full responsibility for what he did without blaming her. He did not say things like, "But you shouldn't have…" or "This was your fault too." How many times in our lives would we have benefited from others simply taking responsibility for their behaviour without blaming us? Ray said Tammy's decision to call the police was totally justified. He recognized that involving the police was a "wake-up call" for him to change his behaviour.

When people have been wronged, they can be paralysed by grief and hurt. They may even contemplate retaliation. Apologies are transformative. When someone offers the graciousness of an apology, it invites the possibility for the person who was harmed to find graciousness in forgiveness. The power of an apology allows discussion to happen, amends to be made and trust to be restored.

EXERCISE: Creating Your Own Perfect World

Think of an interaction or situation where you may have behaved poorly.

1) What action did you do that you regret?

2) What harm did you inflict? (What are you sorry for?)

3) How could you share your apology? (Write out a draft of what you will say.)

Chapter 22
Problem-Solving: From Me to We

The Tree Story

One morning I was faced with an issue. It was 7:20 a.m. and I was in a hurry because I was late for a two-day workshop I was leading. As I loaded materials into my car on the driveway, my next-door neighbour Elaine spied me as she approached her vehicle. She stopped and the following interaction took place:

Elaine: Good morning, Pat! How are you today?

Me: Fine, thanks.

Dianne: Glad to hear it! Say, Rob and I have a teeny-weeny problem with that tree in your back yard, so if you would cut it down, that would be great! (She was pointing to a silver maple that was about three feet from the fence between our properties. I looked at her blankly trying to figure what the problem was with the tree.)

Elaine: Well, would you?

Me: Would I what?

Elaine: Cut down the tree?

Me: No, I don't think so.

(Hoping to avoid a confrontation, I hurriedly jumped into my vehicle and sped off.)

Yes You Will — No I Won't!

When faced with conflict, there are several tools at our disposal to facilitate resolution. We can assess the situation and make choices about the importance of the issue or situation. We can minimize damage when we control our emotions and act calmly. When we find someone's behaviour difficult or troubling, we can ask for a change. If we are unsure of someone's intentions or motives, we can perspective-check. When any of us show our human foibles and act imperfectly and hurt someone, we can choose to apologize as the first step in mending the relationship. Many challenges in our lives can be resolved through the use of these tools and techniques that clarify misunderstandings and miscommunication. However, there will always be real issues that won't go away.

Problems that need solving appear daily. He wants a big wedding; she wants a small and intimate one. The boss wants the project done in seven months; the team believes it will take ten. *She* gets a promotion that will take the family from the mid-west to the west coast, and *his* family lives on the east coast. Suzy needs a new saxophone for next semester and there is no spare cash. Your neighbour is angry because he thinks your garage is on his property and you believe it is not. The list of issues goes on and on.

In daily life, substantive issues arise that are not just perceptual. They are real issues that affect the quality of our lives, and our relationships at home, at work and in the community. If these situations go unresolved it can ruin our relationships. We need to resolve issues as soon as possible so we don't get sidetracked and miss the important things in life. If we can use a problem-solving approach, we will save time, money and energy in resolving disagreements.

This is more easily said than done. When faced with a dilemma that is our own and doesn't involve others, we are often good problem-solvers. However, when confronted with a problem where we need the buy-in or agreement from someone else, we tend to shift into a war-like mentality. When someone has an opinion or solution different from ours, we see the other person as an enemy who needs to be defeated.

We take a competitive mindset: "If I get my way, I win and the other party loses" or "If they get their way, they win and I lose." When we are concerned with winning or losing, we don't listen well. We refuse to share important information that could be instrumental in solving the problem.

A helpful approach to solving disagreements is shifting from a positional approach to an interest-based approach. This approach is based on the premise that when we choose a solution to a problem, we are doing so to satisfy the interests we have.

One of the barriers to effective problem-solving is our tendency to keep information to ourselves. We tell people what we want, but we don't tell them *why* we want what we want. When we withhold information, it is difficult to solve the problem.

CHANGING THE GAME TO WIN-WIN

When Elaine and I started to talk about the tree, we entered into a classic conflict with a substantive problem. The tree was the problem. We had each taken a different position on what to do with it.

Conflict can be framed using the iceberg metaphor:

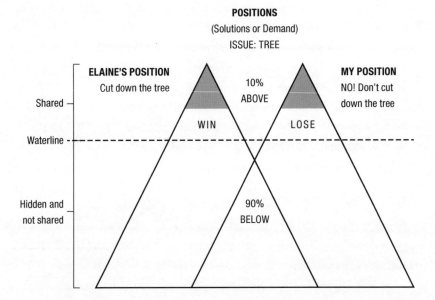

The iceberg analogy is premised on the idea that only 10% of an iceberg sticks up above the surface of the water. The other 90% is hidden beneath the water's surface. Conflicts and problems are like that. We tend to share our position or solution (only 10% of the information), but hide *why* we want what we want, which is the other 90% of the information. Would you knowingly agree to a solution to a problem if you knew you only possessed 10% of the information? Most people would not; they prefer to have as much information as possible. But when we are trying to solve a problem and we don't share what we are thinking, it is like hiding the information beneath the surface of the water.

Most of us choose a solution or position based on our interests. Interests are our needs, wants, fears, hopes, concerns and expectations. While these interests are based on our own views and choices, we also have imposed interests — those things we did not necessarily choose. For example, if you want to drive a car, you are supposed to have a valid driver's license. You did not choose that, it is imposed by law. Similarly, an organization or community has policies, laws and by-laws that are imposed on those who work or live within them.

The problem with a positional approach is it sets us up for a win-lose outcome. If the tree gets cut down, Elaine wins and I lose. If the tree stays up, she loses and I win. Positional, competitive approaches by definition lead to win-lose solutions. In addition, when we interact this way, we only think about our own point of view and what *we* want. We don't think about the other party. How can we possibly come up with a solution that would work for the other party when we disregard his viewpoint? The answer is, we can't.

However, when we use an interest-based approach, we end up sharing almost all the information in a situation. When we share information we find out things we didn't know before. This information gives us the power to brainstorm new solutions we didn't think of before.

I value cooperation and I prefer to have good relationships with neighbours, so once I returned home after my workshop, I went to Elaine's house. My intention was to discuss the tree problem with her, determine her concerns, and see if we could work out a solution together. Here is how the conversation went after I knocked on her door one evening:

Elaine: Oh — it's you!

Me (smiling and ignoring her negative tone): Hi, Elaine. I came over because I wondered if you had time to talk to me about the tree. The other day you said you had a problem with it. I'm not sure what the problem is, but I would like to see what we could do to resolve the issue.

Elaine (doubtfully): Come on in.

Me (getting seated): Thanks! Now — could you tell me what concerns you about the tree?

Elaine: You're darn right I could! That tree is right beside the fence. My garden is on the other side. The branches are so long that when I work in the garden, I whack my head on them! The other thing is the roots are so big they come right under the fence and they're choking my tomatoes. That tree makes it really hard to garden!

Me: Oh, I see — it's the branches and the roots that are giving you the problem?

Elaine: Yes, that's right. Now, won't you cut it down?

Me: Well, before we decide anything, can I tell you why I don't want to cut it down?

Elaine: Sure, go ahead.

Me: That tree is right at the south side of my yard. If we cut it down, we won't have any shade. I want to enjoy my yard but cutting down the tree would give us bright sun all day. As well, the tree is old and beautiful; your kids play in it and mine do, too. It also makes oxygen. I would prefer a solution where the tree stays alive.

(This is how Elaine and I shared our individual interests. We talked about what was underneath the tip of our iceberg so that we could understand why each of us had taken the positions we had.)

Elaine: What do we do now?

Me: Well, given what we've talked about, what ideas do *you* have?

Elaine: Well, first of all, I think I want to thank you for coming over. You did not have to do that. To me it shows some respect, that you respect me as a person. As well, you are so calm; it makes it easier to talk.

The following iceberg shows Elaine's and my interests and how we have exposed information beneath the surface that metaphorically lowers the water line:

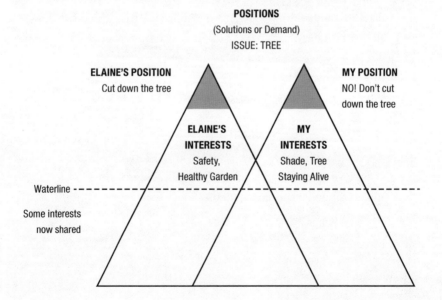

After Elaine thanked me, we started talking about common interests. When you look at icebergs from above the surface of the water, it looks as though there are many icebergs. In fact, usually what you see from the surface are a number of peaks that are really not individual but are connected underneath the surface, sticking up from the same iceberg. Conflicts and problems are like that. Even though it seems from our opposite positions that we have nothing in common, if we go beneath the surface we find we want the same things, but have different ways of approaching the problem.

Elaine and I continued our conversation and agreed that, in addition to the common interest of respect, we both valued responsibility. We were willing to take responsibility for our kids, trees, pets and whatever else we needed to in order to honour our neighbours. We also agreed we valued having a neighbourly relationship. It didn't mean we would have coffee together all the time, but we would like to have a relationship where, if problems arose, we could talk to each other to try to work it out rather than calling the civic offices or the police.

This figure shows the common interests we shared, as well as our own interests:

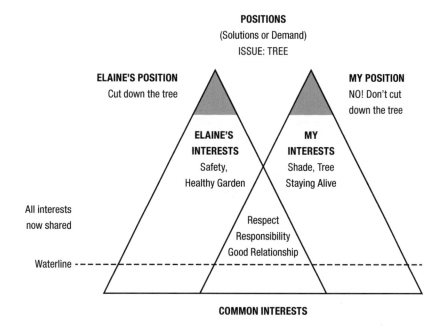

The wonderful thing about common interests is they remind us we care about some of the same things and we therefore agree at some level. When we highlight our common interests it makes us more able to see we can both win if we get our interests met. Common interests motivate us to cooperate.

Elaine and I went on to generate options. Options are just possible solutions to a problem. When we started to brainstorm, we came up with three options:

- Option 1 – Elaine could move her garden to the back of her yard and I would lend her our garden tiller to make this possible.

- Option 2 – Move the tree.

- Option 3 – Modify the tree.

Here is what our options looked like. They are the three horizontal arrows that take into account both of our interests:

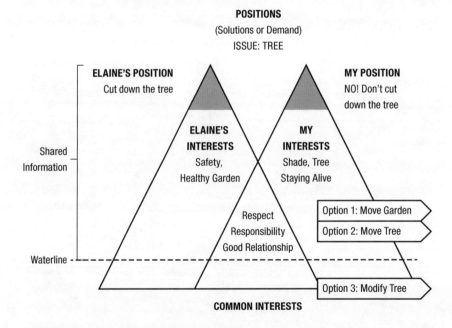

When there is a problem-solving discussion, the parties involved eventually need to come up with some kind of agreement. Elaine and I agreed we would go with Option 3 and modify the tree. She offered that she and her husband would take care of the roots on their side of the fence by cutting them and removing them. Similarly, I agreed that I would cut the branches off the tree from the top of the fence upwards to twenty feet and remove the refuse. That would give them plenty of clearance in the garden.

The other thing to remember about problem solving is sometimes our solutions don't work or might need modifying.

I recommend a final step, I refer to as follow-up. This means setting a time in the future to check in to see how things are going. This gives both parties a chance to experience the agreed change, analyse it and ask for further modifications, if required. Elaine and I agreed to check in each spring and fall to see if anything else needed to be done with the tree.

The exciting part about using an interest-based approach is that it is logical, rich with information and respects both parties. Collaboration is more likely to happen when this approach is used because it exposes both parties' interests. If interests are known, a creative solution can be developed that satisfies each party's interests. When both parties' interests are met because each was part of the solution and is invested in the outcomes, both parties win and are able to support the commitment they made to uphold the agreement.

Many people prefer a win-lose approach because they enjoy debating and believe their best defence is a good offence. In debating, we state our opinion and keep repeating it. We only listen to our opponent's view so that we can disagree, discredit or disprove their position. In an interest-based approach, we listen to understand. Through understanding we are empowered with information to be creative problem-solvers.

Police Mommy and Daddy

When my daughter Jessica was five years old, she loved her dolls and played with them every day. She also loved playing with Tristan, a boy next door who was her age.

Tristan loved playing policeman. He had a badge and a toy gun and would sit on a footstool in our living room pretending to drive a police cruiser.

A problem arose one day when Tristan refused to play house with Jessica and be the dad to her dollies. They started talking and decided that the best thing would be for both of them to do what they wanted. Hence, "Police Mom and Dad" was born. The game was played with each of them taking a baby doll under one arm and a gun in the opposite hand. They both sat on the footstool and rode the

cruiser together. They collaborated with pure joy, and many
criminals were caught while babies were burped. — *PH*

OPTIONS: THE GAME CHANGER

Problem solving happens when we are willing to generate options. When
two parties have opposing solutions, one party will win and one will lose. In
interest-based problem solving, we get all the information on the table and then
generate options or solutions that work for both parties. These solutions tend
to be different from the ones either party offered before the discussion because
initially each party was concerned only about themselves. When collaboration
happens, new options emerge that work for both parties, creating the possibility
of win-win.

With Elaine and me, the two positions were: cut the tree down or leave it
up and do nothing. We were able to work together to brainstorm three options
that led to a solution that worked for both of us. The process of discussion and
creating a solution improved our relationship and built trust.

COOPERATION: THE KEY INGREDIENT
FOR GOOD SOLUTIONS

The most successful hockey team is not the one with the best player on it. It
is the team that works together, plays great defence and scores goals to win.
Everyone on the team is responsible for results. However, what happens to the
team when one person plays for himself instead of for the team? For example,
imagine a defensive player who chooses to charge up the ice to try and score
instead of covering his position and clearing the puck to his teammates. By concentrating on his own goal of getting noticed by scouts to get drafted to another
team he may not play the position the team needs him to play and can contribute to a loss.

Cooperation means working together towards common goals rather than
our own individual goal. One thing that prevents people from cooperating is
selfishness. Some people cannot get past themselves and what they want. Why
is cooperation important?

Like the hockey team that loses, families and companies lose when one person ignores the needs of others for their own gain. We show regard for those who are important to us when we cooperate and consider others.

Tips to Create Win-Win Solutions:

- Listen to the other person to understand their interests and maintain curiosity.

- Ask questions to get more information.

- Share your interests.

- Be prepared to brainstorm other ways (options) to solve the problem that would work for both parties.

SUMMARY

People have tremendous capacity to problem-solve and think creatively. When we are faced with a problem involving another party, our best abilities go out the window because we can become combative. We need to remind ourselves it makes sense to cooperate with those we are in key relationships with, rather than competing with them. When we work together and consider both people's needs, we can come up with a solution that works for everyone. We can be partners in problem-solving.

Tom's Epiphany

When I facilitated a conflict resolution workshop I met a young man named Tom. His co-workers knew him as a hotheaded guy who had a competitive view of how the world works. Many of his co-workers would say things just to get a reaction from him and then laugh at how angry he became.

During my explanation of the iceberg model, Tom stood up, looked around and then left the workshop. His absence was noticeable. After the session I went outside looking for him. As I stood in the parking lot, I noticed Tom sitting in his car. I waved. He waved back and then came out to talk to me.

I asked him if he was okay. He replied, "Yes, I am. I just needed some time to figure things out. I can't believe what you said in there, actually. If I understand you correctly, Pat, what you are trying to tell me is, I don't have to fight with everyone all the time. It doesn't have to be my way or their way. We could actually talk about things and see what each of us wants, and then we could pick a new way that would work for both of us."

"That's exactly it, Tom," I said.

"You know, I think this might change my marriage. I was always thinking either I had to have my way or my wife had to have her way and there was nothing else we could do. This idea of doing what is good for both of us is so simple I can't understand why I didn't think of it before. I'm excited to go home and see what we can do together that will be better for us and for our kids. We don't have to fight so much."

Tom smiled at me, slapped me on the back and turned and shook his head. He walked back into the building standing taller, with a new confidence, and I had a feeling that over the next few weeks people were going to be surprised by a different kind of Tom.

We all have the opportunity to make wise choices and move away from the futility of a win-lose mindset.

EXERCISE: Creating Your Own Perfect World

Problem-Solving Preparation Checklist:

1) What is the issue?

2) What is your position or solution?

3) What is the other party's position?

4) Why do you want what you want? (your interests — needs, wants, fears, hopes, concerns and imposed restrictions)

5) Why do you think the other party wants what he wants? (his interests — needs, wants, fears, hopes, concerns and imposed restrictions or considerations)

6) What options can you think of that would work for both of you?

Chapter 23
Enough is Enough: Exploring Other Methods to Solve Problems

One thing is sure. We have to do something.
We have to do the best we know how at the
moment. — *Franklin D. Roosevelt*

The Break-Up

When Karen and Rick began living together, it was like a second marriage for both of them. Both had previously been married. They sold their homes and pooled their resources to buy a big, beautiful house in which to start a new life together.

After a year of co-habitation, Karen noticed that Rick was taking more shifts at work. He no longer wanted to go out and she felt more like a mother — making meals and cleaning house — than she did a partner. Rick did not want to have friends over and he seemed to resent it when Karen's children came for a visit or a meal. Karen tried to talk to Rick several times to see how they could create a relationship that would work for both of them. Rick sat and listened but his behaviour did not change.

On top of the day-to-day concerns was a financial issue: a couple of years into their new life, Rick had still not given Karen back the $50,000 left over from the proceeds of Karen's house that had been temporarily put into Rick's account to cover the purchase of their new home. Karen asked Rick to transfer the money into her account as they had agreed.

Rick became angry and started listing all the things he had paid for. He felt he should keep the money as compensation for the repairs he had done around the house. Karen and Rick argued for months. Even though they had loved each other and cared enough to move in together, they felt they couldn't overcome their disagreements. Ultimately, it was their lawyers who worked out a deal to divide their assets, as Rick and Karen's relationship dissolved.

As described in this book, effective communication can go a long way in creating the types of relationships we want with those closest to us. When we do encounter difficulties, there are many techniques and tools we can use to work through issues. However, despite our skill level, best intentions or persistence, there are times when our best efforts do not give us the results we want and a problem remains. Sometimes "it is what it is." So the question becomes, what can be done to end the problem?

OPTIONS FOR DEALING WITH PERSISTENT AND UNRESOLVED PROBLEMS

1) **Working Things Out Together: Negotiation**

We have explored resolving conflict directly with the person with whom we have the problem. Negotiation is the term given to a process where the people involved in the conflict communicate with each other directly in order to resolve the dispute between them.

At home, negotiating would mean two siblings solve a problem themselves rather than bringing in a parent to decide who is right. Or, a couple would have a discussion to work through their own difficulties rather than seeing a counsellor. At school, classmates would resolve their own problems without asking their teachers to referee. At work, two co-workers would sort out a conflict without asking the boss to make a decision or enforce a rule.

Negotiating isn't always the answer. Sometimes solving problems involves getting help from other parties or authorities. Resolution does not mean that we will all live happily ever after together. It can also mean ending relationships or associations and changing how we do things. We have the power to assess and choose.

Working out our own problems within a relationship is ideal because it gives us control of the direction of our lives. As well, when we can work out our problems with others, even in difficult circumstances, it can strengthen the relationship, build trust and increase understanding. The process might be uncomfortable, but worthwhile if we make it through to resolution.

However, not all differences and disputes are within our power to resolve. We are not always the right instrument to solve our own problems. There are several options other than negotiation to help us deal with issues, and all other processes have benefits.

2) **Getting Help from a Third Party: Conciliation**

At some point in our lives we all need help. One way a third party can help us when we have problems is to act as a sounding board. Getting help in this way means we talk through our problem with someone who does not have a vested interest in the conflict. We can get a fresh perspective on the issue and maybe even suggestions or coaching on options for dealing with it.

Professionals in your field, trusted colleagues, counsellors, friends, physicians, lawyers or even your local clergy can provide a safe and objective place to test your thinking. If you seek someone else's view, it is imperative you trust the person is not taking your side simply to maintain the relationship. If this person never disagrees with you, then find someone else who will give you an objective opinion.

Sometimes we ask a third party to help in a particular way. For example, Karen and Rick did try getting help from a third party in the form of a relationship counsellor. This counsellor did not tell them what to do. Rather, she helped them have a discussion about what was concerning each of them and provided a process so they could work together to come up with solutions. This process did not work for them, but they tried.

Receiving help from a third party to solve a problem is often referred to as conciliation. In many families where the children are adult, one sibling may play the conciliator role to work things out between parents and children, or between siblings. Often when two employees are having a dispute in the workplace, a co-worker steps in to try to help resolve their differences. There may be times when a boss acts in a conciliatory way, supporting employees while they have a discussion, rather than arbitrating a decision.

Help from third parties seems to occur spontaneously in situations where bystanders are negatively affected by other people's disputes and want it to stop. Conciliation may be a voluntary process, where disputants willingly accept the assistance of a third party to resolve their differences. Often the conciliator is known to the disputants and may or may not have a vested interest in the outcome of the dispute or disagreement. Conciliation occurs when the conciliator works with each disputant separately or with both disputants together. The disputants decide the outcome of their disagreement while the conciliator helps them through the conversation.

In unionized environments, the conciliation process is often written into the union agreement and is more of a formal process; it can be mandatory.

3) **Working Through a Process: Mediation**

In workplace disputes, when conflicts have been going on for a long time and are disruptive to the workplace, mediation is often used to resolve differences.

My view of mediation is that it is a voluntary process, where disputants involve the assistance of a third-party mediator. The mediator is typically an outsider who is unknown to the disputants and provides a process by which each party can share concerns, perspectives and solutions.

The mediator ensures both people in the conflict have an equal chance to express their views. A mediator does not decide what the solution is to the problem. The disputants decide what they are willing to do to solve the problem, while the mediator provides a process to help the parties discuss things in a way they are not able to do themselves.

One case I worked on involved two workers who had to be separated because they were causing an extreme problem in their workplace. They would either yell at each other or give each other the silent treatment. It was uncomfortable for their co-workers to be around them because they hated each other. They both did the same job, but their animosity resulted in no productivity. As I worked with the two parties regarding their relationship, it was obvious that they did not care about each other and did not want to listen to each other. They were only thinking of themselves and protecting their own jobs.

Mediation allowed this pair to have a discussion they were unable to have on their own. When one party heard from the other how much harm he had done, a sincere apology came easily and naturally. When these two individuals decided to try a different approach, each took responsibility for what he said and did, and communicated with a view to treating his colleague with consideration and respect. In the end, they developed a very productive working relationship and were an example to their colleagues of how a professional relationship gone wrong could recover and even improve.

Mediation is often used in disputes between union and management. During the NHL lockout of 2012, mediation was attempted. Today, across Canada and the United States, several organizations offer mediation services in workplaces and to families. If you are interested in mediation services, check the

Web or the phone listings in your area. Many lawyers now provide mediation services. The benefit of mediation is that, through dialogue facilitated by the mediator, people can have a better conversation than they would have on their own. In addition, mediation can feel safer and be less prone to escalate than having a conversation directly with your antagonist.

Mediators are often brought in if conciliation is unsuccessful. A mediator usually meets with both sides individually first, and then facilitates a way to bring both parties to the table to discuss interests and needs, and to encourage open communication.

Hiring a mediator is often quicker and less expensive than going through the courts. Mediation allows for more information to be shared and for restitution to take place.

Mediators and mediation lawyers offer a service that is designed to resolve differences in a fair and non-confrontational way. Many couples who are divorcing look to mediation as a way to resolve issues on child custody, property division and other factors that could escalate if negotiated with a positional view. Do your homework to discover what philosophy a lawyer subscribes to. Mediation is also used within the legal system to resolve some disputes.

4) **Letting Someone Else Decide: Arbitration**

Arbitration is a process in which the disputants provide information on their perspective to a third party. An arbitrator is typically a person in a position of authority who decides the outcome of the dispute. Neighbours arguing over property lines or ownership of a tree between properties may call on their city or town representatives to come and zone the area and provide a ruling on the property lines. The decision of the authority is final in many cases.

In the workplace, a person who has a complaint with a co-worker may go to the human resources department to look for guidance and a ruling on whether safety legislation or performance issues are being compromised. An employee may file a complaint with a Human Rights Commission or some other government or non-government entity to receive a ruling on who is right or wrong and how to solve the problem. In union environments and other formal settings an arbitrator may be used to resolve a dispute.

5) **The Courts: Litigation**

The law in Canada is designed to balance individual rights and freedoms with the obligations people have as members of a larger society. The law is a means to protect us and to maintain order. People who break laws may be subject to sanctions ranging from fines to imprisonment, or other penalties. The criminal justice system deals with issues that arise in families, workplaces or neighbourhoods where there may be evidence the law has been broken. In Canada, a criminal case involves prosecution by the Crown.

In situations of theft, violence, a restraining or custody order being broken, child neglect, abuse, assault or murder, we rely on the justice system to facilitate a resolution. Some problems are well beyond the capacity of an individual to work out with the other person without police or judicial intervention.

The legal process continues when, after a police investigation, someone is charged with a crime and the case proceeds through the criminal justice system, which involves lawyers, judges and sometimes juries.

Civil law deals with the resolution of disputes between parties, including individuals, corporations, partnerships and other legal entities. The civil process involves private lawsuits between individuals or groups who disagree on a matter. One of them might take action to sue the other party for damages, a declaration as to the rights and obligations of the parties, or whatever type of resolution is called for.

Family law relates to issues such as divorce, child custody and child support. For example in divorce situations, if a couple has not been able to agree on workable options, the parties may end up going to court. There a judge makes the decision about property division, financial matters, child custody and access.

CHOOSING A NEW PATH

There are some disputes that will never be resolved to everyone's satisfaction. The interesting outcome of trying to work through disputes with someone is that you often become aware of a person's true beliefs and values, and you might discover you do not like them. There will be times in life when the best strategy for resolution is to change your own circumstances.

Change sometimes needs to happen in our personal lives. Today the term "frenemy" refers to a person who purports to be your friend but does not act like it. This is the person who does not take joy in your good fortune, who gives you back-handed compliments and who may even do things that make you look bad. The mark of a true friend is someone who loves you unconditionally, who shares your joy and supports you. When a person who is supposed to be your friend commits undermining, negative and hurtful acts, it may be time to get a new friend. You don't need to retaliate by being mean and hurtful to this frenemy; simply distance yourself from the relationship. A colleague of mine has a less subtle approach. On his answering machine he says, "Sorry I can't come to the phone right now. I am busy making changes in my life. If I don't return your call — you're one of the changes!"

It is impossible to know everything about the person you marry. In Canada today, approximately 40% of marriages end in divorce. The ending of a relationship can be challenging, especially if there are children involved. However, separation and divorce may be a healthier solution than constant fighting, strife or violence.

Change happens in the workplace. If you cannot see eye-to-eye with a manager, or you have a major problem with a co-worker and it doesn't look as though things will change even after you've exhausted all the problem-solving avenues, your best choice may be to look for a new job.

Change is not bad in these circumstances; it can be a strategy to move forward after trying to resolve differences and after a careful assessment of the choices before you.

RED FLAGS AND CHALLENGING CIRCUMSTANCES

The guidelines, practices and skills outlined in this book have the potential to improve your relationships. However, a premise of these approaches is that the people you interact with are healthy. If a person is not healthy, he or she may not respond to the practices in the way most people would. If you are living or working with people who are experiencing challenging circumstances, then basic communication and conflict resolution techniques may not be enough to support these relationships. The special ways to support people who have health issues are outside the scope of this book. However, below you will find some ideas about how to address these issues.

Awareness of something different going on is the first step. Patience is required as you learn the different communication and relationship needs of the person who is experiencing challenging circumstances.

Addictions

People can experience several types of addiction: gambling, alcoholism, drug use, sex addiction and even shopping addiction. The red flags that indicate possible alcohol or drug use include the smell of alcohol or drugs, slurred speech, confusion or erratic behaviour, change in speech patterns or mood swings. For signs of addictions and help in dealing with people you believe may have addiction issues, talk to your family doctor or contact a crisis line or addictions agency in your community. Another consideration is that many employees have access to an EAP (Employee Assistance Program). These programs offer confidential help accessing professionals to support you and your family. These programs usually provide access to counsellors, lawyers and accountants and other professionals.

Mental Illness

At one time or another, we will all be affected by mental illness through our family or friends, or our own experience. Mental illness affects people of all ages, all education and income levels and all cultures.

Symptoms of mental illness may include depression, difficulty in communicating or withdrawal from social situations, and difficulty being on time for school or work. People who are experiencing mental illness may not respond to communication techniques the way that others will. The point is that communication isn't the problem. Getting help is the opportunity. You can help others by calmly talking to them about what you have observed and asking them how they feel. You can encourage them to see their doctor or other mental health professionals for treatment and support.

Dementia

Forgetfulness, a change in personality, irritability, problems with remembering words or names and losing things are all potential signs of dementia. Most people know someone with dementia or may be caring for someone with this health issue.

Dealing with a person with dementia is challenging. The rules for regular communication do not apply. It takes patience, understanding and caring to communicate with dementia sufferers.

Often people see signs of change but are reluctant to speak about it. Dementia impacts the sufferers' ability to care for and to make choices for themselves. In addition, the normal practices of manners, behaviour and communication go out the window.

Addictions, mental illness and dementia are real complications people deal with every day. In addition, we might be in relationships with people who have fetal alcohol syndrome, learning disabilities or autism. Each person we meet is unique. When people have illnesses or conditions, we have to learn about them — their needs, their abilities and their perceptions — in order to adjust and adapt our style of communicating with them effectively.

Illness

Serious, debilitating illnesses such as cancer, heart disease, asthma, arthritis and diabetes are common in North America. Dealing with people who have acute or chronic conditions can be challenging, as the stress of the disease may affect their ability to communicate and to handle conflict.

Dealing with a loved one who has an illness can take a toll on us and make it harder for us to communicate effectively when we are stressed and tired.

Checking in your community, you may find several organizations, both governmental and volunteer, that provide services and assistance for people dealing with various illnesses. Services are provided to those who are sick as well as their families.

Major Life Change

While it can be challenging to deal with people who have circumstances described above, it can also be challenging to deal with people who are going through major life changes. Circumstances such as the death of a loved one, a change in relationship or marital status, a home move, the birth of a child, a temporary illness or injury or a change in job all put stress on a person. These stressors can make communicating more difficult. It all takes patience. Seeking resources to help people cope with the change can help people and relationships.

ENOUGH IS ENOUGH

When you become involved in a conflict, think about who can help you and the processes you can use to resolve it.

When people are faced with counsellors or lawyers and unfamiliar processes, tempers can flare and people can lose control. However, sometimes more formal techniques need to be employed if people are unable to resolve issues between themselves.

Before you commit to using a more formal approach or involving third parties, it is a good idea to familiarize yourself with the process. For example, if you are thinking about lodging a complaint through your human resources department at work, talk to someone in a hypothetical fashion to find out how the process will work, before you engage in it.

Similarly, if you and your spouse are thinking of splitting, talk to a lawyer to get advice about the law, your assets and child custody arrangements. You can have this kind of conversation without actually launching into a formal process. It is a matter of educating yourself with accurate information before you make a choice to proceed.

Remember you will have to live with whatever consequences arise from your actions. At some point, enough is enough and we need to make a decision to resolve an issue so that we can move on.

PART SIX
The Best is Yet to Come:
Forgiveness, Letting Go
and the Rest of Your Life

Hurts and injuries have a power to divert us
from what is good in life.
The things you feed take your energy and grow.
Choose to grow love and joy.
Live your life and let your light shine. — PH

Chapter 24
The Freedom of Forgiveness

To err is human; to forgive, divine. — *Alexander Pope*

A Broken Heart

A few months ago, my friend Lorne was crushed after his mother told him she was redoing her will and leaving her house and all her belongings to her other son, Martin, who had lived with her all of his life. The original will divided everything equally between Lorne and Martin. While Martin may have lived with his mother, it was Lorne who drove her to doctors' appointments, helped her with her finances, took her grocery shopping, repaired her house and hosted family meals. Lorne's mother said to him, "You have done very well for yourself, but Martin needs help, so I am leaving everything to him."

Lorne was beside himself. He felt neglected and unloved. Even though he understood his mother's property was hers to do with as she liked, he couldn't help but feel betrayed by her unfairness and lack of regard for him and his family.

So goes the story of families. We hurt each other in various ways. Spouses cheat. Children or parents betray each other's trust. Mental, physical, verbal or sexual abuse occurs. People are belittled or manipulated through guilt and blame. Family members are neglected, shunned, discredited and disowned.

Our workplace can also be the source of pain. Co-workers spread rumours, sabotage others' projects, withhold information and bully others. How many people have been sidelined as "problem" employees, or have lost hope when they did not receive a much-needed raise or promotion without any feedback about how they could improve their performance.

Coming To Terms

It is a truth of the human condition that those who are closest to us can hurt us the most. They know our vulnerable spots and their actions hurt all the more because we expect them to protect us and be loyal. When those closest betray us, it is a deep cut that takes time to heal.

Some people are so hurt by the actions of others and what others are "doing to them" or have done to them that they develop ulcers, need to go on stress leave, see psychologists and take medications for stress or depression. In addition, carrying this kind of upset or hatred and focusing all one's energy on the "enemy" means that important family and personal relationships often disintegrate. The person who wronged us is the first thing we think about in the morning. We hold negative thoughts about him through the day and he is the last thing we think about before our restless sleep. We vent to partners and close friends, sharing endless complaints. Important things are ignored. Life grinds to a halt.

In holding onto our grievances and not finding a way to forgive the transgressions of others, it is ourselves we hurt the most. In most cases the perpetrator does not feel any discomfort from our misery.

We miss out on good things in life when we make the choice to focus all our energy on a conflict or a difficult circumstance. We focus on the injustice of it and the bad feelings and hate for the person we feel is responsible. We are held captive by our resentment and pain. When we can move away from these feelings, we find freedom. However, not all violations are equal. Each person's process of forgiving is an individual journey. Forgiveness happens on our terms, on our timetable and at our discretion.

Holding onto our grievances is like clutching a piece of broken glass in our hand and holding it tight. As we grip it, we are further hurt. We have no room for anything else in our hand. When we quit hanging on tight and decide to open our hand, the glass will fall out. We release it. We feel relief and our hand is open to embrace better things such as peace and joy.

When we are faced with difficult circumstances it is helpful to remember the
Serenity Prayer:

Lord, give me the courage to change the things I can,
the patience to accept the things I can't,
and the wisdom to know the difference.

Coming to terms with difficult issues and letting go are not easy. There
are numerous options and modalities to help people process what they
have experienced.

1) **Professional Counselling**

   Counsellors or psychiatrists can be instruments to help people
   deal with their issues. These professionals provide a safe place to
   talk about feelings, explore facts and issues, and look at options
   to deal with what has happened and how to move positively
   forward in our lives. Many companies provide access to a counsellor through an Employee Assistance Program. Access to professionals can be made through a doctor or through programs
   in your area. Remember professionals are people and we don't
   always click with everyone. If you meet a counsellor or physician
   that you don't like, don't give up on getting help. Try someone
   else in the profession that you may feel more comfortable with.

2) **Self-Help Groups**

   There are as many self-help groups as there are illnesses and
   issues. Groups for single parents, dementia support groups,
   and cancer related organizations are examples. The benefit of
   such groups is that individuals can connect with others who
   understand their situation and can offer first-hand advice about
   options to deal with it. It can also be comforting to talk to
   others who understand your experience because they have been
   through similar circumstances.

3) **Self-Help Books**

If you have experienced a problem or issue it is safe to bet someone has written a book on it. Books are available on every topic imaginable. Going to your local library, shopping online or visiting a bookstore will expose you to volumes of ideas about how to handle problems. Sometimes you can take comfort in and learn from someone else's experience.

4) **Releasing Techniques**

Journaling is one form of purging thoughts that keep us stuck. Some people use the burning technique, where they write down on a piece of paper the problems they want to release. They go through their own ritual (usually outdoors) to burn the papers and let go of the issues that have dragged them down.

5) **Spiritual Approaches**

For some, healing and forgiveness can be found through joining an organized religious group that provides support to manage problems and find peace and freedom. Some people choose other spiritual avenues such as meditation, yoga, reiki and therapeutic touch to help them overcome stressful, pivotal events in their lives. You can search for practitioners or classes online or at special trade shows that feature spiritual practitioners.

6) **Focusing on the Good**

When Terry Fox was diagnosed with cancer in 1977, he was shocked. He later turned his problem into an opportunity and started the Marathon of Hope in an effort to raise money to find a cure for cancer. Many people have coped with their difficulties in a similar way, starting foundations to help other people who have had problems, or writing books as a way to share their experiences and help others. A man I know was devastated his father had abandoned him when he was a child. The man found solace in joining Big Brothers to help fill a gap that others were experiencing.

7) **Facing the One Who Wronged You**

This process is not for everyone. Some people have found the only way to come to terms with a grievance is to meet with the person who wronged them to discuss what happened. Sometimes it results in an apology. Sometimes it results in the person denying the situation and their responsibility. Some victims feel better just for trying. For example, some families who have been victims of a crime meet with the perpetrator to discuss what happened and get an understanding of the circumstances. There are several ways to deal with hurt and harm. But there is no magic formula.

Lorne's Peace

A few months later, I talked to my friend Lorne and asked him how things were going with his mom. He said the last few months had been very painful. He had felt betrayed and hurt, and had come to hate his brother, who had sponged off his mother all his life. Lorne said his family had given credence to the saying, "No good deed goes unpunished." He had done so much for his mother and she was returning his kindness with indifference.

In the past, when his mom needed help, Lorne had always obliged with a feeling of happiness at being useful. Given the changes she had made to the will, he felt those good feelings dissipate. He still helped her, but grudgingly. Lorne's wife was concerned his health was at stake. They talked about the situation repeatedly and discussed options to deal with it. Should they have more conversations with Mom to get her to change her mind? Should they think about legal proceedings to block this change or challenge the will at a later time? Should he have a conversation with his brother Martin to try to get him to change their mother's mind?

Lorne realized he was being eaten alive by the issue, partly because his mother's action made him feel differently about his actions as a son. He looked after his mother in a way that was in line with his values and who he was. Now he felt like a sucker, being taken in by someone who did not value him. Ultimately, it made him angry with himself.

Part of the forgiveness process is forgiving ourselves. We chastise ourselves, thinking, "I should have known better," "I should have seen this coming." The truth is, we cannot anticipate everything. We need to forgive ourselves and realize things will always happen in our lives that are outside of our control. We cannot control others; we can only control ourselves.

Lorne finally came to a place where, regardless of his mother's actions, he believed he was conducting himself in a way that reflected his values. He was living his integrity in the way that he cared for his mother.

Lorne decided that ultimately he did not want to spend his time and energy trying to convince his mother to do what he thought was right. He also did not want to spend his time fighting with his brother. He wanted to spend his time in positive ways.

He told me he would never agree with her decision. He felt fair treatment would consist of him and his family being considered in the will. He also felt that the special treatment that Martin was receiving with the will was a carry-over of the special treatment Martin had received in childhood. Some habits die hard. However, Lorne decided to accept the fact that his mother had the right to decide what to do with her money and her property.

LETTING IT GO

Lorne said that once he decided to forgive and let go, he was able to sleep, he quit wasting time and energy and, more importantly, he quit being angry. He said he would never think what his mother did was right. However, he couldn't change it. He and his wife promised each other they would treat their own children equally.

His story is not one of reconciliation; it is one of self-awareness and recognizing the ability to choose. He could have spent the rest of his life being consumed by the power of the hurt he felt from his mother's decision. He realized it was a bad place to be. We all have a choice to focus on what matters to us and on the things that are in our realm of influence. He chose to change the family legacy of inequity to one of caring and fairness.

Forgiveness is not about approving of what the person who harmed you did. It is about finding a way to accept that as humans we all make mistakes. Finding forgiveness can help us move forward.

EXERCISE: Creating Your Own Perfect World

1) What grievance caused by another are you hanging on to that you have been unable to forgive?

2) What actions have you tried so that you can forgive?

3) What else would you be willing to do?

4) How could your life improve if you were able to forgive?

Chapter 25
Letting Go and Moving On

*One cannot walk and stare at the stars
when one has a stone in his shoe. — Ancient Chinese Proverb*

Hindsight

Several years ago, a workshop participant named Steve told the class a story. He said he wanted everyone to repeat his story to others because it had an important message and the more people who knew it, the better.

His story began with building a house. He and his wife were excited about their new home. Finally, they had a bedroom for themselves and one for each of their children. But, after the first rainfall, their joy turned to anger and frustration. They discovered that when it rained, their sewer system backed up and flooded the basement. It was unbelievable they could have this problem with a brand new house.

Steve immediately went to the builders and demanded they fix the problem. When the builders examined the situation, they told Steve they had done everything according to code. The problem, they said, must lie with the City zoning department and the specifications they were given for the depth of the basement.

Steve was furious. He went to the City department that had given the specifications about depth and yelled at them for ruining his home. He wanted the City to fix his problem. He found no one from the department was interested in helping him.

Steve was at his wit's end. He had put all his money into the house and, the way he saw it, his home was ruined yet no one wanted to help him. He went back to the builders and demanded they do something or he would sue them. He also wrote letters to the City saying they needed to help him find a remedy or he would sue them as well.

Eventually, all of Steve's waking minutes were embroiled in the issue with the house. He was always busy writing letters, making phone calls and telling anyone who would listen about the mistake that had been made and how no one cared. Soon his wife and children became frustrated with his obsession. His neighbours quit coming by and did not want to be in his company. Weeks went by, then months, and then years and the problem remained unresolved. Steve's wife begged him to pay the money to have the sewer redone, take the loss and move on. But Steve would not hear of it. He was determined to have justice.

About four years into the situation, Steve's wife could not take it any longer, so she left Steve and took their children with her. Steve was sad to see them go, but he was not about to give up on what was rightfully his. Someone was going to fix his problem and someone was going to pay.

Steve pursued the issue until, finally, eight years later, he was going to have his day in court — face the builders and the City and demand justice. He was excited that his case would finally be heard. Just minutes before the trial was about to start, the builders' lawyer came over and offered Steve a large sum of money to settle and stop the court proceedings. Even though the offer was more than fair, Steve would not accept it. He said, "Forget it!" He wanted everyone to hear of his pain and suffering and did not want the builders or the City to *get away with it*!

When the opportunity came for the builders' lawyer to address the court, he stated that Steve was being totally unreasonable. He produced evidence that a more than reasonable offer had been made to Steve and it was rejected. This evidence made the judge angry, as he, too, believed Steve was being unreasonable by not accepting the offer and was wasting the court's time. He threw out the case and made Steve pay for the legal fees, including those of the builders. So the injustice and unfairness towards Steve continued.

Steve practically wept as he continued telling us his story. He said that, looking back, he was very sorry for the position he'd taken. He had acted with such aggression and anger that he had alienated everyone — the builders, the City, his friends, and most importantly, his family. In hindsight, he felt had he used a more conciliatory approach with the builders and the City and not made threats and demands, the issue could have been resolved years before.

He also said he couldn't believe he had thrown everything away that was important to him because he could not let go of the problem. He said he still struggled with regret. He lost everything that was dear to him — his wife, his children — and almost a decade of his life. His message was that life is precious and your loved ones are precious. He didn't want anyone else to make the same mistake he had — to get so preoccupied with a problem that you lose everything. He could see clearly at that point the situation with the house was not nearly as important as the welfare of his family. He felt he had squandered his life.

Woulda-Coulda-Shoulda

Just as a dog takes a bone and won't let it go, many of us fixate on certain problems or issues in our lives. Like Steve, we may grab onto a problem and put all of our time, energy and focus into it while everything else falls to the wayside. Steve had the awareness to reflect on his experience and determine that if he could have a do-over, it would be letting the house problem go before he lost what was important to him.

EXERCISE: Creating Your Own Perfect World

1) Are you hanging on to something that is stealing your life?

2) How can you let it go?

This poem by ee cummings encourages us to let go of that which does not serve us.

let it go — the
smashed word broken
open vow or
the oath cracked length
wise — let it go it
was sworn to
go

let them go — the
truthful liars and
the false fair friends
and the boths and
neithers — you must let them go they
were born
to go

let all go — the
big small middling
tall bigger really
the biggest and all
things — let all go
dear

so comes love

Chapter 26
Your Own Perfect World

Life is what you make it. It is a privilege to live
it. Some days are really bad, but good days are
always on the horizon. — *Zoe Peckover*

Lifting the Anchor

At a conference, a woman came up to me after I had spoken. Years back, she
had attended a workshop I had facilitated. I was going through a divorce at the
time, raising two young children, running my own business and looking after ill
parents. As usual, throughout that workshop I had used a few of my life experiences to illustrate points and to let people know we are all working on *something*.
The woman told me that my being candid and sharing my story had made her
think. At the time of the workshop, she was living with a man who was abusive.
Her mindset had been that being with him was her only option in life, and her
future had looked depressing and unfulfilling.

After the workshop she had started to challenge that thinking. There were no
children in the relationship and she had no debt. She had asked herself, "Why
am I accepting this man and his ill treatment of me as *my life*?"

After pondering this for several days she finally mustered the courage to
leave him. It was not the struggle she'd thought it would be. He did not threaten
her. He let her go.

Her intention in talking to me after the conference was to thank me for
sharing my story in that earlier workshop. She said knowing someone else
had made a difficult decision and had found happiness gave her the courage
and faith to do the same. She was happy to explain she was now married to a

wonderful man and they were living a happy and loving life along with their children. She shudders to think what her life would be like now if she had not changed her mindset.

Her decision to give herself permission to change her attitude to life had set her free. She pulled up the anchor from a bad situation and sailed freely into a future that allowed her to pursue a life of possibilities, love and abundance. She was courageous in leaving her past behind.

This woman approaching me and sharing her story was a real blessing for me. So often we don't know what impact we have had on others. She encouraged me to keep doing what I am doing. She also reminded me of the importance of connecting with others and being present every day. It is never too soon or too late to change the course of our lives.

Creating Your Own Perfect World

In this book I have shared ideas how you too can create the types of relationships and life that you want. Here is a summary of the key points from each section.

1) **Starting with Yourself**

   You are the architect of your life. Whatever you believe influences what you say and do, and ultimately what you experience. Discover your values and live by them. Your values are who you are. Realize you see things from your own frame of reference.

   Move through life assertively knowing it is your own. Choose to be positive. Have faith in yourself and treat yourself with a loving kindness allowing you to learn, make mistakes, enjoy and grow. Each choice you make has the potential to elicit both positive and negative consequences. Choose wisely.

2) **The Anatomy of Communication**

   Communication is the vehicle we use to do everything in life. We use it to express our goals, ask for what we want, direct others, build relationships and nurture others.

   Communication has two sides. The inside, which is our own voice, our own thinking and our own view, is what we keep to ourselves. The public realm is where we exchange information, ideas and opinions with others. Our behaviour and words are observed and interpreted by others. Do your best to speak your truth to others. Understand the impact of what you say. Realize that as we interact with others, we each share a piece of the conversation.

The words we choose, the tone we use and the supporting body language are all elements of the message. Be prepared to learn and develop your skills.

3) **Relationships and Communicating with Others**

So much of our happiness comes from our relationships. Decide which relationships are your closest and most important. Nurture and invest in those relationships. Be a part of the cycle of giving and receiving. As you give you can find joy and service. As you receive you create the opportunity for others to be empowered to fulfil their legacy.

Connect with others. Listen with your heart for understanding. Use manners and show others respect. Be lavish with your praise to bolster and affirm others. Take the time to listen and understand. No one is an island. We need the shelter of one another. Communicate your needs, hopes and dreams. The circle of support and love around us determines so much of our future.

4) **The Challenges and Hurdles of Interacting**

We are all different and most of us have a preference for our style of interacting. Just because we are different doesn't mean someone is right and someone is wrong. Be willing to adapt your style to be more connected and accessible to others.

When we adapt, we show graciousness and we increase the odds others will understand us and that we will understand them.

As we deal with difficult circumstances, learning to control our anger and other emotions will help us connect. *Feel* your feelings, express them in respectful ways, and let others do the same.

In this world of electronic devices, take the time to choose a medium that is appropriate to your message. Take the time to talk to people. Look them in the eye and connect.

5) **Now this is Awkward! Dealing with Differences and Conflict**

Ultimately we will all experience differences with others that will leave us angry, hurt and conflicted. Start with seeking understanding and sharing perspectives. Don't assume. Convey your piece of the conversation and allow others to speak for themselves.

Ask for a change in behaviour when you would prefer to be treated in a different way. When you wrong someone, make it right. Apologize and make amends. Be willing to problem-solve and work things out. If that doesn't work, look at other processes or people to help you find a way.

6) **The Best is Yet to Come: Forgiveness, Letting Go and the Rest of Your Life**

We will encounter all kinds of challenges, strife and hurt. We can hang onto it or we can let it go. We can wither with hate and resentment or we can do the best we can to move on.

The future starts now. Where your life takes you will depend on what you say and what you don't say; what you do and what you don't do. The power of choice is yours each day. Think about where you want to be and who you want to be. What choices can you make and where will they take you? What is the power of choice? Consider this:

- A choice you make can change your life.

- Your actions affect others.

- Choices allow you to live a more fulfilled life.

- It is important to focus on the people and things that will have a positive impact on your life.

- Extraordinary opportunities are not thrust on you — you have to find them.

- Everything is a choice.

A Life Well Lived

My Great-Aunt Annie was an amazing woman. As far back as I can remember, she was a part of my life. Her visits to our home were always a special occasion. My dad was always excited to see his aunt and treated her with a kindness and gentleness that was special to see.

Annie was remarkable not only because she was always happy, kind and enthusiastic but also because she had lived such a long life. She was old! Born in England in 1892, she immigrated to Canada with her family in the early 1900s and died in 2000 at the age of one hundred and seven.

Her life touched three centuries and two millennia. She experienced first-hand events that many of us only read about. I'm sure she did not expect to live that long. She thrived by taking one day at a time. I believe that her secret to a long life was living each day to the fullest and having her family and friends close to her. Loving relationships are her legacy. None of us knows how long the journey will be. Where will yours take you?

It's a New Day

Every morning when I wake up, I feel energized. It's true! I love my work, I love my family, I have extraordinary friends, and life excites me. Each morning I think, "Wow, I get to go and do what I love today." I wonder who will I meet and what I'll learn. What new opportunity or adventure will come my way as a result of those I connect with and listen to?

It was not always that way. I have had my days of being stifled by what I cannot change. I have been angry and fixated on the hurts of the past. I am human and imperfect yet able to make mistakes and learn.

What a remarkable gift it is to get a clean slate and fresh start every morning. The sun comes up; the day is ripe with possibilities. After eight hours of unconsciousness we are reborn with new energy and the opportunity to fulfil our destiny. We do not need to be stifled by what happened yesterday or ten years ago. Each day is a new start.

WHAT NEXT?

Today really is the first day of the rest of your life. What are *your* thoughts when you awaken? What did you do today that excited you? Who did you see and connect with that brought joy and love to your heart? Do you have passion for your work? Does it bring you satisfaction and the opportunity to use the gifts and skills you were given? Are you leaving the kind of legacy that you want to leave?

I feel constant amazement at the gift of life and the possibilities that bubble before us. I revel in the goodness that is around me. Each of us has knowledge, talents and abilities. We also have unexplored potential to develop new skills, achieve new goals and reach new heights. For these things each day I close my eyes and utter a blessing of thanks:

I am grateful for all that I am, all that I have, and all that I can be.

Do not wait for fate to divine your future. Use your gifts, find your strengths and take a step each day to create your own perfect world.

Acknowledgements

I will be eternally grateful to many people who supported and helped me distil and clarify my thoughts for this book.

Thanks to my book coach Les Kletke for freeing me to understand that writing is a process.

Special thanks to George Poritsanos and Julie DesLauriers, who provided a first reaction, insight and perspective, as well as suggestions about content and wording. Their kindness, enthusiasm, generosity and effort are appreciated.

Thanks to Brenda, Ken, Shirley, buddy Barb and my siblings, in-laws and extended family, who always had faith in the project and listened patiently as ideas bloomed. With sincere appreciation to Louise McNaughton-Filion for her anchoring quote.

To my editor Lois Braun, whose insight, candour, passion and common sense helped me find my voice. Thank you to Rhonda Kezema for her work on the manuscript. Special thanks to Tanice Houston whose final read inspired and energized me and the manuscript at the end of a long road. Thank you to John Myers and Cynthia Lau who provided advice on content. Thanks to Elizabeth Falk, proofreader extraordinaire, whose final review let me sleep at night.

I have so much gratitude and love for my family, Dennis, Matt, Jess, Steph and Jeff for supporting me in this process. They shared ideas, listened and were patient and flexible for the two-year period while this book was being created.

To the FriesenPress Team, my appreciation for your partnership in getting this book completed.

And finally, thank you to Lorella DePieri, who facilitated the workshop that changed my life.

Endnotes

Introduction

[1] Dr. Louise McNaughton-Filion. (Used with permission)

[2] P. J. Zak, *The Moral Molecule: The Source of Love and Prosperity,* (New York. Dutton Penguin Books, 2012), 205. (Used with permission)

Chapter 2

[3] The Wisconsin Council on Children and Families (WCCF), *Quality Matters,* A Policy Brief Series on Early Care & Education, (Madison Wisconsin: Winter 2007 Newsletter, Volume 1), (Used with permission) *The WCCF is a "a multi-issue advocacy group working to ensure that every child in the state grows up in a safe and healthy family and community."*

Chapter 3

[4] Notes from an interview with Dr. Lee Berk. (Used with permission) Lee Berk, DrPH, MPH, FACSM, FAAIM, CHES, CLS is a psychoneuro-immunologist and Director of Clinical Molecular Research at Loma Linda University, Loma Linda, CA.
For further information email: lberk@LLU.edu

Chapter 5

[5] L. H. Chiu, (1972). *A Cross-Cultural Comparison of Cognitive Styles in Chinese and American Children.* (Taylor and Francis: International Journal of Psychology, 7(4), 235-242. (Used with permission under license)

Chapter 7

[6] Lorella DePieri, Results by Design Consulting Inc. (Used with permission) To contact Lorella, see: http://www.rbdconsultants.com/contact.php

Chapter 9

[7] Article reference: Chiefs quarterback Brady Quinn on Jovan Belcher murder-suicide: 'It was an eerie feeling after a win', (Associated Press: 2012/12/03) Used with permission of The Associated Press Copyright© 2012. (All rights reserved)

[8] Tom Rath, and Donald O. Clifton, *How Full is Your Bucket? Positive Strategies for Work and Life* (New York: Gallup Press, 2004), 55 & 57. (Used with permission)

[9] Robin Dunbar, *How Many Friends Does One Person Need?* (London: Faber and Faber, 2010), 21.

[10] Gary Chapman, *The 5 Love Languages: The Secret to Love That Lasts.* (Chicago: Northfield Publishing, 2010), 10 & 16. (Used with publisher's permission)

Chapter 10

[11] International Listening Association's definition of listening. (Used with permission)

For more information visit: www.listen.org or info@listen.org

Chapter 12

[12] Quote used with permission of The Emily Post Institute, Inc.

For more information contact: http://www.emilypost.com

Chapter 14

[13] William Marston, *The Emotions of Normal People.* (London: Kegan Paul, Trench, Trubner & Co. Ltd., 1928), 107, 108 & 109. (Used with permission) (Taylor & Francis Books, UK)

Chapter 16

[14] Marshall McLuhan, *Understanding Media*, (Routledge, London, 1964, 2003), 6. (Used with permission) (Copyright: the estate of Marshall McLuhan)

Author's note: McLuhan, a Canadian professor and writer, also coined the term *global village* in his book, *The Gutenburg Galaxy: The Making of Typographic Man*, (1962)

[15] Leanne Schmidt, Secret Handshake interview. (Used with permission)
For more information visit: www.meetup.com/secrethandshake

Chapter 17

[16] Dr. Brad McRae, Director of the Atlantic Leadership Development Institute located in Halifax, Nova Scotia.
Excerpt and 3 x 3 Feedback Exercise. (Used with permission)
For more information visit: www.bradmcrae.com

Chapter 21

[17] Lynn Johnston, *For Better for Worse*. (Used with permission)

About the Author
Pat Hirst
B. Comm. (Hons.) CAE

Pat Hirst is a speaker, trainer, and mediator. She believes that evolving our communication skills and resolving conflict is the key to great relationships. Through workshops, retreats and keynotes she shares strategies and tools to coach people to create the life they chose.

Pat received her Bachelor of Commerce (Honours) from the University of Manitoba and her Certificate in Adult Education from St. Francis Xavier University. She has instructed with the Schulich Executive Education Centre, York University in Toronto, and the University of Winnipeg. She received her training in conflict resolution from Mediation Services in Winnipeg.

Her client list includes private and public organizations in a variety of sectors. She is also a member of the Canadian Association of Professional Speakers. Pat lives in Winnipeg and spends her spare time reading, being outdoors, and connecting with friends.

For Information visit www.pathirst.com

Look for future *"In a Perfect World"* titles.